Delinquents and Nondelinquents
in Perspective

Delinquents and

Nondelinquents

in Perspective

Sheldon and Eleanor Glueck

HARVARD UNIVERSITY PRESS

CAMBRIDGE, MASSACHUSETTS 1968

To devoted associates
connected with this research
from its inception

Mildred P. Cunningham

George F. McGrath

Rose W. Kneznek

John E. Burke

Mary H. Moran

Sheila Murphrey

Contents

PART II   AS THEY ARE AS MEN

PART III "THE PAST IS PROLOGUE"

Tables

Authors' Preface

This is the first of a new series of volumes to grow out of the combined data of *Unraveling Juvenile Delinquency*[1] and a tracing of its delinquents — first to age 25 and then to age 31.

The present work encompasses, on a descriptive level and at a stage of tentative interpretation, the findings of a detailed follow-up inquiry into the conduct of the juvenile offenders and the matched nonoffenders of *Unraveling* as they grew into adolescence and early adulthood. Later on, a more intensive analysis of these assessments will be made through cross-correlation of some of the follow-up data presented here with some of the original data of *Unraveling*. In the meantime, the information gleaned from *Unraveling* and from the two follow-up spans analyzed in the present work is valuable not only in itself but as a basis for explorations into the establishment of an etiologic-treatment typology of delinquents as well as of a recidivistic typology.

The particular research to which this volume is devoted has been somewhat restricted by the difficulty of securing sufficient funds to follow the life histories of all the 500 delinquents and the 500 nondelinquents who were compared in detail in *Unraveling*. We think the reader will agree, however, that there is a sufficient number of cases and verified information on which to present reliable findings (438 delinquents and 442 nondelinquents). As best we can ascertain, this is the first time in the history of Criminology that a substantial number of delinquents and their matched nondelinquent controls have been followed to an age beyond temporal adolescence.[2] The inquiry covers

1. Sheldon and Eleanor Glueck (New York: The Commonwealth Fund, 1950; Cambridge, Mass.: Harvard University Press, 1951).

2. Cf. L. N. Robins, *Deviant Children Grown Up: A Sociological and Psychiatric Study of Sociopathic Personality* (Baltimore: Williams & Wilkins, 1966). This compares the adult status of 524 persons originally seen as children in a child guidance clinic with 100 "normal control subjects."

not only subsequent criminality but the conduct of the two groups in many of the major activities of life.

When, in 1948, we undertook to trace into adulthood the delinquents and nondelinquents whose make-up and background we described in *Unraveling*, the plan was to cut off the investigation when the boys, grown to manhood, had attained age 25. However, when that stage was reached, the challenge of the findings impelled us to go on; and we sought additional support to continue the follow-up to age 31.

Begun in 1948 and completed in 1965 (the field investigations in 1963), the follow-up inquiries derived their earliest support from the Nathan Hofheimer Foundation and from the Field Foundation. From January 1953, and extending until December 31, 1963, funds were available from the Ford Foundation; and beginning September 1, 1957, supplementary funds were made available by the National Institute of Mental Health (M 1817), for a five-year period, toward completion of the second of the two follow-up spans. This was succeeded in 1963 by another grant from NIMH (MH 07286) which, though focused on the development of a typology of delinquents referred to above, necessitated tabulation and interpretation of the already-gathered field data, together with the findings of *Unraveling Juvenile Delinquency*, as a basis on which to construct the sought-after typologies of delinquents.

It is always pleasant to acknowledge the aid received from our staff. We owe a special debt of gratitude to those members who have been actively connected with this research project in various capacities from its inception. To all these devoted associates we dedicate this volume: Mrs. Mildred P. Cunningham, case collator, a member of the staff from the time we began our work in 1925 until her retirement in 1963; Mr. George F. McGrath, who was associated with us for eighteen years as chief field investigator and who is now, we are proud to say, Commissioner of Correction of New York City; Mr. John E. Burke, who has been a skillful interviewer throughout the period of this project; Mrs. Rose W. Kneznek, our statistical consultant, who has supervised and checked the statistical details of this work; Mrs. Mary H. Moran, who has patiently consulted hundreds upon hundreds of case records in welfare agencies and gleaned information from various other recorded sources; Mrs. Sheila Murphrey, our administrative secretary, who also has been associated with the follow-up project from its beginnings and who has been patiently helpful in a variety of ways in connection with it.

We owe a debt also to Mr. A. Perry Holt, who carefully gathered the criminal record data from the courts of Massachusetts, and to other associates who have participated in one way or another in the preparation of the manuscript and in computational and other work, especially Miss Lillian Buller, our Research Assistant who joined our staff in 1960, Mrs. Ruth Banen, and Mrs. Ida Selkowitz.

We alone are responsible for the design of the research, its general supervision, the analysis of the case materials, and the interpretation of the findings.

Our gratitude extends not only to the members of our staff, but to a great many agencies, public and private, in and out of Massachusetts, with which we have had contact during the course of the research, by letter, by examination of their records, or by personal interviews. They are so numerous that we cannot possibly thank them all; but here in Massachusetts we want especially to express our appreciation to the Massachusetts Department of Correction, Massachusetts Department of Vital Statistics, Massachusetts Board of Probation, Massachusetts Department of Public Safety, Massachusetts Department of Mental Health, branches of the American Red Cross, Boston Social Service Index, Boston Department of Public Welfare, Family Society of Greater Boston, Boston Juvenile Court, the various District Courts and Probate Courts of Massachusetts, and the Suffolk Superior Court. The many probation and parole officers with whom interviews were held and who provided information from their records, we can hardly thank in person; their contributions, together with those of a great many others, have been vast.

There have also been a great many out-of-state agencies and individual sources of information. Here again we can only say a blanket "thank you." For example, there were out-of-state bureaus of vital statistics which sent us whatever information we asked for, many social service exchanges, many penal and correctional institutions, many departments of public welfare, police departments, the Army, the Navy, and a miscellany of public and private agencies. Some reflection of the extent of our contacts for information outside Massachusetts may be gleaned from the fact that inquiries went to 37 states, and even to Great Britain, Canada, and Mexico. The most numerous inquiries went to California (115), New York (112), New Hampshire (76), Florida (40), Illinois (35).

We have been fortunate indeed throughout the years to have the confidence of the public and private agencies with which we have had to deal, and to have been able to function with only very occasional and minor frustrations.

We are indebted to the Harvard Law School for sponsoring and housing our project and especially to Dean Erwin N. Griswold, for his recognition of the importance of the researches we are conducting into the causes, treatment, prediction, and prevention of juvenile delinquency.

This volume is divided into three parts:
One: As They Were as Boys
Two: As They Are as Men
Three: "The Past is Prologue."

Sheldon and Eleanor Glueck

Westengard House
Harvard Law School
Cambridge, Massachusetts

May 15, 1967

PART I   AS THEY WERE AS BOYS

"I grow daily to honor facts more and more, and theory less and less." — Carlyle

"It is certainly not the least charm of a theory that it is refutable." — Nietzsche

I Some Highlights of *Unraveling Juvenile Delinquency:* Parental Background

INTRODUCTORY

It is common knowledge that the great majority of children growing up in urban slums do *not* become delinquents despite the deprivations of a vicious environment, despite the fact that they and their parents have not had access to fruitful economic opportunities, despite the fact that they are swimming around in the same antisocial subculture in which delinquents and gang members are said to thrive.

Why?

Some light has been thrown on this question in a detailed and painstaking comparison of a sample of 500 white delinquents and 500 white nondelinquents — all boys — matched by residence in underprivileged areas, age, ethnic origin, and global intelligence. *All* of them spent their early years in highly underprivileged areas of Greater Boston. These were regions of much physical and moral deterioration and antisocial deviance.[1] They were usually adjacent to areas of industry and commerce; houses were dilapidated, rents low; there were dirty alleys; there was much economic dependency and downright poverty. But something which many recent writers on the causes and patterns of delinquency seem to shut their eyes to in the enthusiastic quest for some oversimplified, all-embracing, unilateral theory of etiology is illustrated by such facts as that *both* the delinquents and the nondelinquents of *Unraveling Juvenile Delinquency* were selected from such slum areas. This is evidenced by the closeness of the incidence of delinquency rates: 59% of the delinquents and 55% of the nondelinquents lived in neighborhoods in which the delinquency rate was 10–24.9 per thousand; 20% of the former and 23% of the latter came from regions in which the delinquency rate was 25–49.9 per thousand; and 15% of the antisocial boys and 17% of the youngsters in the control group resided in areas in which the delinquency rate was 50–100 per thousand.

In order to bring into focus certain other underlying sources of possible difference, the two sets of boys were originally also matched with respect to age, ethnico-racial distribution, and intelligence.

First, as to age: the delinquents averaged 14 years, 8 months, and the nondelinquents, 14 years, 6 months, when taken on for study, with an age range of 9 to 17 years. Second, as to ethnico-racial composition; a fourth of both groups were of English background; another fourth, Italian; a fifth, Irish; less than a tenth were old American, or Slavic, or French; smaller percentages were Near Eastern or Portuguese, Spanish, Scandinavian, German, or Jewish. The differences between the delinquents and the controls were negligible. Third, regarding intelligence, as measured by the Wechsler-Bellevue Test: the delinquents had an average I.Q. of 92; the nondelinquents, 94; and while 21 delinquents and 10 nondelinquents had intelligence quotients of under 70, only a few of each group rated over 120.

Obviously, the fact that 500 of these boys were persistent delinquents and 500 somehow managed to avoid delinquency in childhood cannot be attributed significantly to (a) residence in urban slum areas, (b) age differences, (c) ethnico-racial variation, or (d) significant variation in general intelligence.

What, then, is a set of reasonable explanations, one that accounts for the divergence in the behavior of the two groups of juveniles and also accounts, if we may anticipate the following chapters, for their *continued divergence* during adolescence and early adulthood?

BIOLOGICAL AND CULTURAL LEGACY OF THE PARENTS

To seek the answers to these questions, we first take a look into the families and homes in which the parents of the delinquents and those of the nondelinquents were themselves reared. From what kind of people did the parents of our two sets of boys spring? In what kind of environment were they reared? Such questions seem to us to be much more directly relevant than a search for the characteristics of a "delinquency subculture" or of slum or "ghetto" regions; for childhood maladjustments begin early in life, and the parents of our two sets of boys must have carried into the process of caring for and disciplining their children the ideational, emotional, spiritual, characterial, and behavioral residues of their own upbringing.

In certain respects, the families from which the parents came did not differ very much: both groups lived in conditions of poverty or near-poverty. Both sets of parents had been reared by fathers and mothers with little formal schooling. Moreover, little difference be-

4

tween the parental situation of the fathers and mothers of our delinquents and nondelinquents was established in respect to the presence of severe diseases (cancer, tuberculosis, diabetes, disorders of the cardiovascular system and renal system, syphilis, certain glandular disturbances, and diseases of the central nervous system). One or another of these serious ailments was found to have existed in over half the families of the fathers and mothers of both the delinquent and the nondelinquent boys.[2]

As to intelligence, a condition of varying grades of mental "dullness" (including occasional instances of diagnosed feeblemindedness) was found to be present in about a tenth of both delinquents' and nondelinquents' paternal families.

There were differences, however: while mental backwardness existed in one fourth of the delinquents' maternal families, it had been found in only one seventh of the nondelinquents' maternal families. More significantly however, such severe emotional abnormalities as psychoses, psychopathies, psychoneuroses, epilepsies, sex inversions, marked emotional instability, and pronounced temperamental deviation existed in one or more members of at least a fourth of the families from which the delinquents' fathers sprang, compared to but one-sixth of the nondelinquents' paternal families. The maternal families of the delinquents were also found to be far more pathological emotionally than those of the nondelinquents, the proportionate incidence being three-and-a-half to two.

Another microscopic look at possible explanations for the divergence of the two groups *ab initio* revealed that 37.0% of the fathers of the delinquents and 31.4% of the fathers of the nondelinquents had been reared in families in which one or more members were reported to have drunk to the point of intoxication, and 46.8% of the mothers of the delinquents, compared to 35.4% of the mothers of the nondelinquents, had been brought up in such homes.

The families in which the parents of our youngsters were reared were also not without criminalism. But this was definitely more prevalent in the homes of the delinquents' parents and considerably more so in the households of the boys' mothers than in the paternal family groups. Four out of ten of the fathers of the delinquents had their start in life in homes in which one or more of the immediate family group were delinquents or criminals, compared to 32.2% of the fathers of nondelinquents; and over half (54.8%) the maternal families of the former contained one or more criminalistic members, compared to 36.2% of the latter.

Here again we must pause to inquire whether residence of our boys in urban slum areas or in delinquency subcultures is more likely to explain the divergence between the delinquents and the nondelinquents than the differences noted in the families in which their parents were reared. Certainly, human experience suggests the hypothesis that, since the parents of our delinquents — especially the mothers — came from more sordid homes than did those of the nondelinquents — bad as these were — the childhood influences upon our delinquents must have had much to do with their maladjustments.

Not only the parental families, but the parents of the two groups of boys varied significantly.

PARENTAL MAKE-UP AND BEHAVIOR

First, we may ask how adequate the parents of the delinquents and nondelinquents were for marriage and parenthood; for these are matters which, again, experience suggests were very likely to determine the attitudes, standards, and conduct of the children whom they brought into the world. Laying aside certain factors in which the parents of the two groups were quite similar — very little schooling and age at marriage (half the mothers of both delinquents and nondelinquents were under 21) — we turn to significant differences.

While almost four in ten of the marriages of the delinquents' parents were "forced," almost three in ten of the marriages of the parents of the nondelinquents were also forced. Unexpected and often unwanted propulsion into marriage because of illegitimate pregnancy can hardly be regarded, even in these times of changing sex mores, as an auspicious beginning for the assumption of family responsibilities, especially the rearing of children.

As with the grandparents of our subjects, it was found that a far higher proportion of the mothers of the delinquents than of the nondelinquents suffered from serious physical ailments, intellectual retardation, emotional disturbances, drunkenness; and, during their girlhood years or later, an excessive percentage of the delinquents' mothers had committed offenses which society labels delinquent or criminal. So, also, the fathers of the delinquents were as a group more burdened with physical, intellectual, emotional, and behavioral disturbances than were the fathers of the nondelinquents.

Can it be doubted that such an array of handicaps to wholesome and intelligent parenthood leaves a deposit in the hearts and minds of children? It is to be noted that these influences left their mark long before the boys of our study spent much of their time in the streets with equally deprived children.

But there is more to the personality and character distortions imposed by the under-the-roof culture.

In coping with poverty and dependency, which burdened both sets of families, the greater inability of the parents of the delinquents to fulfill their familial obligations is also strikingly evident, adding one more significant datum to the strangely overlooked situation that it is not merely external environment, but the selective, differential response to it, that is involved in determining outcomes in terms of standards, attitudes, and behavior. Nine out of ten of the delinquents' families, compared to less than seven out of ten of the nondelinquents', called upon welfare agencies for financial aid. Moreover, apart from the equal proportion of families (almost one in six) in which the chief reason for financial help was the physical or mental illness of the breadwinner, the main cause for resort to outside aid in the families of delinquents was the unwillingness of the breadwinner to assume his responsibilities, while inadequacy of income stemming from general economic depression and seasonal unemployment mainly accounted for need of financial assistance in the families of nondelinquents. All this assumes greater significance in light of the fact that there was little difference among the two groups in the nature of the occupations of the principal breadwinners.[3]

Turning now to the more subtle aspects of family life, it was found that the families of the delinquents were far more inclined than those of the nondelinquents to live from hand to mouth and from day to day, borrowing without thought of their ability to reimburse and showing little comprehension of the need to limit expenditures to conform to their meager incomes. These irresponsible and budgetless expenditures involved not only food, rent, medical care and insurance, but installment purchasing.

The greater inadequacy of the delinquents' families compared to the others was noted also in more planlessness and confusion in daily living as reflected in irregularity of mealtimes and bedtimes of children, hours for doing home lessons, and the like: Almost twice as many families of the delinquents as of the nondelinquents were found to be completely slipshod in their way of life.

Regarding ambition and a sense of responsibility in the two groups of families — as revealed by the attitude of the elders toward protecting the good name of the family, by their embarrassment over irregularities in behavior and status of any members, and by preference for self-help as opposed to outside sources of financial aid — the families of the delinquents, with more than four in ten showing little evidence of family pride, were inferior to the families of the non-delinquents, among whom but one in ten was definitely lacking in the aforementioned attributes of self-respect.

Relatedly, concerning ambitiousness of the families — as reflected in realistic desires on the part of the parents that their children should have higher education, or that the family should move to a better neighborhood in order to remove the children from the excessive hazards of economically and morally blighted regions, or in saving to buy a house, or in plans to establish a small business — while it was found that both sets of families were inadequate in these respects, this was true of nine-tenths of the delinquents' families, compared to seven-tenths of the nondelinquents'.

Reviewing next the conduct standards of these homes, a marked contrast between those of the delinquents and those of the nondelin-quents was found. To determine behavior standards, evidences of immorality, alcoholism, and criminality were looked for among mem-bers of the family. As was true of their own parents, such unwhole-some practices were found to exist in a considerably higher propor-tion of the parents of the delinquents than of the nondelinquents: nine-tenths of the former had low conduct standards, compared to somewhat over five-tenths of the latter.

Since the tenor of family life is set by the parents and their relation-ship to one another, it is significant that for one in three of the delinquents' families, compared to only one in seven of those of the nondelinquents, the inharmonious relationship of the parents had resulted in an open breach, one or the other parent (usually the father) having left or deserted the family; and in another third of the delin-quents' families, compared to a fifth of the nondelinquents', the parents were in fact incompatible although no final separation had occurred.

Much has been written in recent years about the modern matriarchate, the dominant and domineering position of the mother in the American household. The families being described appear to follow the prevalent pattern, for in five-tenths of the families of both groups the mother was the obvious head, assuming in large measure the practical direction of the family — disciplining the children, controlling expenditures, and in general managing the household affairs. Yet many more of the delinquent boys were deprived of maternal supervision, a situation explainable by the fact that a greater proportion of delinquents' mothers worked outside the home in jobs which absorbed most of their energies. A much lower percentage of the delinquents' than of the nondelinquents' mothers arranged suitable supervision for their children during absences from home (fewer than one in ten, compared to two thirds). Some evidence of the laxity in supervision of the children is disclosed by the fact that as many as a third of the delinquent boys, as compared with a mere handful of the nondelinquents, were street beggars.

Maternal neglect and careless oversight of children are being more and more recognized as among the major sources of youthful maladjustment and delinquency and clearly the mothers of the delinquents were far more remiss in the care of their children than were the mothers of the control group.

FAMILY LIFE

In fewer of the families to which the delinquent boys belonged than in the others was there provision by the parents for recreational activities of the members as a group, such as going on picnics or to the beach together, visiting relatives, attending movies. Group recreational activities were not at all common among two thirds of the delinquents' families, in contrast to somewhat more than a third of the others. Such neglect of opportunities to develop family solidarity and a community of interests must tend to increase the likelihood of "go-it-alone" conduct which shows little regard for the family and its wishes.

Reliance of the delinquent boys upon their own devices for their frequently antisocial recreational outlets was aggravated by the failure of their parents to give any serious thought to making the home attractive enough to encourage the children to bring in their playmates; for only two in ten of the delinquents' families, compared to almost four in ten of the nondelinquents', were hospitable to their children's friends. The greater inclination of the delinquents to derive security from gang membership may well be partially attributable to the unattractiveness and inhospitality of their homes.

There is already evidence that the forces of disruption found excessively in the families of the delinquents were greater and stronger than those making for cohesiveness. In addition, it should be pointed out that less than two in ten of the families of the delinquents, compared to six in ten of the families of the control group, evinced strong and steady affectional ties among the members, shared joint interests, took pride in their homes, and felt themselves to be "one for all and all for one." Thus, in the highly important quality that is both expressive of loyalty to the blood group and supportive of the individual in his sense of security and in devotion to others, the delinquents were far more deprived than the nondelinquents.

By now the definitely poorer quality of the family life of the delinquents must be evident. There was less effective household management and routine, less cultural refinement; parents were less self-respecting and less ambitious to improve their social and economic status or that of their children; conduct standards were much lower in the homes in which the delinquents were reared. Nor was the quality of family life of the delinquent boys as wholesome as that of the nondelinquents in regard to the relationships between the parents, supervision of the children, provision for recreation in the home, and, especially, closeness of family ties.

With all this evidence, amply supported by thorough investigation and collation of medical and social data from many sources, it seems surprising that so many writers on Criminology continue to attribute all or most criminogenic influences to the characteristics of the urban slums or a delinquency subculture. Can it be doubted that the human environment inside the homes in which the delinquent boys grew up was far less conducive to the rearing of wholesome, happy, and law-abiding children than that in which the nondelinquents were reared? Since the two groups of youngsters had been matched at the outset, not only with respect to age and general intelligence (traits involving only the boys themselves), but also with respect to ethnico-racial derivation and residence in underprivileged urban neighborhoods, the differences between the families of the delinquents and those of the nondelinquents revealed in the foregoing analysis[4] are all the more significant.

However, even the array of facts presented above, disclosing the poorer quality of family life, is not sufficient to account for the dismal destination of the delinquent children; for it will be recalled that quite a number of nondelinquent boys had been reared under equally unfavorable conditions. In order to achieve a more comprehensive explanation — and there is more information both about the families and the boys that can add to understanding — one should assuredly view the boys in their principal theaters of action: the home, the school, the neighborhood. But before considering the make-up and conduct of the two sets of youths, it is in order to take a look at a few family statistics about the parents.

HOME LIFE

With respect to one factor frequently mentioned as significant in contributing to delinquency — the conflict of cultures between native-born children and foreign-born parents — the two sets of families were essentially similar; at least one of the parents of six-tenths of both delinquents and nondelinquents had been born abroad and had resided in America for similar lengths of time. Thus, potentials for conflict between the foreign culture of the parents and the local culture of their American-born sons — as reflected in the boys' rebellion over the exclusive use of a foreign language in the home, over foreign customs, traditions, disciplinary practices, cookery, and the like — evidently played little or no role in criminogenesis.[5]

It has frequently been stated that delinquents stem from larger families than nondelinquents. On the whole, our delinquents did come from somewhat larger families, the average being seven children as compared to six in the households of the control group.[6] The greater number of children in the homes of the delinquents is explainable partially by the fact that a higher proportion of one or the other of their parents had remarried.[7]

Only children, first-born children, and youngest children are said to be especially vulnerable to the development of behavioral difficulties, because they are in a pampered position in the family constellation. However, *lower* proportions of the delinquent group than of the nondelinquent were found to be in these supposedly vulnerable categories.

Although there was little difference in the size of the households of which the two groups of boys were a part, there was in fact somewhat more crowding of living quarters in the delinquents' homes. It seems reasonable to infer that this resulted in greater likelihood of emotional tension and friction; that it meant loss of privacy, and thereby might have induced sexual and other emotional shocks. Actually, 32.6% of the homes of the delinquents as contrasted with 24.8% of the homes of the nondelinquents were overcrowded as determined by the fact that three or more persons shared a bedroom; while at the other extreme, only 8.5% of the homes of the delinquents as contrasted with 14.8% of the homes of the nondelinquents provided a bedroom for each member.

The stability of the early home is one of the most significant social factors to be looked into from the point of view of wholesome family life; for here are involved a child's insecurities, confusions about standards of behavior, and other interferences with efforts at adaptation.

Uprooting is bound to make excessive demands upon powers of adaptation; it raises fears and doubts regarding parental reliability, understanding, protection, affection, and one's relationship to the authoritarian adult world and to the suggestions and taunts of one's peers.

Before presenting the findings, it should be stated that we defined a stable household as one in which preferably both parents, but at least one, remained in unbroken physical and affectional relationship to the children except for brief and expectable absences. The measure of household instability was determined by the number of removals of a boy from the particular family group of which he was naturally a part — that is, the home of his parents — or in the event of disruption of the home because of death, desertion, separation, divorce, and the like, the home of the remaining parent, usually the mother.[8] By this standard there is no question but that, generally speaking, the delinquents grew up in a far less stable setting than did the nondelinquents, for a much higher proportion of them than of the control group (half the former, in contrast to only a tenth of the latter) were exposed to one or more radical household changes. No fewer than six out of every ten homes of the delinquents, compared to three and one-half in ten of those of the nondelinquents, had been broken by separation, divorce, death, or the prolonged absence of the parents; and somewhat over half these among the delinquents (56.8%) and somewhat less than half these among the nondelinquents (47.3%) were still under five years of age when the initial break occurred. It is probable that the first definitive breach in the organic structure of the family is crucial, because it is likely to deal the greatest emotional blow to a child's conception of the solidarity and reliability of the parental team and to disrupt his general sense of security as well as of family stability. In some cases, also, a breach in the family pattern may seriously distort the process of emotional-intellectual identification of a boy with his father as a hero-ideal.

In respect to the causes of disruption of the family circle, too, the delinquents' families presented a much more dismal picture than did those of the control group; for in every type of family breach there was an excess among the homes of the delinquents, the principal causes being abandonment of the boy at birth or shortly thereafter by unmarried parents, desertion of the family by one or both parents, temporary separation of the parents, prolonged imprisonment of a parent. Among the nondelinquents the initial family fracture resulted more typically from death of a parent, separation or divorce, or hospitalization. Moreover, as the years passed, there was a more rapid disintegration of the families of the delinquents. Only half the group of delinquents had the normal experience of being reared continuously by both or one of their own parents, in contrast to nine-tenths of the control group.

Such findings reveal the greater instability of the family matrix of the boys who got into trouble with the law, and again reflect the more extensive and intensive emotional handicaps under which they grew up and which, as it were, readied them for irresponsible and defiant behavior.

Not unrelated to the foregoing is an aspect of family life that perhaps transcends in significance even those malign conditions already noted: namely, the affectional relationships between parents and children. There is no doubt that a warm tie between father and son is of great consequence in inducing a boy to develop a set of ideals and standards through the process of emotional-intellectual "identification." Should the boy–father bond not be close, the growing child may seek a substitute in companionship with other disadvantaged children in the streets; or he may pass through a stage of grave puzzlement and insecurity, of frustration or resentment, with resultant psychoneurotic symptoms. It is therefore highly revealing that only four out of every ten of the fathers of the delinquents, in contrast to eight in ten of the fathers of the control group, evinced warmth, sympathy, and consistent affection toward their boys.

So, also, a substantially lower percentage of the mothers of the delinquents (72.1%, compared with 95.5% of the nondelinquents' mothers) held their sons in affectional warmth. And while one out of four of the delinquents' mothers showed clear evidence of being cripplingly overprotective of the boys, this was true of only one in seven of the other mothers. Also, a far higher proportion of the mothers of the delinquents than of the nondelinquents were openly indifferent or hostile to the boys, often to the point of rejection.

Since parent–child relations are a two-way emotional street, it is important to note the affectional attitudes of the boys toward their parents. There is widespread acceptance nowadays of the Freudian formulation of the role of close affectional ties between parents and children and the favorable or unfavorable "solution" of that well-known family triangle, the "Oedipus situation," as constituting the very root of personality formation. "It is clear," write English and Pearson, "why Freud says that the Oedipus situation is the nuclear complex of all the neuroses. The reaction pattern which the little boy forms to solve these difficult relations with his parents, particularly with his father, serves as the pattern for all his future human relations, whether in the field of love or of business competition. If the solution has been healthy, so will his future human relationships be healthy and be undertaken in the light of their reality. If the solution has been unhealthy, he will approach his future relationships with an unhealthy pattern and meet them by this rather than by an intelligent understanding of the real situation."[9] But whether one accepts or rejects the Freudian formulation, the emotional attitude of a boy toward his parents is a strong indicator of his personality. In this respect, the findings assume great significance; for a far lower proportion of the delinquents than of the nondelinquents (some one-third, as contrasted with two-thirds) were found to have close affectional ties to their fathers; and fewer delinquents than nondelinquents had an affectional attachment to their mothers (two-thirds as compared with nine-tenths).

As has been noted, dynamic psychiatry teaches that the process of identification of the growing boy with his father, whom he consciously or unconsciously tries to emulate, is highly significant in the development of personality and character. The extent to which a boy's father was acceptable as a figure with whom to identify is revealed in the finding that fewer than two out of ten of the delinquents, as contrasted with more than half the nondelinquents, considered the father to be the kind of man that the boy himself would like to be, and had respect for the father's vocational and social standing as well as some sort of common understanding with him.

As to siblings, in three out of ten of the delinquent group compared to less than one in ten of the nondelinquent, the brothers and sisters were indifferent or openly hostile to the boy.

Psychiatrists and psychologists, and more and more juvenile court judges, realize the extent to which a child's attitudes and deportment are influenced by his feeling, justified or not, of the genuineness of his parents' interest in his well-being. Whatever the outward manifestations of interest may be, it is the feeling of the authenticity of the parental concern, its abiding affectional motivation, and its sincerity that leave a wholesome precipitate in the structure of personality and character. It is particularly striking that, while only about two in ten of the delinquents felt that their mothers and fathers were genuinely concerned about them, the far larger proportion of seven in ten nondelinquents were confident of their parents' interest.

Objective evidence of the lesser concern of the delinquents' parents is reflected in the vagueness of their plans for the youngsters' future: in more than six out of ten of the delinquent group, as compared with four in ten of the parents of the nondelinquents, parents had devoted no thought to this all-important matter. Further evidence of the lesser concern of the parents of the delinquent group for the welfare of the boys derives from the discrepancy between the information given the psychiatrist by the boys themselves as to how they used their leisure and that given by their parents (usually the mother) to the field investigators. Either the delinquents' parents knew far less about how the boys spent their spare time or preferred not to admit that their sons' habits were bad or that they were running around with questionable companions. The home investigators got the distinct impression that the parents of the delinquents were actually unaware of many of the boys' activities.

A further reflection of wholesome or unwholesome parent–child relationships is seen in the disciplinary attitudes and practices of mothers and fathers. These parental initiatives are important in directing children toward clear and consistent guidelines of right and wrong and the varying consequences of different types of behavior. But apart from this process of socialization through definition of moral-legal prohibitions, unsuitable disciplinary practices may have serious results in the development of a child's personality, character, and habit systems. Inconsistency between the parents in disciplining a child, excessive anger, unfairness, or other forms of overemotional response to the numerous peccadilloes normally engaged in by children during the early years when they are testing a developing sense of power may be baneful sources of emotional distortion and ultimately result in ambivalence toward or defiance of the authority of the parents and later of school and law.

Here, again, the delinquents were excessively handicapped in that they were victims of far more permissiveness on the part of their mothers than were the nondelinquents: 56.8%, compared to 11.7% of the mothers paid little attention to the boy's misbehavior; and only a handful (4.2%) of the delinquents' mothers, in sharp contrast to 65.6% of the nondelinquents', met the happy and wholesome standard of both firmness and kindliness in their disciplinary practices. The fathers were generally more inclined than the mothers to be overstrict with the boys, this being true of one-fourth of the delinquents' fathers and less than one tenth of the nondelinquents'. Inconsistent disciplinary practices were more than twice as prevalent among the fathers of the delinquents as among the other fathers (41.6% vs. 17.9%).

An outstanding difference between the disciplinary practices of the delinquents' and nondelinquents' parents was found in the considerably greater resort of the former to physical punishment and the lesser extent to which they calmly reasoned with the boy about his misconduct. There is a reciprocal mechanism here: it may well be that the delinquent boys, being so continuously involved in acts of misconduct, called forth more rigid or more impulsive and erratic controls on the part of the parents.

SUMMARY AND COMMENT

Although in respect to poverty and lack of formal schooling the grandparents of our two sets of boys were very similar, the families of the delinquents' parents were more extensively characterized than those of the nondelinquents' by mental retardation, emotional disturbances, drunkenness, and criminalism.

Apart from these differences in the grandparental well-springs, the qualitative deficiencies in the immediate families of the delinquents are reflected in a lesser capacity of the fathers to earn an honest living, in less effective household management, in less refinement of cultural atmosphere, in less self-respect on the part of the parents, in less adequate oversight of the children, and in weaker family ties.

More of the delinquents than of the control group were victims of the indifference or downright hostility of their parents; and they, in turn, were less attached to their parents. This greater emotional deprivation of the boys who developed into delinquents is reflected also in a more frequently expressed feeling on their part that their parents were not concerned about their welfare. Not nearly so many of the delinquents as of the control group identified with or sought to emulate their fathers. Disciplinary practices were more erratic, and physical punishment was more frequent, among the delinquents' fathers and more lax among their mothers. Fewer of both parents of the delinquents than of the nondelinquents met a desirable disciplinary standard of firmness accompanied by kindness and lack of temper.

Other significant differences between the personal and familial backgrounds were noted in the preceding pages; but from this brief summary, there is considerable evidence at the very threshold of the inquiry, for the inference that the lawbreakers, far more than the control group of nondelinquents, derived from a family background and were reared in a home atmosphere not conducive to development of emotionally-integrated, happy youngsters, conditioned to obey legitimate authority in school and society.

Notes

1. Clifford H. Shaw, in *Delinquency Areas* (University of Chicago Press, 1929), long ago pointed out that "High [delinquency] rates occur in the areas which are characterized by physical deterioration and declining populations.

The areas in which the greatest concentrations and highest rates are found have many characteristics which differentiate them from the outlying residential communities. . . . these areas are in a process of transition from residence to business and industry and are characterized by physical deterioration, decreasing population, and the disintegration of the conventional neighborhood culture and organization." *Ibid.*, pp. 203 and 204.

2. Complete data were impossible to secure because records pertaining to the older generation had not been kept as adequately by hospitals, courts, and social agencies as are those of more recent years, and because data obtainable regarding relatives born and reared abroad were not sufficiently reliable. While not always seeking information about every member of the family group, we made a determined effort to search for positive evidence of the presence of serious physical and mental disorders in at least one member. The intensity and extent of the search for such family data were the same for the nondelinquents as for the delinquents. See Sheldon and Eleanor Glueck, *Unraveling Juvenile Delinquency* (New York: The Commonwealth Fund, 1950; Cambridge, Mass.: Harvard University Press, 1951), chap. V, "Exploring Family and Personal Background."

3. Few of the fathers were engaged in a business of their own, or were in clerical positions, or in such public utility services as motorman, mailman, and the like. A third were unskilled laborers; a tenth were truck drivers or teamsters; less than a third had skilled or semiskilled occupations.

4. The above analysis is a condensation of much of the family background materials of *Unraveling Juvenile Delinquency*, but certain data have been omitted for the present purpose.

5. There are, of course, other sources of culture conflict than those deriving from the foreign background of the parents.

6. Although many other variables, such as religious persuasion, economic underprivilege, and immigrant parentage, may partially account for the size of families, this is less likely to be so in the study on which *Unraveling Juvenile Delinquency* is based than in the usual researches on size of family, since the delinquents and nondelinquents had been matched at the outset in respect to ethnico-racial derivation and residence in underprivileged areas.

7. Almost a third of the delinquents, compared to half that proportion of the nondelinquents, had half- or step-brothers and -sisters.

8. If a boy was removed from the home of his own parents to live in a foster home for more than a brief period (a few days to a few months), or if he was sent to live with relatives for more than a short time under circumstances representing a break with home ties, this was deemed a household change. Temporary departures from home — on vacation, or brief commitment to a penocorrectional institution or to a hospital for treatment of a physical or mental condition — were not looked upon as a breach with the original household.

9. O. S. English and G. H. J. Pearson, *Common Neuroses of Children and Adults* (New York: W. W. Norton, 1937), p. 38.

II Some Highlights of *Unraveling Juvenile Delinquency:* Characteristics of Delinquents and Nondelinquents

INTRODUCTORY

In seeking the answer to the question why some children of families subjected to the pressures of underprivileged urban regions develop a tendency to antisocial behavior while others manage to comply essentially with the rules of society and law, one must not confine the inquiry to a study of intellectual and personality traits. Such characteristics do not express themselves in a human vacuum. They are at least partially anchored in bodily constitution; they are not all due to life's experiences. The bodily constitution is, moreover, not only basic but first in point of time in the history of the individual.

While it is risky to generalize about the exact participation of heredity and environment in the end-product of human personality and character, it may safely be said that bodily constitution embraces the more fixed and permanent core of the human being (anatomically and physiologically); and in essential structure it is probably determined genetically, although affected, also, by early intra- or extra-uterine environmental influences.

But, in addition to body type, certain findings from psychologic (especially Rorschach) and psychiatric tests and interviews are relevant to an adequate assessment of the two sets of youths we are concerned with. For details and supporting data the reader is referred to *Unraveling Juvenile Delinquency* and two derivative works: *Physique and Delinquency*[1] and *Family Environment and Delinquency*.[2] In the present work we present a bare outline of the materials as part of the necessary briefing preliminary to setting forth the data of the follow-up investigations of the two sets of human beings under comparison.

BODY BUILD

Do our delinquents differ significantly in physical composition from the nondelinquents? And, if so, how?[3]

Comparison of the physiques of the 500 delinquents and 500 non-delinquents disclosed certain findings that cannot be ignored in any comprehensive analysis of the etiologic roots involved in delinquency, just as the under-the-roof culture of the two sets of boys cannot be ignored. First, as a group, the law-violating boys have sturdier bodies than the law-abiding ones. Second, their bodily structure is more harmonious. Third, they are generally somewhat more masculine. Most important, if one reflects on the anthropologic findings regarding bodily indices and physique types, one is forced to the conclusion that the majority of persistent juvenile delinquents tend to be of the *mesomorphic* (muscular, well-knit) type. This is important not only in itself but because the various physique types into which human beings can be classified[4] tend to be related to certain traits and factors which can be plotted along a biosocial continuum.[5] When certain characteristics especially conducive to the commission of antisocial acts are found, for example, to characterize mesomorphs, this constitutional type *and* the related traits must somehow be involved in etiology, though several stages removed from the acts of persistent delinquency. To illustrate: it was found that the mesomorphic physique type is more highly characterized by such traits suitable to aggressive acts as physical strength, energy, insensitivity, the tendency to express tensions and frustrations in action; and the mesomorphic type was also found to be relatively free from such *inhibitions* to antisocial adventures as feelings of inadequacy, marked submissiveness to authority, emotional instability, and the like.[6]

It is not unreasonable to assume that the basic reason for the excess of mesomorphs among delinquents may be that boys of predominantly mesomorphic physique are endowed with traits that equip them especially for a delinquent role when under the pressure of malign sociocultural conditions, while endomorphs (to cite a body type in which the incidence of delinquents and nondelinquents in our samples is similar), being less energetic and less likely to act out their drives, have a lower *delinquency potential* than mesomorphs. True, other traits investigated, such as aggressiveness, adventurousness, acquisitiveness — although etiologically involved in the end-product of delinquency — do not vary significantly in incidence among body types. Nevertheless, boys who possess certain other characteristics, such as excessive energy and a tendency to act out tensions, frustrations, feelings of aggression, thirst for adventure, acquisitive impulses, and the like, are especially prone to delinquency, particularly if they live in the exciting and culturally deprived regions of underprivileged urban areas.

But there are other characteristics of the two sets of boys we are discussing that may also be relevant to etiology.

HEALTH

No clinical study of delinquents is deemed complete without a physical examination, but the reason for requiring exploration into the health of maladjusted youth is not always clear. It is obvious that there may be endocrinologic and other deficiencies related to symptoms of fatigue, irritability, and the like; or sensory or muscular handicaps, which have not only a physiologic but a psychologic significance for attitude and behavior. Apart from this, there are special emotional attributes, such as the frequently alluded to "inferiority complex," with its over-compensatory reactive behavior, which may be significant in analyzing the roots of maladjustment and delinquency.

At all events, the aim in *Unraveling Juvenile Delinquency* was to leave no stone unturned in the baffling search for the roots and dynamics of causation.[7] Summarizing the chief findings of the medical examination which was given to both groups of boys by a competent physician-psychiatrist on the staff,[8] it was found that the view that delinquents are in poorer health than nondelinquents from similar general environments is not justified; little difference was discovered on standard physical examination between the two groups.

With respect to their health as infants and young children, no differences between the two sets of boys were revealed from careful inquiry of their mothers and consultation of early medical records, except for the two important facts that a considerably higher proportion of the delinquents were reported to have been enuretic and extremely restless (hyperkinetic) children. In their susceptibility to disease and infection and their immunity to contagious diseases, the two groups resembled each other.

More significant, and in harmony with the low incidence of ectomorphs among the delinquents, a *lower* percentage of them than of the control group of nondelinquents were found to have various neurologic handicaps (63.7% vs. 72.7%).

Although there is no over-all difference between the two groups in observable evidences of functional deviations, a few differences in the incidence of certain of these deviations might be mentioned: tics and ambidexterity are less prevalent among the delinquents (3.0% vs.

8.4%), while extreme nailbiting is more characteristic of them (21.4% vs. 15.6%).

INTELLIGENCE

It will be recalled that at the outset of the inquiry into the differences and similarities between the 500 delinquent boys and 500 nondelinquents we matched the two groups, pair by pair, in respect to *general* (global) intelligence. The 500 pairs encompassed a wide range of intelligence quotients. Thus, 140 of the delinquents and 152 of the nondelinquents had an I.Q. of 100 or over on the Wechsler-Bellevue Full Scale Intelligence Test; at the other end of the scale, 359 of the former and 346 of the latter ranged downward in I.Q. from 99 to 60. The average intelligence quotient of the two groups was 92 for the delinquents and 94 for the nondelinquents.[9]

Yet the two sets of boys could well differ in respect to the specific skills and abilities that enter into the composition of global intelligence, and it was indeed found that there were differences in respect to the *composition* of global intelligence. These were determined through application of the Wechsler-Bellevue Test and, in part, of the Rorschach Test. It was found that the delinquent group was somewhat more apt in those intellectual tasks in which the approach to meaning is by direct physical relationships with a minimal dependence on intermediate symbols or abstract thinking. This may in part explain their inferior school achievement and their more general dislike of the usual classroom tasks. Also, the delinquents were found to be more erratic in their intellectual capacities than the more consistent and steady nondelinquents.

While the two groups tend to resemble each other in many of the more qualitative and creative expressions of intelligence (such as originality, intuition, phantasy), they differ somewhat in others which would seem to be closely associated with capacity or incapacity to make adequate conventional adjustments to the demands of social life. Thus, fewer delinquents than nondelinquents have adequate powers of observation and fewer show a potential capacity for objective interests; and to a greater extent than the control group, the delinquents are unrealistic thinkers, lack "common sense," and are unmethodical in approaching their problems. Reflection upon these differences, especially the ones involving the deeper intellectual tendencies of the two groups, suggests that such strivings are the ones which are especially interwoven with deep-rooted emotional dynamics. They are, therefore, the very mental tendencies likely to be involved not only in ability to cope with ordinary school tasks but also in the general processes of socialization and adjustment to the realistic demands of life.

PSYCHIATRIC SIZE-UP

To the experienced and skillful psychiatrist, children often reveal their emotional stresses and strains much more readily than do adults. Through long experience in interviewing boys, the psychiatric member of our staff had developed a special flair for gaining quick and sympathetic rapport with the boys.

The aim of this portion of the inquiry was to obtain as objective an estimate of the emotional make-up of the 500 delinquent and 500 nondelinquent boys as could be revealed by the psychiatrist's diagnostic art. Therefore, following the original plan of the research to avoid possible circular reasoning, the psychiatrist, in interviewing the boys, did not have access to data about them from other areas of the inquiry.

Briefly, the lawbreakers were found to function on a less efficient level and were less stable emotionally than the nondelinquents. At the same time, they were more dynamic and energetic; more aggressive, adventurous, suggestible, and stubborn. This combination is likely to result in inability or unwillingness to abide by the law's restrictions; for such boys were much inclined to impulsive, unreflective discharge of their energy drives, thereby breaking through the bonds imposed upon them by societal custom and law but not adequately internalized by them. Certain sources of motivation can get such boys into troublesome conflict with society's codes. The delinquents were, for example, much more inclined than the other boys to immediate indulgence of their appetites and were more eager to acquire material possessions.

To such a system of internal forces, which impels toward self-centered satisfaction of impulse irrespective of the prohibitions of custom and law, should be added the finding that basic personality orientations among the delinquents made it more difficult for them to conform to acceptable standards. As a group, they were found to be less conventional than the law-abiding boys, and not nearly so conscientious in achieving their goals. They were also, as already noted, less realistic in facing situations; less practical in considering the feasibility of a contemplated course of conduct; far less critical of themselves and, correspondingly, more self-centered.

Moreover, as we have seen, there is much more in the family background of the delinquents than of the nondelinquents that is stress-producing, so that a far higher proportion of them than of the other boys displayed emotional tensions arising from faulty father–son or mother–son relationships. More of the delinquents than of the boys of the control group had marked conflicts arising out of faulty adjustment of their problems of sexual identification, out of poor relations with companions, out of inability to make a satisfactory compromise between ambition and reality, and out of feelings of inferiority. Significantly, the delinquents tended to resolve their mental struggles through "acting out" their difficulties (extroversive behavior), the nondelinquents through turning them inward (introversion).

These psychiatric findings, so obviously related to the mechanisms tending to inadequate and improper social adjustment, are in general harmony with those revealed independently by the other avenues of exploration. Standing alone, they are highly suggestive hints — though not complete explanations — of why one set of boys inclined to persistent delinquency, while the other, in similar external environmental settings, managed somehow to get along acceptably. When fitted into the total picture, they gain significantly in etiologic relevancy. They tend not only to show that there is much more to the causal explanation of delinquency than indiscriminate and nondiscriminating attribution of etiology to "living in slums," or the "deprivation of opportunity," or other generalized external cultural matrices, but they tend also to confirm, in many respects, the findings derived from the deep-probing Rorschach personality-character tests.

PERSONALITY-CHARACTER STRUCTURE

It is often taken for granted that the way a person gets along in life is almost wholly dependent on his "brains,' that is, his intelligence. But probings of the mainsprings of conduct and social relations tend more and more to stress the role of temperamental and emotional forces in the development of personality and character[10] and the channeling of conduct. Intelligence is of course a powerful instrument of adaptation and for the solution of life's problems; but the way a person *employs* his intellect depends a great deal on the deeper dynamics of the organism — the ebb and flow of feelings, the trends, thrusts, and tensions of emotion that pull the levers behind the scenes of personality and character. So it becomes of the utmost importance to obtain insights into the subsurface forces that influence individual make-up and behavior tendencies. To some extent this has been done in the foregoing section on the psychiatric diagnoses of the boys. There are other techniques for plumbing the depths of psychic structure and dynamics:

psychoanalysis, hypnoanalysis, narcoanalysis and others. A systematic and relatively simple means, however, is furnished by a number of "projective tests," including the Rorschach Test, selected at the time our research was decided upon as most suited to the purpose.

In earlier pages, in which the bodily types of delinquents and non-delinquents were compared, the concern was with biologic and essentially hereditary traits, and with a great variety of sociocultural forces that played upon the basic organism of the boys. Now we shall draw in the dynamic emotional moorings of personality and character revealed by the Rorschach Test. For the personality and characterial traits revealed by such a test are, in a sense, the admixtures of the interplay of original endowment and repeated experiences, particularly those of the first few affectively charged years of life.

The Rorschach Test consists of ten symmetrical ink-blots (most of them black, some colored) which look as if they had been made by throwing drops of ink on a paper and folding it in the middle, this resulting in a design often reminiscent of a butterfly. Through long clinical employment of the test on various groups of persons in different countries, its significance has been found to be fairly dependable in revealing the inner mental life; it has established its value as a prober of personality and character. The subject's reaction to the blots is projected out of the depths of his personality without his being able successfully to disguise his inner feelings and emotional attitudes. These responses are then scored according to a standard scheme and interpreted by a skilled psychologist, in respect to *apperception* — that is, the subject's general size-up of the blots, the *quality* of his reactions, and their *content*.[11] The subject is scored on these various aspects of his responses in accordance with established standards, and his score is tabulated to yield a Rorschach *psychogram*, which provides a panoramic view of his temperamental-emotional topography, including both surface and subsurface features. In other words, the diagnosis is not based upon any single response; it is the patterning of responses that is significant. The Rorschach Test thus projects the deeper, often subconscious, elements of mental activity in such a manner that to the expert they reveal highly significant features of structure, tensions, and dynamics of personality and character.

Briefly summarizing the results of comparisons of the delinquents and the control group in respect to the Rorschach Test, the first category is that of basic attitudes toward authority and society; and in the traits here encompassed, it was found that the delinquents were markedly distinguishable from the law-abiding boys by their unwillingness or inability to tame their natural impulses toward self-indulgent behavior in order to bring their drives into line with the authoritative demands of the home, the school, and the larger society. While only slightly more self-assertive than the nondelinquents, the boys who got into trouble were found to be far more socially defiant, far less submissive, and more ambivalent, to authority.

In regard to feelings of insecurity, anxiety, inferiority, frustration, a significantly higher proportion of the delinquents than of the control group were found to be subject to feelings of not being recognized or appreciated, and of resentment. However, the delinquents as a group had an appreciably *lower* incidence of other handicapping emotional attitudes, such as feelings of anxiety or insecurity, of helplessness, of fear of failure.

Surprisingly little difference was found between the two groups in the degree to which they felt unwanted or unloved, or not taken care of, or not being taken seriously. It may be that, in the rough and tough milieu in which the two sets of boys lived, such feelings are quite common among children. While this situation is to be deplored and ought certainly to be coped with in a responsible society, the similar incidence among delinquents and nondelinquents of such emotional attitudes makes it unlikely that they have any close causal relationship to persistent delinquency, although they may act as differentiative catalytic agents when other psychologic factors are brought into play.

With respect to kindliness and hostility, it was found that the delinquent boys were markedly less cooperative in their relationships with those with whom they were closely associated; a substantially greater proportion of them than of the nondelinquents had conscious or unconscious hostile impulses; they were more suspicious of the motives of others; they were more destructive. And more of the delinquents than of the nondelinquents were armed with an exaggeratedly defensive attitude toward life.

As to traits subsumed under the heading of dependence and independence, it was found that the delinquents felt far less dependent than did the nondelinquents; they were less conforming, far less conventional, and more confident of their ability to handle their own problems.

As to the goals of strivings, it was found that the law violators as a group were more narcissistic, more orally receptive (parasitic), and more destructive-sadistic (cruel) than the boys who conformed to the legal order. Correlatively, the delinquents were far less masochistic (self-punishing) than the law-abiding boys.

With respect to certain general qualities of personality, the delinquents again were found to possess qualities which made it difficult for them to adapt to society's prohibitions. They were considerably more impulsive and vivacious than the law-abiding boys, less self-controlled, and they tended to act out their emotional tensions.

Finally, it was apparent that there were some differences between delinquents and nondelinquents in the extent and nature of mental abnormality or pathology.[12] A somewhat higher proportion of the law-breakers than of the law-abiding youngsters were found to have a mental abnormality of one kind or another (51.4% vs. 44.3%). Many more delinquents than boys in the control group were described by the Rorschach analysis as "poorly adjusted, asocial, poorly adapted," or "primitive," apart from their acts of delinquency (16.9% vs. 5.9%). On the other hand, neither definite psychoses nor disturbances of the central nervous system played a significant role in the lives of these two sets of boys. Although it is often claimed that many delinquents are "psychopathic"[13] or show marked trends toward such a condition, only 7.3% of the delinquents and 0.4% of the nondelinquents were so diagnosed.[14]

Severe neuroticism was found to exist in only 3.2% of the delinquents and 5.1% of the other boys. However, mild neuroticism (a condition in which the neurosis does not prevent the individual from quite efficient and not too painful social adaptation) was found among 16.3% of the former and 23.2% of the latter; and youths with distinct neurotic trends but not classifiable in the two former categories amounted to 5.1% among the delinquents and 7.5% among the nondelinquents. Totaling the boys diagnosed as markedly or mildly neurotic, or with neurotic trends, it becomes clearer that there is less neuroticism among the delinquents than among the control group (24.6% vs. 35.8%).

To summarize the findings of the Rorschach Test, it is clear that the delinquents possessed to an excessive degree certain traits and tendencies likely to interfere with adequate and wholesome adjustment to the requirements of the social order. In much greater proportion than their nondelinquent counterparts they were defiant, and they were ambivalent toward or nonsubmissive to authority. They were more resentful. They were far more hostile, suspicious, and destructive. The goals of their drives were to a far greater extent both parasitic and destructive-sadistic. They were definitely more impulsive and less self-controlled. They were far less cooperative and markedly less conventional in their ideas, feelings, and behavior than the nondelinquents.

Some of the traits possessed in excess by the delinquents are of a kind which, if guided into socially acceptable channels, are far from undesirable. Such characteristics as a tendency to "act out" their difficulties (extroversion), greater freedom from fear of failure and defeat, and less dependence on others, might, under proper circumstances and influential guidance, be assets rather than liabilities.

SUMMARY

The variations in physique type and derivative traits, and the marked differences in incidence of so many of the personality-character traits of boys growing up in underprivileged urban areas should convince the reader that, while the study of environmental pressures is important, examination of how and why different children respond to these external pressures is indispensable. It is not alone exposure to unwholesome environmental experiences that can explain delinquency, but rather what these experiences mean, selectively, in the shaping of personality and character and the canalizing or sublimating of primitive impulses.

If one reflects on the differences between the two groups of boys in their basic character traits, it becomes apparent that these variations are not altogether haphazard but tend to fall into a general, meaningful personality pattern, despite the fact that there are hints here and there of subpatterns. Among the delinquents, they form themselves into a cluster of associated energy-expressing and emotion-discharging characteristics of the uninhibited, untamed, unreflective child; and there is little mystery about the "causes" of persistent maladapted behavior when one considers the ease with which modern urban conditions supply the theater of action for boys of this nature.

However, one must not ignore the familial backgrounds which helped to differentiate between the two sets of boys. All these influences contribute to the distinction between the two, and one would make a serious mistake to reach for some simple general abstraction to account for this.

Notes

1. Sheldon and Eleanor Glueck (New York: Harper, 1956; New York: Kraus Reprint, 1965).

2. Sheldon and Eleanor Glueck (London: Routledge & Kegan Paul; Boston: Houghton Mifflin, 1962).

3. As a basis for this part of the original inquiry, full-length photographs (front, side, rear) of the 500 delinquents and 500 nondelinquents were taken. (For detailed method of taking the photographs and of analyzing them anthropologically, see *Unraveling Juvenile Delinquency*, Appendix C, p. 307, prepared by Carl C. Seltzer.) The reader is reminded that our delinquents and nondelinquents were originally matched in accordance with their ethnic origins (Italian delinquent with Italian nondelinquent, Irish with Irish, Greek with Greek,

etc.). This precludes the possibilty that any dfferences in the physique of delinquents and that of nondelinquents are due to basic differences in racial stock.

4. Dominance of the *mesomorphic* component among the delinquents is shown by the fact that, while 60.4% of that group could be so classified, only 30.8% of the nondelinquents were mesomorphic. Dominance of the *ectomorphic* component among the *nondelinquents* was found in the fact that while 39.4% of such boys were so classifiable, only 14.4% of the delinquents were. The numbers involved in the other somatotypes (*endomorphic* and *balanced*) were small. See *Unraveling Juvenile Delinquency*, p. 193.

5. Glueck, *Physique and Delinquency*.

6. *Ibid.*, chap. XI.

7. One of the lines of investigation we wanted to carry out was to compare the electro-encephalograms of the two sets of boys; but when *Unraveling* was begun the standards of the indications of this type of inquiry had not yet been sufficiently worked out for the "normal."

8. Dr. Bryant E. Moulton, previously with the Judge Baker Guidance Center of Boston.

9. See *Unraveling Juvenile Delinquency*, Table IV-7 and Appendix B. Dr. David Wechsler, originator of the test, regarded this as a very close match.

10. These two concepts are often related, combined, or used interchangeably in the literature, stemming largely, we suppose, from the difficulty of dividing personality and character patterns into their constituent traits and of determining the typical affinities of individual traits to temperamental and characterial types. It is clarifying if one conceives personality to be the totality of physical, temperamental, affective, and intellectual make-up of an individual. Personality is neutral so far as character is concerned; character is personality plus the ingredients of ethico-religious, parental, and other ideals or goals that typically guide or dictate an individual's conduct. A man may have a strong or weak personality, and a judgment of his personality would be similar regardless of his parental inculcation of one or another set of values and regardless of his ethical views or religious convictions. A man may have a good or bad character, and the judgment as to this depends upon the extent to which his actions typically conform to a set of ethical or religious standards within which he is judged. However, character type is related more or less to the nature of personality structure.

11. In regard to apperception, responses are noted and evaluated as being to the *whole* blot, to *details*, and the like. In respect to quality, three types of basic mental responses are set down: *form*, *movement*, and *color*. In regard to content, the subject may, for example, recognize the form of an animal, or a human being, or an object, a landscape, some anatomical pattern, or some abstract design. Originality and banality of his responses also are noted and integrated into the total personality size-up.

12. These diagnoses were corroborated by independent classifications made by the staff psychiatrist. See *Unraveling Juvenile Delinquency*, p. 242, n. 8.

13. The Rorschach experts used this term to designate all marked mental and emotional deviations that did not clearly belong in any one of the other diagnostic groupings.

14. The telltale marks that justify an incontrovertible diagnosis of psychopathic personality — difficult to ascertain even in adulthood — may not be fully apparent in boyhood.

III Some Highlights of *Unraveling Juvenile Delinquency:* Behavior of Delinquents and Nondelinquents

INTRODUCTORY

Having considered the family background and traits of the two sets of boys under comparison, we turn next to an account of their behavior in school and in the streets.

THE BOY IN SCHOOL

Since knowledge is one thing, and its efficient and socially acceptable employment another, "book learning" does not play as important a role in the development of character and related conduct as may once have been supposed. The child's instinctual drives, his emotional moods and impulses, his temperamental slant, are inevitably involved in his use of the instruments given him by the learning process. Yet schooling can provide a sense of emotional satisfaction in achievement of skills; it can arouse socially acceptable ambitions; it can place the pupil in contact with adults with whom he might identify and whom he might strive to emulate, just as, *per contra*, schooling can leave scars in the psyche which may well enhance the development of resentful antisocial attitudes and defiance not only of the authority of the teacher but of other wielders of society's authority.

Moreover, the school is the child's first proving-ground outside the home. It supplies the first proof of his adaptability and capacity for socialization in a theater of action in which there are strict rules enforced by nonparental authority. Outside the familiar home atmosphere, the child is forced to face reality and prove his capacity to sink or swim.

Here, then, are some basic facts regarding conduct and achievement in the school situation. Although the delinquents and nondelinquents had been matched by age and general intelligence at the time of the first investigation, twice as many of the delinquents as of the control group had not yet gone beyond the sixth grade (36.4% vs.

17.2%), and excessive numbers of the former were below the sixth grade or had been placed in special classes (24.2% vs. 9.8%) when we first studied them. Moreover, little more than half as many delinquents as nondelinquents (22.2% vs. 38.2%) had reached junior high or high school. As a group the former were a year behind the latter in educational achievement, the average grade attained by the delinquents being the seventh, by the nondelinquents, the eighth. While the juvenile delinquents may have had to repeat grades because of removal from school and commitment to correctional institutions, this does not wholly explain the difference in the grade achieved; the excessive moving of the delinquents' families also accounts for uprootings from school. More than four-tenths of the delinquents had been in more than five different schools, as compared with less than two-tenths of the nondelinquents.

Regarding backwardness, twice as many delinquents as nondelinquents were two or more years behind the proper grade for their age (41.0% vs. 21.2%). Also, twice as many delinquents (two in ten as compared with one in ten) had been in special classes for retarded children. Some of the reasons for the greater educational retardation of the delinquents were derived from interviews with their most recent teachers. From them it was determined that half the delinquent group manifested a lack of interest in school work, as compared with one-sixth of the nondelinquents; half the former and only a fifth of the latter were "inattentive"; almost half (44.8%) the delinquents in contrast with one-fifth of the control group were "careless"; two in five contrasted with one in five were "lazy." The teachers also reported that a fifth of the delinquents and a tenth of the nondelinquents were frequently tardy. And almost two in ten of the delinquents as contrasted with one in ten of the nondelinquents were described by their most recent teachers as "restless."

Some of the distaste for school is no doubt due to certain aspects of the curriculum; that is why our staff psychiatrist sought to determine from the boys which school studies they especially liked, recording only those for which a boy could give definite reasons. Both groups of boys expressed strong preferences for courses in the manual arts (64.5% and 58.7%), and both showed little enthusiasm for arithmetic, social studies, art courses, English (including reading and spelling), science courses, commercial subjects, foreign languages. Perhaps this is generally true of boys of limited cultural background reared in the submerged areas of our larger cities.

As to scholarship, the school records disclosed that four in ten of the delinquents compared with fewer than one in ten of the nondelinquents were poor or indifferent students, as reflected by grades of D and E in most or all subjects; and while a mere handful (1%) of each group achieved an all-A record, less than six-tenths of the delinquents compared to nine-tenths of the nondelinquents were average pupils (the B and C groups).

On the whole, therefore, despite the essential similarity in age and intelligence quotient between the two groups, and taking into account the greater irregularities in school attendance on the part of the delinquents, their educational attainment was below that of the nondelinquents. This fact is confirmed by comparing their average reading quotients on the Stanford Achievement Tests.[1] This showed a five-point difference between the two sets of boys in favor of the nondelinquents, which, though not large, is statistically significant; so, also, the delinquents were inferior to the control group in arithmetical achievement.

Many a delinquent interviewed by the psychiatrist spontaneously exclaimed, "I hate school because I am always left back," or "It is too hard," or "I want to go to work"; and only one-tenth of the delinquents readily accepted schooling, as compared with two-thirds of the nondelinquents. While the reasons the delinquents gave for their marked dislike of school are largely reflective of temperamental and emotional difficulties and, to some extent, perhaps intellectual inadequacy, the essential causes for resisting school are difficulties in learning, lack of interest in subject matter, resentment of restriction and routine. With respect to academic and vocational ambitions, a far higher proportion of the delinquents than of the control group (over four in ten, in contrast to less than one in ten) wanted to stop school immediately; and a much lower proportion of the former than of the latter (three-tenths compared to two-thirds) wanted to go on to high or trade school.

When questioned about the kind of pursuits they would like to follow after completing their schooling, three out of ten of the delinquents compared to less than two in ten of the nondelinquents expressed only vague, superficial, childish, or unrealistic notions. However, the delinquents were more inclined than the nondelinquents to adventurous occupations, such as aviation, going to sea, joining the armed services (21.3% vs. 12.2%); and a lower proportion wished to learn a trade (40.7% vs. 58.3%) or wanted to engage in intellectual or aesthetic pursuits (1.2% vs. 6.5%).

Questioned regarding the boys' relationships to their schoolmates, recent teachers gave information which placed a considerably lower proportion of the delinquents than of the nondelinquents in the *good*[2] category (four and a half in ten compared to two-thirds); and a higher proportion of the former than of the latter (two in ten compared to less than one in ten) in the *poor* category.

No fewer than 95.6% of the delinquents, in contrast to 17.2% of the nondelinquents, persistently (and often seriously) misconducted themselves in school.[3] Three-tenths of the delinquents were under eight years of age when first showing signs of maladapted behavior in school. The difficulties in social adaptation as manifested by school misconduct were clearly evident among the delinquents prior to puberty, while the school behavioral difficulties of the few nondelinquents who misbehaved did not show up until puberty and early adolescence.

While the vast majority (94.8%) of the delinquents truanted at one time or another, only one in ten of the nondelinquents ever truanted and then only occasionally.

Thus it is clear that social maladjustment expressed itself excessively throughout the school careers of the juvenile delinquents, not only by disobedience, unruliness, defiance, stubbornness, temper tantrums, and the like, but by running away from difficult or unpleasant social situations and obligations.

THE BOY IN THE STREETS

It has already been seen that the homes of the delinquents were far less adequate than those of the law-abiding boys both in physical attributes and in more subtle qualitative aspects. The delinquents had less reason than the nondelinquents to be attached to their homes and more reason to seek satisfactions in the streets. It is to be remembered that *all* the boys — nondelinquents as well as delinquents — lived in economically and culturally underprivileged neighborhoods, so that if we would learn how and why a similar cultural matrix has somehow squeezed some boys into different shapes of law-violators while permitting others to remain law-abiding, we must dig deeper and look farther. Selected for the study from badly deteriorated or rapidly deteriorating areas of a large city, a great proportion of both groups were found to have lived in such malign neighborhoods all their lives (94.2%, 92.0%). If they were removed from such regions, it was only for brief periods: in the case of 88 delinquents, because of placement in foster homes by courts, social agencies, and occasionally by their own families in an effort to counteract deleterious home and street influences; in the case of 17 nondelinquents, generally because of their placement by welfare agencies necessitated by illness of parents or disruption of the home.

Frequent moving about means relative anonymity and the likelihood of failure to develop a loyalty and responsibility to neighbors; it tends to develop a sense of instability rather than a relative identification with certain cultural values and a socially induced disciplinary influence on conduct. While four-fifths of the families of the delinquents had moved from region to region five or more times, only two-fifths in the control group had done so; one in three of the former had changed residence eleven or more times, compared to only one in ten of the latter. Thus, the delinquents had far less chance than the other boys to develop neighborhood ties and loyalties. The delinquent boys were also more markedly subjected to unusual environmental contacts: while seven in ten experienced "bunking out," placement in foster homes, removal to orphanages and other protective institutions, placement in schools for the feebleminded, and commitment to correctional schools, such uprootings occurred among only one in ten of the nondelinquents.

All in all, some two-thirds of the delinquents compared to only a tenth of the nondelinquents first left the parental household before age 17. In the case of the delinquents, the causes for the first departure from home were related to the boy's own misconduct (delinquency, running away, bunking out). As regards the small group of nondelinquents who were separated from their parental homes, their first departure resulted from situations beyond their control (disruption of the home, parents' financial inability to care for them, unsuitability of the home, illness of parents or of the boys themselves).

Working after school hours is in the American tradition, but it can have either desirable consequences in teaching business practices and contributing to a sense of economic responsibility or harmful ones in developing a premature sophistication and subjecting a boy too early to the hazards of life in the city streets. The great majority of both groups of boys (85.0% of the delinquents, 78.7% of the nondelinquents) worked after school, most of them deriving their spending money entirely from their earnings. In relatively the same proportions, boys of both groups took jobs because they wanted spending money, or because urged to do so by their families, or because they enjoyed the prestige of being wage-earners, or wanted to help their families. More of the delinquents than of the nondelinquents worked only occasionally, almost six-tenths of the delinquents as compared with a third of the nondelinquents gravitating principally to such street trades as peddling, bootblacking, selling newspapers. This means that the delinquents were more often exposed to street influences. A considerably lower proportion of the delinquents than of the other boys

(8% vs. 25%) were mainly engaged in jobs in which some supervision and protection were provided (as office boy, errand boy, messenger, store helper), but few of either group worked in factories. On the whole, then, the delinquents were employed in the more hazardous and adventuresome jobs, in which they were less subject to protection from vicious street influences.

Despite their after-school work, there was time for some household duties; yet 45.6% of the delinquents and 33.9% of the nondelinquents were not required by their families to do household chores. Only one-fifth of the delinquents and a little over two-fifths of the nondelinquents were assigned any regular household tasks, such as running errands, making their own beds, emptying garbage and ashcans.

Interviews with the boys and their parents (usually the mother) and sometimes with older brothers and sisters, as well as interviews with their most recent teachers, and consultation of records of settlement houses, boys' clubs, and family welfare agencies disclosed the following facts regarding the manner in which delinquents and nondelinquents preferred to spend their leisure time — the information being grouped under the headings of adventurous, competitive, active noncompetitive, nonactive.[4] The most striking, although foreseeable, finding was that a much higher proportion of the delinquents than of the control group preferred *adventurous* activities (50.2% vs. 10.1%). A lower percentage of the former than of the latter preferred sports free of the competitive element (38.7% vs. 50.0%); far fewer of the delinquents than of the nondelinquents (8.3% vs. 31.4%) chose competitive sports or games; and fewer were content with quiet amusements. A greater thirst for excitement among the delinquents — this time expressed vicariously — was also disclosed in the finding that almost half the group, compared to a tenth of the law-abiding boys, attended movies excessively (three or more times a week). Thus, not only in real life, but also in phantasy, the delinquent boys showed a much more powerful urge for exciting outlets.

Their greater desire for adventure is indicated by the various risk-entailing activities in which the delinquents exceeded the nondelinquents: over nine-tenths of them, compared to less than a fourth of the other boys, were in the habit of stealing rides, hopping trucks, and the like; over nine-tenths, compared to less than a tenth of the nondelinquents, kept late hours, roaming about the streets after dark; 90.0% and 22.8%, respectively, began to smoke at an early age; 29.2%, compared to less than one percent, began to drink before or during their early teens; 66.8%, compared to 10.0%, made a practice of sneaking into movies; 61.8% of the juvenile delinquents, but only 3.8% of the nondelinquents, indulged in various acts of destructive mischief; strikingly, 59.0% of the delinquents, in contrast to only 1.2% of the nonoffenders, ran away from home; 58.8%, compared to 1.6%, "bunked out"; 53.0%, as compared to 9.0%, gambled (largely "shooting craps"); and 13.2% of the delinquents, compared to 0.4% of the nondelinquents, set fires.

The foregoing evidence leaves little doubt that in virtually all major forms of exciting activity offered to boys by the deteriorated American urban area, the delinquents as a group greatly exceeded the youngsters who remained essentially law-abiding. Once again, therefore, one must point to the superficiality of generalizations that the slum itself is a major "cause" of delinquency; for here we have another illustration of the *selective* influence of the urban deteriorated area and of wide *individual differences* in susceptibility, immunity, and vulnerability of those who live in a "delinquency area," or a "delinquency subculture," or a "ghetto."

But there is still more evidence: Almost all the delinquents (95.2%), compared with some three-fifths (58.4%) of the nondelinquents, were in the habit of hanging around street corners; 86.8%, compared to 14.2%, sought their recreations in regions considerably distant from their own homes; many more delinquents than nondelinquents played in vacant lots, on waterfronts, in railroad yards; more spent time in poolrooms, dance halls, and similar places of commercialized recreation. By contrast, a much *lower* proportion of the delinquents than of the other youngsters spent at least some of their leisure hours at home (41.8% vs. 93.2%), or on playgrounds (29.4% vs. 61.0%).

A craving for risky adventure partially accounts for the fact that a considerably higher proportion of the delinquents than of the other boys met with serious accidents, mostly in the streets: 14% of the delinquents, compared with 5% of the nondelinquents, were struck down by vehicles; 19%, compared to 10%, suffered from other serious accidents, such as falling from moving vehicles, or from roofs, windows, fences, bridges, lamp posts, and other such places.

In view of the high degree of organization of club activities for boys in the Boston area, it is to be expected that both groups of boys had had contacts at one time or another with boys' clubs, settlement houses, or similar supervised recreational services; but of the 344 delinquents and 334 nondelinquents from whom information was elicited concerning regularity of their use of supervised recreational facilities, 59.6% of the delinquents, as compared with 72.7% of the control group, attended clubs two or more times a week, and 24.7% of the former compared to 9.6% of the latter attended on special occasions only, as when a movie was shown or an athletic contest was held. Moreover, it turned out that a fourth of the delinquents attended boys' clubs only upon the insistence of probation or parole officers. An additional third of the delinquents (as well as almost a third of the nondelinquents) who visited boys' clubs did so on the urging of parents or other relatives, or of teachers, while a much lower proportion of the delinquents than the nondelinquents (36.1% vs. 56.5%) became members because urged to do so by companions or brothers or sisters. Actually, very few of either group joined clubs on their own initiative (8.0% vs. 13.5%).

The lesser desire among delinquents for organized and supervised recreational activities reflects their general attitude toward controlled recreation. Thus, twice as many of them as of the nondelinquents (21.3% vs. 11.6%) expressed marked dislike or contempt for the supervised activities provided in clubs, playgrounds, and school gymnasiums, while many more nondelinquents than delinquents (37.9% vs. 18.1%) were enthusiastic about controlled recreation. However, three-fifths of the delinquents and half of the nondelinquents (60.6% vs. 50.6%) were vague in their attitude toward supervised play, either because they had not given any thought to the matter or were indifferent; or they indicated that their like or dislike of group activities depended on whether or not their friends participated. The difference between the delinquents and the boys of the control group in acceptance of supervised recreation is suggestive and in harmony with other findings in the study.

It has been taken for granted that, living in slums, most boys would be "infected" by the bad companion who plays the role of the proverbial rotten apple in the barrel. But boys are not apples, and they tend to be attracted to, or to choose, companions who are congenial to them. Thus, while over half the delinquent boys (56.0%) became members of gangs, only three of the youngsters who remained nondelinquent despite residence in the slum areas joined gangs. The troublesome boys seemed far less content than the nondelinquents with a few friends or even with a "crowd" as opposed to a formalized gang; however, by and large, they were seriously maladjusted and delinquent children long before they were gang members. Gang membership may have multiplied their antisocial activities; it rarely generated persistent delinquency.

While the delinquents almost without exception chummed largely with other delinquents (98.4%), the boys of the control group, despite the fact that they too lived in the slums, had few intimates among delinquents (7.4%). The evidence would suggest that the tendency to develop companionships selectively is a much more fundamental fact in any analysis of the etiology of juvenile crime than the theory that "differential association" of nondelinquent boys with delinquents is a basic cause of delinquency.

Almost half the delinquent group were attracted to youths older than themselves, compared to only one in ten of the nondelinquents, a tendency which suggests the search for a substitute "ego-ideal" to admire and emulate; for, as was shown, their fathers were less sympathetic and less acceptable as admired models than were the fathers of the nondelinquents.

Although the majority of both groups were not as yet particularly "girl-minded," a higher proportion of the delinquents (16.4% vs. 10.6%) sought the companionship of girls. While this may be due partly to the fact that they were not as well supervised by their parents as the nondelinquents, their greater interest in companions of the opposite sex may also reflect their greater sexual precocity, since at least 19.4% of the delinquents compared with only 1.8% of the control group had already had heterosexual experiences when taken on for study; 21.2% of the former and 1.2% of the latter had indulged in various forms of sex play; and, as disclosed by psychiatric interview, 29.4% of the delinquents, compared to 2.8% of the nondelinquents, were excessive masturbators.

CHURCH ATTENDANCE

Some four in ten of the delinquents, in contrast with two-thirds of the nondelinquents, attended church once a week. Church attendance alone, however, especially by children, is not a sufficient criterion of adherence to religious tenets. No intensive exploration was made of the reasons for the lesser church attendance of the delinquent boys; so all that can be vouchsafed is that this reflects parental attitudes.

SUMMARY AND COMMENT

It is necessary to touch upon only a few of the outstanding differences in behavior in school and neighborhood between the delinquents and nondelinquents to conclude that very early in life there were signals of rough seas ahead for the boys who became delinquent. They were as a group more retarded scholastically, disliked school more markedly, resented its restrictions, and were eager to drop out. They were less friendly and more pugnacious toward their schoolmates. A larger proportion of them than of the control group truanted; they misbehaved seriously or persistently; and, as some indication of the deep-rootedness of their emotional difficulties, their misconduct occurred at a much earlier age than among the small number of misbehaving nondelinquents.

While all came from urban slums, their response to environmental enticements and pressures varied. Many more of the delinquents than of the control group hopped trucks, kept late hours, smoked and drank at an early age, committed destructive mischief, ran away from home and school, bunked out, begged and the like. Many more of them expressed dislike of organized recreational centers such as boys' clubs and other places of supervised recreation.

The delinquents gravitated toward gangs while the nondelinquents avoided such antisocial groups; the chums of the former tended to be other delinquents; of the latter, law-abiding boys like themselves.

When facts of which the foregoing are only a sample are reflected upon, it becomes clear that in order to understand the impact of the milieu on those who live and act therein, gross findings regarding the various delinquency rates in different zones of a city, or descriptions of slum areas in general, or generalizations about "lack of opportunity," offer only dim and superficial illumination of forces making for delinquency. For, given a similar deteriorated and disadvantaged general environment, the response of different *individuals* to its elements is selective and varied. The assumption that the mass social stimulus to behavior, as reflected in the particular culture of a region is alone, or primarily, the significant causal force in conduct or misconduct runs counter to another undeniable fact: that in every society — whether largely rural or largely urban, whether in the unwholesome milieu of the "ghetto" or in the externally pleasant reaches of suburbiana, whether agricultural or industrial, whether composed essentially of one ethnico-racial group or of several, whether existing at one historic period or another — there have been *individuals* who would not or could not conform to the taboos and laws prohibiting particular forms of behavior.

Enough of the background and makeup of the delinquents and nondelinquents has been presented in the foregoing pages to make it clear that study of the varying impact of general social forces on individuals must focus on the biologic status and childhood conditioning.

In the succeeding chapters we shall examine the history of the two sets of persons we are concerned with, as they grew from boyhood to manhood. The first of these chapters is concerned with the aims and techniques of the follow-up inquiry.

Notes

1. While it is impossible to say that any test can distinguish sharply between inherited and acquired abilities, achievement tests are designed to elicit the degree of learning actually reached following a period of instruction. We do not overlook the fact that inadequacies in achievement involve, on the one hand, innate deficiencies and, on the other, many extraneous factors such as emotional distress, poor study habits, truancy, dislike of school and so on. See Chapter II for a summary of the intellectual traits of the two sets of boys.

2. *Good:* gets on well with other children, is friendly, makes effort to please and hold friends. *Fair:* though not seeking companions, not actively antagonistic. *Poor:* pugnacious and unfriendly and not liked by other children.

3. This encompasses truancy, stealing, persistent attempts to attract attention, inattention, mischievousness, disobedience, defiance, stubbornness, lying, underhandedness, smoking, sexual misconduct.

4. *Adventurous:* amusements involving risk, excitement, daring, such as "hopping trucks." *Competitive:* sports or games in which there is rivalry between individuals and teams, such as baseball, football, basketball. *Active noncompetitive:* amusements involving much bodily action without competition, such as swimming, hiking, bicycling. *Nonactive:* quiet amusements lacking in action or competition, such as being a spectator at events, movies, reading, indoor hobbies.

PART II   AS THEY ARE AS MEN

IV   Aims and Techniques of Follow-Up Inquiries to Age 31

INTRODUCTORY

The longitudinal study of development from boyhood to manhood, and the attendant conduct of our subjects in various aspects of life, not only makes it possible to determine much of the life-graph of typical delinquents as compared with their matched nondelinquents, but should also yield clues regarding the age-spans at which vulnerability to delinquency and to repetitive crime patterns tends to diminish From various prior researches, as well as the present one, we are convinced that the first few years of life are of major significance in molding character under the influence of the adults with whom the child identifies emotionally and intellectually. But this does not mean that character-formation and character-distortion cease after the age of five or six. There are of course other biologic stages at which the organism has to perform great feats of adaptation to the surrounding cultural demands — puberty, adolescence, adulthood, old age; and we surmise that the follow-up materials which have been assembled, verified, and collated over a long span of years will throw some light on a substantial segment of the life-cycle of delinquents in comparison with their matched nondelinquents; on how, and to some extent perhaps why, the delinquents differ from the nondelinquents in the crucial task of adaptation to the demands and challenges of the physiologic-psychologic age-spans during which the evolving personalities play their roles in home, neighborhood, and society.

We hope that this detailed follow-up of delinquents and the control group of nondelinquents will contribute to a better understanding of the typical and atypical. Our interpretation of the tables discussed in the present work may of course not be sufficiently revealing; much of the significance of the findings can only be in the nature of clues, or of incomplete segments of a total picture to be rounded out when, in a contemplated subsequent work, the factors of the follow-up are systematically interrelated with the materials of *Unraveling Juvenile Delinquency*. But we hope that most readers will find the descriptive follow-up data of the present volume meaningful and intellectually challenging.

PURPOSE OF THE STUDY

Certain major weaknesses have too often marred research into problems of deviant behavior which the law identifies as "criminal." First, there has been neglect of an elementary principle of relevant scientific method — comparison of the experimental sample with a matched control group. Second, there has been a failure to follow the careers of delinquents and nondelinquents over a substantial segment of the life-span, in order to note the vicissitudes of time and their relationship to some assumed working hypothesis of the etiology of deviant behavior. Third, there has been too great a tendency to evade the tough and tangled skein of biological and sociocultural forces involved in criminogenesis by spinning facile unilateral theories labeled by catch titles and accompanied by little factual support.

Regarding this last weakness of much criminologic research, one is tempted to apply the wise dictum of the distinguished Russian physiologist-psychologist, Ivan Pavlov, who, shortly before his death in 1936, underscored a lesson which it would be well for criminologists to have ever before them: "Perfect as is the wing of a bird, it never would raise the bird up without resting on air. Facts are the air of a scientist. Without them your 'theories' are vain efforts."

Now a word about how the present follow-up study originated. Toward the end of the research which resulted in the many-faceted study, *Unraveling Juvenile Delinquency*, we evolved a plan to pursue the careers of the original group of juvenile offenders and their matched nondelinquents over a considerable portion of the life-cycle. The aim was to uncover the changes in conduct that occurred with the passage of the years. We wanted to find out what happened, not only from the obvious point of view of recidivism and nonrecidivism, but also with respect to family life, employment history, recreational activities, and the like. Had it been feasible, we would have checked on the behavior of our two groups well into middle life. As it is, we followed the careers of the delinquents and nondelinquents from the time they were originally taken on for study in connection with *Unraveling* (when they ranged in age between 9 and 17) to the age of 31. This means that the story of their initially divergent status can now be told as they emerged into adolescence (with its familiar physiological and psychological variations) and into early adulthood.

Although we have made other follow-up studies,[1] the investigation reported in the present volume is the most significant of our vertical, or historical, studies of delinquents and criminals; for unlike the prior follow-up inquiries, which were limited to delinquents, the present one pursued the careers of the *nondelinquents* with whom the delinquent boys had been originally matched, pair by pair, in respect to age, ethnico-racial derivation, general (global) intelligence, and residence in economically underprivileged areas of Greater Boston. The use of a control group should make possible a clearer understanding of the careers of delinquents than has been provided by other long-term investigations, in which knowledge of the changing status and behavior of the delinquents, in the absence of a control group to serve as a yardstick, could only occasionally be contrasted with the general population. Now we are able to focus attention systematically on the differences and resemblances among delinquents and nondelinquents in the perspective of time.

SOME METHODOLOGICAL PROBLEMS

Obviously, to follow up almost a thousand boys to the age of 31, who were only 9 to 17 years old when first encountered, is a task of no mean proportions. It could not have been accomplished without the rich background of case-investigational experience that we and the key members of our staff had already gained. The most important staff members had been with the project since the days of the original accumulation of the raw materials for *Unraveling*. Although the investigation was unique among the several we had already conducted (because of its inclusion of nondelinquents), the techniques of follow-up developed from prior researches were all relevant.[2] It is on the basis of this total experience that the latest follow-up inquiry was constructed.

To provide some conception of the "machinery" of our investigations, we present in Appendix A *The Case of Henry W. Part I* was first published as Appendix A of *Family Environment and Delinquency*[3] and tells the detailed story of the investigation of Henry at the time he was included in *Unraveling Juvenile Delinquency*. Part II continues the inquiry to age 31. From a careful reading of this case investigation, the reader should gain a conception of the method and the many facets of the inquiry.

Field investigations, begun in 1949 and completed in 1963, were initiated as each boy approached his 25th birthday. This check-up not only routinely spanned the years from 17 to 25 (17 being the limit of juvenile court jurisdiction in Massachusetts), but retrospectively filled in the history of delinquency on all the boys up to the age of 17, because most of them were much younger when first studied.[4] In addition, certain information was retrospectively derived which could not always be completed in connection with the original *Unraveling* study. This was so as regards: age of subject at death of father and of mother; nature of first departure from home, age boy first left home, and reasons for leaving; nature of first breach in family life and age of subject at first breach; school grade attained, age boy first left school, and major reason for stopping school; age subject first began to work. The second follow-up of the men, begun when each reached age 31, continued the history beyond the twenty-fifth birthday.

One of the major objectives in the construction of schedules (and later of codes) to furnish the investigators with directives for securing the desired information was to make the data comparable wherever possible with the findings of *Unraveling Juvenile Delinquency* and the materials of our prior follow-up studies (most particularly *500 Criminal Careers, Later Criminal Careers, Criminal Careers in Retrospect,* and *One Thousand Juvenile Delinquents* and *Juvenile Delinquents Grown Up*), but of course adding other data to enrich the present inquiry.

Although *Unraveling Juvenile Delinquency* encompassed 500 delinquents and 500 nondelinquents, the exigencies of time and limitations of funds did not make possible the tracing and check-up of the entire number (24 delinquents and 11 nondelinquents were deceased by the end of the follow-up periods); but actually the substantial number of 463 delinquents and 466 nondelinquents were studied during the first period (to age 25) and 438 delinquents and 442 nondelinquents during the second (to age 31). To avoid any confusion that might arise from the use of different samples (*e.g.*, 463 delinquents up to the age of 25 and 438 delinquents for the second follow-up period), all the tables presented in this and subsequent chapters are based on the 438 delinquents and 442 nondelinquents for whom it was possible to secure information for the entire period. It should be noted here that complete information was not always available for each case, and therefore not all tables contain data for 438 delinquents and 442 nondelinquents.

In order to test the representativeness of the follow-up sample, a comparison was made — for 110 variables selected from the data of *Unraveling*[5] — between the original sample of boys and the follow-up

TABLE IV-1. NUMBER OF SOURCES OF INFORMATION
ON EACH CASE FOR EACH FOLLOW-UP INVESTIGATION

| | First Follow-Up Period | | | | Second Follow-Up Period | | | |
| | Delinquents | | Non-delinquents | | Delinquents | | Non-delinquents | |
	No.	%	No.	%	No.	%	No.	%
Less than 7	6	1.4	92	20.8	119	27.2	256	57.9
7–11	163	37.2	260	58.8	236	53.9	166	37.6
11–15	186	42.5	72	16.3	72	16.4	18	4.1
15 and Over	83	18.9	18	4.1	11	2.5	2	0.4
Total	438	100.0	442	100.0	438	100.0	442	100.0

$$\chi^2 = 189.92; P < .01 \qquad \chi^2 = 100.84; P < .01$$

sample. The data are presented in Appendix B, where it is apparent that there is no instance of a significant difference between the two samples.

As shown in Table IV-1, the sources of information — both personal and recorded — comprised *at least seven* for 98.6% of the delinquents and 79.2% of the nondelinquents in the first follow-up span; and 72.8% of the delinquents and 42.1% of the nondelinquents during the second.

As a further indication of the extent and intensity of the follow-up investigations, it should be noted that, during the first span, personal interviews were held with 66.9% of the delinquents and 81.5% of the nondelinquents (supplemented, of course, by other sources of information); and during the second period, with 55.7% of the former and 79.0% of the latter (see Table IV-2). The greater proportion of

TABLE IV-2. WITH WHOM INTERVIEW HELD CONCERNING EACH FOLLOW-UP
INVESTIGATION[o]

| | First Follow-Up Period | | | | | Second Follow-Up Period | | | | |
| | Delinquents | | Non-delinquents | | P | Delinquents | | Non-delinquents | | P |
	No.	%	No.	%		No.	%	No.	%	
Subject in Person (incl. questionnaire)	293	66.9	360	81.5	< .01	244	55.7	349	79.0	< .01
Parent (incl. step-parent)	161	36.8	214	48.4	< .01	122	27.9	159	36.0	< .01
Wife (or ex-wife)	68	15.5	79	17.9	< .40	139	31.7	205	46.4	< .01
Other Persons	158	36.1	157	35.5	< .90	223	50.9	207	46.8	< .30
Records Only	5	1.1	1	0.2	< .10	25	5.7	0	0.0	< .01
No. of Cases[a]	438	100.0	442	100.0	—	438	100.0	442	100.0	—

[a] This is a multiple-category table; that is, an individual can be included more than once, and therefore the percentages do not total 100.0

direct interviews with the nondelinquent youths was due in part to their readier availability and also to the fact that other sources of information were not as numerous as for the delinquents. The law-abiding men were not, for example, to such an extent known to various welfare agencies as were the delinquents, whose "footprints in the sands of time" were deeper and more frequent.

Although the techniques used in deriving information about the delinquents and nondelinquents were essentially similar to those used in prior researches, there were a few problems and a few areas of inquiry that we had not been concerned with in such force before. First, because of the long spread of the follow-up period (a maximum of 22 years in the case of the youngest boys of *Unraveling Juvenile Delinquency*, and a minimum of 15 years for those who were already 16), we experienced an enhancement of the problem of tracing the men within a city, from city to city, and from state to state; and as they grew older and their economic conditions generally improved (the investigations, it will be remembered, were carried out between 1949 and 1963), there was less recourse by families and individuals to welfare agencies from which we had in past researches (including *Unraveling*) gained so much information.[6]

Even more crucial than in our prior follow-up studies was the problem of not revealing to a newly acquired wife the criminal history of a husband, and of allaying any suspicions on the part of the families of nondelinquents as to our purpose in reinvestigating. We relied a great deal on the rapport initially established by our tactful and highly sensitive field workers who, as already mentioned, were associated with the project from its inception. In an effort to reconstruct the military careers of the delinquents and nondelinquents during the Korean War as well as in the peacetime armed forces, we had to establish a network of contacts with Army and Navy officials, Selective Service Boards, and Veterans Bureaus, being at times handicapped by the restrictions placed upon them by their superiors regarding the furnishing of information for research projects. This often entailed permission of the subject himself to seek information about him, which we were generally able to secure. On the whole, there was marked success in assembling the data from numerous complementary sources.

The gathering of the criminal histories from birth to age 31 entailed reference to the Massachusetts Board of Probation files, records of the Massachusetts Department of Correction, state and federal fingerprint records (through the Massachusetts Department of Public Safety), police department and court records in any place in which we learned "our man" had been, whether as a resident or vagrant or migrant worker. The thoroughness of the findings attests to the persistence of the staff in securing every bit of information available in the particular instance.

It may now be pertinent to sample a few of the instructions given to persons responsible for gathering the data and entering the information onto work sheets and later onto schedules, in order to show how consistency and uniformity were assured in so vast and unprecedented a project. For example, the staff were instructed that in the case of subjects who were *not in the community* on the date of the inquiry and throughout the preceding three years because of confinement in a penal or nonpenal institution, or employment in the armed forces, or vagrancy, all factors pertaining to home and neighborhood and recreation at home were to be considered as "inapplicable." They were also instructed, to cite another example, that if a subject was at sea and had no fixed abode in the community which he could call his home between trips, the situation was also to be considered as "inapplicable" as to place of residence. If, however, he did have a fixed abode in the community, all descriptions concerning his place of residence and neighborhood situation were to be considered as if he were actually living there.

A record of the findings on a carefully tested schedule was made by our highly experienced case collator; then one of the authors reviewed the data, raising questions, asking for additional information where necessary, and finally interpreting and coding each case in accordance with a well-tested set of codes and definitions.

RELIABILITY OF THE ORIGINAL CONTROL GROUP

It is important to examine the control group in the light of information obtained after publication of *Unraveling Juvenile Delinquency*. As already noted, when the 500 *nondelinquents* were first selected for *Unraveling*, they ranged in age from less than 11 up to 17, and were of an average age of 14½. However, 37 of them were found — on restrospective inquiry in connection with the present work — to have developed records as juveniles before they reached the 17th birthday, which is the limit of juvenile court jurisdiction in Massachusetts. Of these 37, three were sentenced (or the case was filed) before they reached the age of 13; three, before their 14th birthday; six, before age 15; seven, before their 16th birthday; and eighteen, during their 16th year. Their "delinquency" must be reviewed in the light of the definition used in selecting the 500 *delinquents* of *Unraveling*: ". . . delinquency refers to repeated acts of a kind which when committed by persons beyond the statutory juvenile court age of sixteen are punishable as crimes. . . ."[7] Of the 37 boys who were sentenced before the age of seventeen, 15 were convicted of a single minor offense as juveniles (truancy, trespassing, occupying street, drunkenness, riding street car, running away, discharging firearms, being a stubborn child); and 16, for one serious offense (larceny, breaking and entering, using auto without authority, assault and battery with dangerous weapon, receiving stolen goods). The remaining six boys were convicted two or three times for serious offenses as juveniles. Had we been "seers," we might have excluded from the original nondelinquent control group the 22 boys convicted of one or more serious offenses as juveniles.

The very small number of boys originally included in the *nondelinquent group* who manifested evidences of *juvenile* delinquency in accordance with the definition adopted for *Unraveling*, is a fact of prime significance in supporting the soundness of the control group of *Unraveling* as the yardstick against which the juvenile delinquents were measured. For the purposes of the present monograph, the relative immunity of the young nondelinquents to the malign influences of the outer environment (neighborhood and community and culture) is a fact of fundamental significance.

We now turn to the findings of the follow-up investigations.

Notes

1. Sheldon and Eleanor Glueck, *500 Criminal Careers* (New York: Alfred Knopf, 1930; New York: Kraus Reprint, 1965); *Five Hundred Delinquent Women* (New York: Alfred Knopf, 1934; New York: Kraus Reprint, 1965); *One Thousand Juvenile Delinquents* (Cambridge, Mass.: Harvard University Press, 1934; New York: Kraus Reprint, 1965); *Juvenile Delinquents Grown Up* (New York: The Commonwealth Fund, 1940; New York: Kraus Reprint, 1966; *Later Criminal Careers* (New York: The Commonwealth Fund, 1937, New York: Kraus Reprint, 1966); *Criminal Careers in Retrospect* (New York: The Commonwealth Fund, 1943; New York: Kraus Reprint, 1966).

2. For descriptions of methodology used in prior researches, see *500 Criminal Careers*, chap. V and Appendices; *Five Hundred Delinquent Women*, Appendices, especially Appendix A; *Juvenile Delinquents Grown Up.* chap. XXI and Appendices; *Criminal Careers in Retrospect*, pp. 7 and 8; *Unraveling Juvenile Delinquency*, chaps. V and VII.

3. Sheldon and Eleanor Glueck (London: Routledge & Kegan Paul; Boston: Houghton Mifflin, 1962). Reprinted by permission.

4. More than half the group were under 15. For age distribution of the boys when originally studied, see *Unraveling Juvenile Delinquency*, p. 37.

5. These variables were originally chosen for the analyses of body type and family environment. See *Physique and Delinquency*, and *Family Environment and Delinquency*.

6. See *Unraveling Juvenile Delinquency*, Tables IX-12 and IX-13, pp. 103 and 104.

7. *Unraveling*, p. 13.

V The Place Called "Home"

INTRODUCTORY

When we first encountered the 500 delinquents and 500 nondelinquents in *Unraveling Juvenile Delinquency*, 92.8% of the former and 95.4% of the latter were residing with one or both of their own parents, while the others were living under the roof of step-parents or other relatives. They were all residents of central Boston. It should be remembered that most of the *delinquents* were actually in the Lyman or Shirley Correctional School when we first met them, but their home base was, of course, with their parents.

Among our follow-up quests, we were interested to determine the nature of the first departure from home of both the delinquents and the nondelinquents. Such a breakaway reflected a disturbed condition — either of the boy himself or of the home, or both — even if for a brief period, such as running away from home. Most of the departures, however, were for longer periods, such as commitment to a correctional school or placement in a foster home because the household of which the boy was a part was broken up or because a court or welfare agency found the boy's own home unsuitable. Another of our quests was to determine how many of the boys were in correctional institutions at ages 17 and 22, and how many were at that time still living under the parental roof.

WHEREABOUTS AT 17 AND 22 YEARS OF AGE

As shown in Table V-1, on their 17th birthday, we found about half the delinquents (53.4%) still living in the Boston or Greater Boston area, as compared with nine-tenths (92.1%) of the nondelinquents. On their 22nd birthday, there was no reduction in the proportion of delinquents residing in the Greater Boston area, but a definite decrease among the nondelinquents, due in large part to service in the Armed Forces. On their 17th birthday, almost a third of the delinquents (30.8%) were

TABLE V-1.   WHEREABOUTS ON 17TH AND 22ND BIRTHDAYS

| | First Follow-Up Period | | | | Second Follow-Up Period | | | |
| | Delinquents | | Non-delinquents | | Delinquents | | Non-delinquents | |
	No.	%	No.	%	No.	%	No.	%
Boston or Greater Boston	234	53.4	407	92.1	233	53.2	275	62.2
Other Places in Massachusetts	14	3.2	5	1.1	8	1.8	9	2.0
Outside Massachusetts	9	2.1	10	2.3	24	5.5	13	3.0
Penal or Correctional Institution	135	30.8	1	0.2	91	20.8	4	0.9
Nonpenal Institution	4	0.9	0	0.0	4	0.9	1	0.2
Armed Forces	16	3.6	12	2.7	49	11.2	139	31.5
At Sea	17	3.9	6	1.4	23	5.2	1	0.2
Wandering About; Fugitive from Justice	9	2.1	1	0.2	6	1.4	0	0.0
Total	438	100.0	442	100.0	438	100.0	442	100.0
	$\chi^2 = 199.22$; P < .01				$\chi^2 = 157.49$; P < .01			

found to be in penocorrectional institutions. The proportion of delinquents in penal institutions on the 22nd birthday was lower than it had been on the 17th birthday, dropping from 30.8% to 20.8%. There was a considerable increase in the proportion of young men in the Armed Forces at age 22: from 3.6% of the delinquents at age 17 to 11.2% at age 22; and from 2.7% of the nondelinquents at age 17 to 31.5% of the nondelinquents at age 22.

We were interested to know with whom the delinquents and nondelinquents who were in the community — that is, not in a correctional institution, or in the Armed Forces, at sea, or wandering about — were making their homes on their 17th birthday (see Table V-2). Actually

TABLE V-2.   WITH WHOM LIVING ON 17TH AND 22ND BIRTHDAYS

| | At Age 17 | | | | At Age 22 | | | |
| | Delinquents | | Non-delinquents | | Delinquents | | Non-delinquents | |
	No.	%	No.	%	No.	%	No.	%
Parents or Relatives	248	96.5	420	99.5	145	54.7	205	69.0
Wife and/or In-Laws	4	1.6	0	0.0	95	35.9	82	27.6
Alone or with a Friend; in Employment Away from Home	5	1.9	2	0.5	25	9.4	10	3.4
Total	257	100.0	422	100.0	265	100.0	297	100.0
	$\chi^2 = 10.10$; P < .01				$\chi^2 = 15.91$; P < .01			

96.5% of these delinquents were found to be living with parents or close relatives, as compared with 99.5% of the nondelinquents. Four delinquents were already living with a wife while none of the non-delinquents was yet married.

On their 22nd birthday — when many more of the nondelinquents were in the Armed Forces — the proportion of delinquent boys in the community actually making their homes with parents or close relatives fell from 96.5% at age 17 to 54.5%; there was a lesser reduction in nondelinquent boys still living with parents or close relatives — from 99.5% at age 17 to 69.0% at age 22. And by then considerably higher proportions than at age 17 were living with a wife (or with a wife in the home of her parents): 35.9% of the delinquents and 27.6% of the nondelinquents.

There is evident an increase in the proportion of delinquent men living alone or with casual acquaintances: 1.9% of the delinquents at 17 years of age and 9.4% at age 22.

WHEREABOUTS AT END OF EACH FOLLOW-UP PERIOD

We turn now to a comparison of the location of the delinquents and nondelinquents at the end of the first follow-up period, when they were 25 years old, and at the close of the second, when they were already 31 years old (see Table V-3).

TABLE V-3.   WHEREABOUTS AT END OF EACH FOLLOW-UP PERIOD

	First Follow-Up Period				Second Follow-Up Period			
	Delinquents		Non-delinquents		Delinquents		Non-delinquents	
	No.	%	No.	%	No.	%	No.	%
Boston or Greater Boston	221	50.5	327	74.0	245	55.9	313	70.8
Other Places in Massachusetts	13	3.0	19	4.3	32	7.3	47	10.6
Outside Massachusetts	32	7.3	39	8.8	63	14.4	58	13.1
Penal or Correctional Institution	89	20.3	2	0.5	49	11.2	2	0.5
Hospital for Mental Disease	0	0.0	0	0.0	3	0.7	1	0.2
Hospital for Physical Disease	1	0.2	0	0.0	0	0.0	0	0.0
Armed Forces	44	10.1	53	12.0	10	2.3	16	3.6
At Sea	19	4.3	1	0.2	11	2.5	2	0.5
Wandering About; Fugitive from Justice	19	4.3	1	0.2	25	5.7	3	0.7
Total	438	100.0	442	100.0	438	100.0	442	100.0
	$\chi^2 = 139.76$; $P < .01$				$\chi^2 = 80.54$; $P < .01$			

By the end of the first follow-up period, 50.5% of the delinquents and 74.0% of the nondelinquents were still living in the Boston or Greater Boston area. It is to be remembered that they were all residents of the core areas of Boston when we first encountered them. Some of them had moved, of course, into peripheral areas, but still within the boundaries of the city of Boston. By the end of the second follow-up period, there was little change: we found that 55.9% of the delinquents and 70.8% of the nondelinquents were residing in the Boston or Greater Boston area. At age 25, 7.3% of the delinquents and 8.8% of the nondelinquents were living outside the State of Massachusetts; and, by the end of the second follow-up period, 14.4% of the delinquents and 13.1% of the nondelinquents were residing outside the state.

It is to be noted that a fifth of the delinquents (20.3%) were in penocorrectional institutions on their 25th birthday, and 11.2% of them at the end of the second follow-up period. While 10.1% of the delinquents and 12.0% of the nondelinquents were in the Armed Forces on their 25th birthday, only 2.3% of the delinquents and 3.6% of the nondelinquents were in the military services on their 31st birthday.

Of those in the community at the end of the first follow-up period (see Table V-4), we found 37.6% of the delinquents and 44.7% of the nondelinquents residing with one or both parents or close blood relations. By the end of the second follow-up period these proportions were reduced: at that time 15.3% of the delinquents and 19.9% of the nondelinquents were living with one or both parents or close relatives. Residing with wife and children at the end of the first follow-up period were 55.3% of the delinquents and 51.2% of the nondelinquents; while at the end of the second, 76.5% of both the delinquents

TABLE V-4. WITH WHOM LIVING AT END OF EACH
FOLLOW-UP PERIOD

| | First Follow-Up Period | | | | Second Follow-Up Period | | | |
| | Delinquents | | Non-delinquents | | Delinquents | | Non-delinquents | |
	No.	%	No.	%	No.	%	No.	%
Wife and Children	147	55.3	197	51.2	260	76.5	320	76.5
Parents or Relatives	100	37.6	172	44.7	52	15.3	83	19.9
Alone or with a Friend; in Employment Away from Home	19	7.1	16	4.1	28	8.2	15	3.6
Total	266	100.0	385	100.0	340	100.0	418	100.0

$\chi^2 = 5.00$; P < .10 $\qquad$ $\chi^2 = 9.32$; P < .01

TABLE V-5. DEPARTURES FROM HOME[a]
DURING EACH FOLLOW-UP PERIOD

| | First Follow-Up Period | | | | Second Follow-Up Period | | | |
| | Delinquents | | Non-delinquents | | Delinquents | | Non-delinquents | |
	No.	%	No.	%	No.	%	No.	%
Some	422	96.3	381	86.4	347	79.2	248	56.2
None	16	3.7	60	13.6	91	20.8	193	43.8
Total	438	100.0	441	100.0	438	100.0	441	100.0

$\chi^2 = 27.56$; P < .01 $\chi^2 = 53.10$; P < .01

[a] Parental home; or, if married during respective periods, home established with wife.

and the nondelinquents were making their homes with a wife and children.

DEPARTURES FROM HOME

As we look back to the first departure from home of the delinquents and nondelinquents up to the time of our original encounter with them in *Unraveling Juvenile Delinquency*, we see that a serious breach in the home ties had already occurred among 71.4% of the delinquents but among only 9.2% of the nondelinquents. (This does not mean that such ties were not in some cases resumed.) It is obvious that this movement away from the family roof (whether it was from the home of the parents, or later from their own homes) had increased significantly and was particularly great during the first follow-up period, for Table V-5 shows that 96.3% of the delinquents and 86.4% of the nondelinquents left the home of their parents, or the home established with a wife, at some time during this period (even if not permanently), some leaving more than once. During the second follow-up period, there was less movement away from the home base, for lower proportions — 79.2% of the delinquents and 56.2% of the nondelinquents — left their homes for a time during this span of years.

What is clear from Table V-6 is that of those who did leave during the first follow-up period — and accounting for all known departures — 46.4% of the delinquents and 53.3% of the nondelinquents, established their own homes. These proportions rose to 57.9% for the delinquents and 70.6% for the nondelinquents during the course of the second follow-up span. A considerably higher proportion of the nondelinquents than of the delinquents entered the Armed Forces during the first follow-up span (70.3% as compared with 43.6% of the delinquents), and a greater percentage of the nondelinquents than of the delinquents entered the Armed Forces at some time during the second follow-up period (28.2% vs. 16.7%). Naturally, a major difference between the delinquents and nondelinquents was found in the proportions who were at one time or another during either span in a penocorrectional institutional — 51.2% of the delinquents, as compared with 4.7% of the nondelinquents during the course of the years from 17 to 25; and about similar proportions in the second follow-up span, when they ranged in age from 25 to 31.

MOBILITY

We are interested next in learning something about the moves made by the young men from one address to another. Was there relative stability of places of residence, or did they move about a great deal? And was there a notable difference between the delinquents and nondelinquents in this regard?

Excluding the delinquents and nondelinquents who were in institutions or at sea or in the Armed Forces, 57.8% of the delinquents, as contrasted with 85.5% of the nondelinquents, either moved less frequently than once a year or they did not move at all during the first follow-up period; this was also the case in respect to 61.7% of the delinquents in the second five-year span, as contrasted with 93.3% of

TABLE V-6. NATURE OF DEPARTURES FROM HOME DURING EACH FOLLOW-UP PERIOD

	First Follow-Up Period					Second Follow-Up Period				
	Delinquents		Non-delinquents		P	Delinquents		Non-delinquents		P
	No.	%	No.	%		No.	%	No.	%	
To Establish or Re-establish Own Home	196	46.4	203	53.3	< .10	201	57.9	175	70.6	< .01
To Live with Relatives	152	36.0	91	23.9	< .01	192	55.3	87	35.1	< .01
Armed Forces	184	43.6	268	70.3	< .01	58	16.7	70	28.2	< .01
Penal or Correctional Institution	216	51.2	18	4.7	< .01	175	50.4	12	4.8	< .01
Hospital for Mental or Physical Disease	23	5.5	11	2.9	< .10	37	10.7	14	5.7	< .05
To Wander About	61	14.5	6	1.6	< .01	71	20.5	10	4.0	< .01
To Go to Sea	44	10.4	5	1.3	< .01	29	8.4	4	1.6	< .01
Other (live with employer, friend, alone)	96	22.7	49	12.9	< .01	167	48.1	55	22.2	< .01
No. of Cases[a]	422	100.0	381	100.0	—	347	100.0	248	100.0	—

[a] This is a multiple-category table; that is, an individual can be included more than once, and therefore the percentages do not add to 100.0.

TABLE V-7. FREQUENCY OF MOVES DURING
EACH FOLLOW-UP PERIOD

	First Follow-Up Period				Second Follow-Up Period			
	Delinquents		Non-delinquents		Delinquents		Non-delinquents	
	No.	%	No.	%	No.	%	No.	%
None	50	15.4	124	31.1	28	7.9	47	11.7
Less Often than Once a Year	138	42.4	217	54.4	192	53.8	329	81.6
Average of Once a Year	9	2.8	11	2.7	13	3.6	4	1.0
More Often than Once a Year (incl. aimless drifting)	128	39.4	47	11.8	124	34.7	23	5.7
Total	325	100.0	399	100.0	357	100.0	403	100.0
	$\chi^2 = 80.01$; P < .01				$\chi^2 = 112.61$; P < .01			

the nondelinquents. Thus, as Table V-7 shows, there was greater mobility among the delinquents than among the nondelinquents.

Of those who moved one or more times during the second period, it is seen from Table V-8 that 52.3% of the delinquents and 48.3% of the nondelinquents moved to different parts of the same city in which they were resident at the beginning of the period (not a significant difference), while 20.4% of the delinquents and 31.5% of the nondelinquents remained in the same neighborhood. Among the delinquents, 12.8% drifted about aimlessly without any fixed abode for at least part of the second follow-up period, but among the nondelinquents, only 2.0% did so.

TABLE V-8. NATURE OF MOBILITY DURING
SECOND FOLLOW-UP PERIOD

	Delinquents		Nondelinquents		
	No.	%	No.	%	P
Remained in Same Section of City	67	20.4	112	31.5	< .01
To Different Part of Same City	172	52.3	172	48.3	< .30
To Different City in Same State	49	14.9	75	21.1	< .05
To Different State	82	24.9	46	12.9	< .01
To Different Country	1	0.3	4	1.1	< .30
Aimless Drifting	42	12.8	7	2.0	< .01
No. of Cases [a]	329	100.0	356	100.0	—

[a] This is a multiple-category table; that is, an individual can be included more than once, and therefore the percentages do not add to 100.0.

TABLE V-9.   KIND OF NEIGHBORHOOD IN WHICH RESIDENT AT END OF EACH FOLLOW-UP PERIOD

	First Follow-Up Period				Second Follow-Up Period			
	Delinquents		Non-delinquents		Delinquents		Non-delinquents	
	No.	%	No.	%	No.	%	No.	%
Poor Residential Area[a]	263	81.4	276	66.7	252	71.6	210	50.6
Fair Residential Area	28	8.7	53	12.8	45	12.8	92	22.2
Good Residential Area	26	8.0	61	14.7	37	10.5	78	18.8
Other (semi-rural, rural, small town)	6	1.9	24	5.8	18	5.1	35	8.4
Total	323	100.0	414	100.0	352	100.0	415	100.0

$$\chi^2 = 22.02; \ P < .01 \qquad\qquad \chi^2 = 35.06; \ P < .01$$

[a] Includes deteriorating tenement, single, or two-family house areas; and factory, interstitial, or lodging-house areas.

NEIGHBORHOOD CONDITIONS

As pointed out in *Unraveling*, both the nondelinquents and the delinquents lived in the slum areas of Greater Boston when we first encountered them. Table V-9 shows that, as time went on, their home environment improved somewhat and that the favorable changes were more frequent among the nondelinquents than the delinquents.

At the end of the first follow-up period, 81.4% of the delinquents in the community, and 66.7% of the control group were still making their homes in poor residential areas; that is, congested urban regions of old and neglected single- or two-family wooden and brick tenements and rundown apartment houses and lodginghouse or factory regions. By the close of the second check-up span, 71.6% of the delinquents — but only 50.6% of the nondelinquents — continued to live in such poor residential areas. Thus, there is an upward movement to better neighborhoods, in favor of the nondelinquents.

Table V-10 shows that 95.9% of the delinquents and 91.1% of the nondelinquents lived in underprivileged areas during all or some of the first follow-up period. However, there was some improvement during the second period in the case of the control group, for by that time 79.1% of the nondelinquents, compared with 91.0% of the delinquents, still resided in such depressed regions. Thus, there was an upward movement — though not very great — among the boys, now young men, originally rated as nondelinquent during the investigations made in connection with *Unraveling*. This would suggest that the nondelinquents made more of an effort than the delinquents to "pull themselves up by their own bootstraps."

TABLE V-10. TIME SPENT IN UNDERPRIVILEGED AREAS DURING EACH FOLLOW-UP PERIOD

	First Follow-Up Period				Second Follow-Up Period			
	Delinquents		Non-delinquents		Delinquents		Non-delinquents	
	No.	%	No.	%	No.	%	No.	%
Some	330	95.9	367	91.1	352	91.0	326	79.1
None	14	4.1	36	8.9	35	9.0	86	20.9
Total	344	100.0	403	100.0	387	100.0	412	100.0
	$\chi^2 = 7.03$; P < .01				$\chi^2 = 21.73$; P < .01			

What of the areas in which the delinquents and nondelinquents were living at the end of the two follow-up periods? What were the probable influences for antisocial behavior in these regions?

Table V-11 shows that 81.2% of the delinquents and 68.1% of the nondelinquents were living in deteriorating slum areas at the end of the first follow-up period; such was the case among 66.7% of the delinquents and 43.9% of the nondelinquents at the end of the second follow-up period. Although some improvement had taken place, only 13.3% of the delinquents and 25.7% of the nondelinquents finally established homes in good neighborhoods (that is, residential areas of apartments or single or two-family houses with a little ground, and free of the unwholesome influences of street life, barrooms, alleys, dumps, railroad yards, hangouts for vagrants). In the improved status of many nondelinquents in respect to the neighborhoods in which they established homes, one begins to get a clue to a continuation of the boyhood divergence between the delinquents and the nondelinquents with the passage of time.

How best describe the poor neighborhoods in which so many of the delinquents and the nondelinquents lived? Table V-12 shows that these

TABLE V-11. EVALUATION OF NEIGHBORHOOD INFLUENCES SURROUNDING HOME AT END OF EACH FOLLOW-UP PERIOD

	First Follow-Up Period				Second Follow-Up Period			
	Delinquents		Non-delinquents		Delinquents		Non-delinquents	
	No.	%	No.	%	No.	%	No.	%
Poor	259	81.2	280	68.1	230	66.7	181	43.9
Fair	42	13.2	58	14.1	69	20.0	125	30.4
Good	18	5.6	73	17.8	46	13.3	106	25.7
Total	319	100.0	411	100.0	345	100.0	412	100.0
	$\chi^2 = 25.44$; P < .01				$\chi^2 = 40.08$; P < .01			

TABLE V-12. NATURE OF POOR NEIGHBORHOOD INFLUENCES
SURROUNDING HOME AT END OF EACH FOLLOW-UP PERIOD

| | First Follow-Up Period | | | | | Second Follow-Up Period | | | | |
| | Delinquents | | Non-delinquents | | P | Delinquents | | Non-delinquents | | P |
	No.	%	No.	%		No.	%	No.	%	
Street Life	248	95.8	273	97.5	< .30	214	93.0	174	96.1	< .40
Barrooms	219	84.6	239	85.3	< .80	185	80.4	163	90.0	< .01
Alleyways, Dumps, Empty Lots	221	85.3	255	91.1	< .05	174	75.7	154	85.1	< .02
Railroad Yards & Tracks	93	35.9	89	31.8	< .40	51	22.2	36	19.9	< .60
Cheap Commercialized Recreation (including hangouts for vagrants)	87	33.6	77	27.5	< .20	42	18.3	32	17.8	< .90
Centers of Vice	76	29.3	73	26.1	< .90	37	16.1	29	16.0	< .99
No. of Cases [a]	259	100.0	280	100.0	—	230	100.0	181	100.0	—

[a] This is a multiple-category table; that is, an individual can be included more than once, and therefore the percentages do not add to 100.0.

neighborhoods were markedly characterized by street life, barrooms, alleyways, dumps, empty lots, and that some of them had the added disadvantages of railroad yards and tracks, hangouts for vagrants, centers of vice.

These, then, were the unfavorable earmarks of the regions in which most of the delinquents and many of the nondelinquents were residing. The malign influences were there, in the external environments in which both groups were living, not only during childhood but in their adult years.

"UNDER-THE-ROOF" CONDITIONS

What was the make-up and character of the households of which our young men were a part, either of their parental families or, if they were married, of the homes they had established with their wives and children? If they were living away from the family home, what was the nature of this home? First of all, what was the size of the household of which our men were a part?

In an earlier table we have shown with whom our young men were making their homes at the end of each follow-up period, but we have not yet indicated the size of the households of which they were a part, or described the interior of these homes.[1] Table V-13 shows that only 6.8% of the delinquents and 2.4% of the nondelinquents were living entirely alone at the end of the first follow-up period, while 9.4% of

TABLE V-13. SIZE OF HOUSEHOLD OF WHICH A MEMBER AT END OF EACH FOLLOW-UP PERIOD

	First Follow-Up Period				Second Follow-Up Period			
	Delinquents		Non-delinquents		Delinquents		Non-delinquents	
	No.	%	No.	%	No.	%	No.	%
Subject Only	23	6.8	10	2.4	35	9.4	13	3.1
2 Persons	40	11.9	87	20.7	50	13.5	45	10.6
3 Persons	92	27.4	132	31.4	61	16.4	95	22.3
4 Persons	74	22.0	89	21.2	76	20.5	105	24.7
5 or More Persons	107	31.9	102	24.3	149	40.2	167	39.3
Total	336	100.0	420	100.0	371	100.0	425	100.0

$$\chi^2 = 22.08; P < .01 \qquad \chi^2 = 19.87; P < .01$$

the delinquents and 3.1% of the nondelinquents were living by themselves at the end of the second follow-up span. At age 25, 31.9% of the delinquents and 24.3% of the nondelinquents were members of households in which there were five or more persons; this was true of 40.2% of the delinquents and 39.3% of the nondelinquents by the end of the second follow-up period. Thus, while more delinquents lived alone or in large families at the end of the first period, the proportion of delinquents living alone or only with one other person was higher at the end of the second period.

But the size of the household is hardly as relevant as overcrowded conditions in the home. It may be recalled that, when originally investigated for the purposes of *Unraveling*, the two groups differed somewhat in the incidence of crowding in the home, 32.6% of the homes of the delinquents being overcrowded (more than two persons — exclud-

TABLE V-14. CROWDING OF HOME AT END OF EACH FOLLOW-UP PERIOD

	First Follow-Up Period				Second Follow-Up Period			
	Delinquents		Non-delinquents		Delinquents		Non-delinquents	
	No.	%	No.	%	No.	%	No.	%
One Person per Bedroom	88	27.3	160	38.7	97	27.4	197	47.1
Two Persons per Bedroom[a]	157	48.8	204	49.4	156	44.1	180	43.1
More than Two Persons per Bedroom	77	23.9	49	11.9	101	28.5	41	9.8
Total	322	100.0	413	100.0	354	100.0	418	100.0

$$\chi^2 = 22.32; P < .01 \qquad \chi^2 = 56.15; P < .01$$

[a] Not including an infant.

ing an infant in the case of a married couple — occupying a bedroom), as contrasted with 24.8% of the homes of the nondelinquents.

It will be seen in Table V-14 that, at the end of the first follow-up period, 23.9% of the homes of the delinquents were found to be over-crowded, as contrasted with 11.9% of the homes of which the nonde-linquents were a part — in both instances an improvement over the crowded conditions of their boyhood homes. There was actually not very much change at the end of the second period, 28.5% of the homes of the delinquents being overcrowded, as contrasted with 9.8% of those of the nondelinquents. However, the nondelinquents had achieved a greater degree of comfort than the delinquents, in that each member of the household had his own bedroom (except for the sharing of a room by a married couple or with an infant); for, by the end of the first period 38.7% of the homes of the nondelinquents were in the "comfortable" category, in contrast to 27.3% of the households of the delinquents; and, by the end of the second span, 47.1% of the non-delinquents, compared to 27.4% of the delinquents, lived in homes in which there was one bedroom for each member. This is a great im-provement over the boyhood years, when only 8.5% of the delinquents and 14.8% of the nondelinquents, and the members of the households of which they were a part, each had a bedroom. This is of course but one index of the comfort of a home, but it does reflect a contrast in the two sets of homes.

The household furnishings surely reflect something of the atmosphere of the home. Did the two households vary in this respect? Table V-15 shows that in respect to home furnishings, and despite the fact that the size of the households of the delinquents and nondelinquents appeared to be similar, a higher proportion of the homes of the delinquents were sparsely furnished. At the end of the first follow-up period, when our

TABLE V-15. FURNISHINGS OF HOME IN WHICH
LIVING AT END OF EACH FOLLOW-UP PERIOD

| | First Follow-Up Period | | | | Second Follow-Up Period | | | |
| | Delinquents | | Non-delinquents | | Delinquents | | Non-delinquents | |
	No.	%	No.	%	No.	%	No.	%
Good	71	23.0	144	36.4	96	31.3	231	56.1
Fair	193	62.4	238	60.1	172	56.0	168	40.8
Poor	45	14.6	14	3.5	39	12.7	13	3.1
Total	309	100.0	396	100.0	307	100.0	412	100.0
	$\chi^2 = 35.58$; P < .01				$\chi^2 = 54.61$; P < .01			

men were 25 years old, 14.6% of the homes of the delinquents, as contrasted with only 3.5% of the homes of the nondelinquents, were found to be drab, threadbare, and with sheer necessities only. These proportions of poorly furnished homes continued to the end of the second follow-up period (12.7% vs. 3.1%). These were homes not only devoid of furniture other than absolute essentials, but of pictures, lamps, bookshelves.

However, 23.0% of the homes of the delinquents were describable as good in the first follow-up period, as contrasted with 36.4% of the homes of the nondelinquents. These were homes in which there was sufficient furniture for all the family's needs, reflecting evidence of planned acquisition. While the proportion of such homes grew in the second follow-up period, when 31.3% of the homes of the delinquents and 56.1% of the homes of the nondelinquents could be categorized as good, it is apparent that the nondelinquents made greater gains. Comparison with the status of their childhood homes shows considerable improvement; when we first encountered the delinquents and nondelinquents in *Unraveling*, only 8.5% of the homes of the delinquents and 12.0% of the homes of the nondelinquents could be described as good. While both groups improved, the progress of the nondelinquents in this one index of improvement is especially notable.

What about the orderliness and cleanliness of their homes at the end of each follow-up period?

Table V-16 indicates that, at the end of the first follow-up period, 67.0% of the homes of the delinquents were found to be orderly and clean, as compared with 79.1% of the homes of the nondelinquents; while, at the end of the second follow-up span, 67.7% of the homes of the delinquents were orderly and clean, as compared with 82.0% of the homes of the nondelinquents. Certainly the *under-the-roof* physi-

TABLE V-16. ORDERLINESS AND CLEANLINESS OF HOME
AT END OF EACH FOLLOW-UP PERIOD

	First Follow-Up Period				Second Follow-Up Period			
	Delinquents		Non-delinquents		Delinquents		Non-delinquents	
	No.	%	No.	%	No.	%	No.	%
Neat and Clean	205	67.0	319	79.1	197	67.7	337	82.0
Fairly Neat and Clean	61	19.9	68	16.9	62	21.3	60	14.6
Disorderly and/or Unclean	40	13.1	16	4.0	32	11.0	14	3.4
Total	306	100.0	403	100.0	291	100.0	411	100.0
	$\chi^2 = 22.62$; P < .01				$\chi^2 = 23.97$; P < .01			

TABLE V-17. HOUSEHOLD ROUTINE DURING
FIRST FOLLOW-UP PERIOD

	Delinquents		Nondelinquents	
	No.	%	No.	%
Planned	165	54.5	322	80.5
Partially Planned	81	26.7	58	14.5
Haphazard	57	18.8	20	5.0
Total	303	100.0	400	100.0

$$\chi^2 = 59.94; P < .01$$

cal conditions were somewhat better, therefore, for the nondelinquents
than the delinquents. Here, too, as with respect to crowding, there was
some betterment of the conditions in which both delinquents and nondelinquents were living when we first encountered them in *Unraveling
Juvenile Delinquency*, for a considerably lower proportion of the
delinquents were, as children, living in clean and neat homes (48.7%),
and a lower proportion of the boyhood homes of the nondelinquents
(65.5%) were neat and clean than in their later years. It may be that
the younger generation of homemakers, having better facilities with
which to keep their homes clean (vacuum cleaners, washing machines,
electric cook stoves), were in a better position to maintain neatness
and cleanliness. (We have noted that installment-buying of kitchen
and other household equipment was resorted to by the families of both
the delinquents and the nondelinquents. The fact of low income did
not deter them from the acquisition of household equipment, and for
this reason the women of the household had many more mechanical aids
to housekeeping than were available to the parental generation.)

Another indication of under-the-roof conditions is reflected in the
household routine maintained by the two groups. This is evidenced in a
systematic concern with specific mealtimes and bedtimes; and, if there
are children, in specific hours for their play, home lessons, and bed-
time. When we first encountered the delinquents and nondelinquents
in *Unraveling*, almost twice as many of the families of the delinquents
as of the control group (29.7% vs. 15.7%) were completely slipshod
in their way of life, but now we find in Table V-17 only 18.8% of
the households of the delinquents in this category and 5.0% of those
of the nondelinquents; so it is already evident that there has been improvement. When they were children, only a fourth of the delinquents
(24.4%) were a part of well-planned households, where the routines
of the day were carefully laid out, as compared with half of the nondelinquents (49.1%). There has (as we see from Table V-17) been

great improvement among both groups in this regard. Nevertheless, a far lesser proportion of the households of the delinquents than of the nondelinquents can be described as maintaining a well-kept routine for the members of the family.

SUMMARY

As might be expected, throughout both follow-up periods, fewer of the original delinquents than nondelinquents were part of normal community living: at age 17, 58.7% vs. 95.5%; at age 22, 60.5% vs. 67.2% (this was a period of substantial involvement in the armed services for the nondelinquents); at age 25, 60.8% vs. 87.1%; and at age 31, 77.6% vs. 94.5%. While the delinquents showed a tendency to earlier marriage, by the end of the second follow-up investigation, similar proportions were living with their wives and children.

Although the delinquents exhibited greater mobility, it was the nondelinquents who showed greater improvement both in the neighborhood to which they moved and in the under-the-roof conditions in which they lived.

From the foregoing analysis it is obvious that, at the very threshold of the follow-up inquiry, the divergence of the two groups under comparison was already evident. It is clear that, while both sets of men improved somewhat in certain aspects of their original status with the passage of the years, the improvement was generally more marked among the nondelinquents than among the delinquents.

Notes

1. The men who were in correctional institutions, in the Armed Forces, or at sea, were omitted in the evaluation of the character of the households.

VI   Health Status

INTRODUCTORY

Under ideal conditions, it would have been feasible to subject the delinquents and nondelinquents — grown to manhood — to the same comprehensive and varied physical and mental examinations originally given them as boys. This was impossible, however, both because of the difficulty of persuading adults to submit to physical, psychiatric, neurological, and psychological examination "merely for the sake of science" and because of the enormous expense involved.

We did the next best thing. All available records in hospitals and clinics were examined and collated, and significant information concerning the health history of the two groups over the years of the successive follow-up studies was thereby obtained.

PHYSICAL HEALTH

In *Unraveling Juvenile Delinquency* it was reported that the general health status of the delinquents varied little from that of the control group[1]: the condition of 92.1% of the delinquents and 88.1% of the nondelinquents was found by the examining physician to be good or excellent; that is, the youths were of sound general development, well-nourished, and at most had only minor, nondisabling defects. Only 1.0% of each group were describable as definitely in poor health, since they were burdened with definite physical handicaps and/or handicapping defects. Thus, the claim made by some that delinquents are definitely inferior in physical health to nondelinquents could not be supported by comparison of the two samples of boys from the slum areas of Greater Boston.

What now, of the situation disclosed by the passage of time?

As shown in Table VI-1, at the close of the first follow-up period, 89.4% of the delinquents and 84.7% of the nondelinquents could be characterized as in general good health. A small divergence in favor

TABLE VI-1. PHYSICAL HEALTH AT END
OF EACH FOLLOW-UP PERIOD

	First Follow-Up Period				Second Follow-Up Period			
	Delinquents		Non-delinquents		Delinquents		Non-delinquents	
	No.	%	No.	%	No.	%	No.	%
Good	388	89.4	371	84.7	349	82.9	404	92.0
Fair	43	9.9	61	13.9	65	15.4	34	7.8
Poor	3	0.7	6	1.4	7	1.7	1	0.2
Total	434	100.0	438	100.0	421	100.0	439	100.0

$\chi^2 = 4.48; P < .20$ $\chi^2 = 17.85; P < .01$

of the nondelinquents was noted, however, at the close of the second period, when the "good" category among the delinquents contained 82.9% of the boys compared to 92.0% among the control group. As during boyhood, there were only very small numbers of men who could be classified as in poor health in either period.

Summarizing the health situation for the two follow-up periods (Table VI-2), it can be said during the first, 85.8% of the delinquents and 85.0% of the nondelinquents had neither severe illnesses nor physical disabilities; during the second, the proportions were 80.7% and 85.9%.

Thus, on the whole, Father Time has not dealt badly with either group so far as their general physical health is concerned. We must therefore look elsewhere for the pressures — internal and external — that have resulted in the diverging ways of conduct that continued among the original juvenile delinquents and their matched nondelinquents.

MENTAL HEALTH

In *Unraveling Juvenile Delinquency*, psychiatric, neurological, and

TABLE VI-2. SEVERE ILLNESS OR PHYSICAL DISABILITIES
DURING EACH FOLLOW-UP PERIOD

	First Follow-Up Period				Second Follow-Up Period			
	Delinquents		Non-delinquents		Delinquents		Non-delinquents	
	No.	%	No.	%	No.	%	No.	%
None	375	85.8	373	85.0	343	80.7	377	85.9
Some	62	14.2	66	15.0	82	19.3	62	14.1
Total	437	100.0	439	100.0	425	100.0	439	100.0

$\chi^2 = 0.12; P < .80$ $\chi^2 = 4.16; P < .02$

Rorschach Test investigations indicated that somewhat more than half of the delinquents (51.4%) and somewhat less than half of the nondelinquents (44.3%) were distributed into neurotics, psychopaths, those with psychotic trends, asocial, primitive, poorly adjusted and unstable persons, those with organic mental disturbances, and those with undifferentiated mental pathology.[2]

One of the larger groups among the pathologic were the psychoneurotics (subdivided into *marked, mild,* and those with *neurotic trends*), and here a significant difference was noted: 24.6% of the boys who were delinquent, compared to 35.8% of the youths in the nondelinquent class, were diagnosed as neurotics. It is to be noted that here is one item in the network of influences we are considering in which there was found a greater incidence among the *nondelinquents.* How does the incidence of neuroticism in early childhood compare with its incidence as determined at the close of each of the follow-up periods, when the boys had grown to manhood? Does the higher proportion of neurotics among the nondelinquents persist?[3]

The first thing to be noted from Table VI-3 is that a divergency occurred between the two groups with the passage of time, the nondelinquents having a substantially higher proportion of mentally normal in both periods. With the passage of the years, also, the incidence of neuroticism tended to equalize among the two groups (although some difficulties of diagnosis may be involved). The incidence of psychotics continued small. It is, however, in the categories of psycho-

TABLE VI-3. TYPE OF MENTAL PATHOLOGY
DURING EACH FOLLOW-UP PERIOD

| | First Follow-Up Period | | | | Second Follow-Up Period | | | |
| | Delinquents | | Non-delinquents | | Delinquents | | Non-delinquents | |
	No.	%	No.	%	No.	%	No.	%
No Conspicuous Mental Pathology	185	42.3	305	69.5	146	33.8	330	74.7
Neuroticism (marked, mild, severe)	101	23.1	99	22.5	68	15.7	63	14.2
Psychoses or Psychotic Trends	19	4.4	9	2.1	21	4.9	7	1.6
Psychopathy	66	15.1	2	0.5	77	17.8	2	0.5
Poor Adjustment	46	10.5	5	1.1	101	23.4	32	7.2
Miscellaneous	20	4.6	19	4.3	19	4.4	8	1.8
Total	437	100.0	439	100.0	432	100.0	442	100.0
	$\chi^2 = 126.21$; P $< .01$				$\chi^2 = 189.68$; P $< .01$			

TABLE VI-4. SOCIAL INEFFICIENCY
DURING FIRST FOLLOW-UP PERIOD

	Delinquents		Nondelinquents	
	No.	%	No.	%
Marked	164	37.6	32	7.3
Mild	87	20.0	102	23.2
None	185	42.4	305	69.5
Total	436	100.0	439	100.0

$$\chi^2 - 119.47; \; P < .01$$

pathic personality and poorly adjusted persons, whose difficulties were largely affective, that as time went on the delinquent group turned out to be more handicapped than the control group. Here, then, is a clue to possible and even probable etiology of delinquency and recidivism, although, as we have previously cautioned and will continue to point out in subsequent chapters, it is hazardous to attribute delinquency and recidivism to one "cause" in isolation from related influences.

As can be inferred from Table VI-3, the less advantageous total situation of the delinquents is shown by the fact that no fewer than 57.7% had — as adults during the first follow-up period — one or another of the conditions deemed on good authority (psychiatric diagnoses in welfare agency, court, and mental hospital records, and other appropriate sources) to be classifiable as involving some mental pathology, while among the nondelinquent control group only 30.5% were so describable. The percentages with noted mental pathology during the second period reflected a distinct advantage on the part of the nondelinquents: delinquents, 66.2%; nondelinquents, only 25.3%. Clearly, then, with the passage of the years, the mental state of the delinquents deteriorated appreciably more than that of the control group.

The effect of mental pathology on social efficiency has been determined for the first follow-up period and is noted in Table VI-4, in which a judgment is presented of actual interference with social functioning (in family life, work, leisure) because of mental pathology.

The more disadvantaged position of the delinquents in respect to the extent to which mental pathology interfered with social activity in work and other respects is seen in Table VI-4. Almost two-fifths of the delinquents as compared with less than a tenth of the nondelinquents, were handicapped in their social efficiency as a result of various forms of mental pathology.

Here again, therefore, the indispensability of considering the individual's personal make-up in any sound assessment of the etiologic involvements in delinquency and recidivism is strikingly evident; and no amount of effort to "place the blame" on the external environment or the culture of the slum area can gainsay the fact.

SUMMARY

The foregoing analysis has shown that, in general *physical* health, the delinquents and nondelinquents did not differ greatly over the years, the high majority of the two groups remaining, as they had been when originally examined as children, in essentially good health.

By the close of the second follow-up span, the original incidence of mental pathology had changed notably. The greater incidence of various classes of neurotics among the nondelinquent group had been reduced to the point where the control group resembled the delinquents in the incidence of neuroticism. With the passage of the years, there was a small increase among the delinquents in the number originally diagnosed as "primitive," poorly adjusted, unstable. There was also a substantial increase in the diagnosis of psychopathic personality among the delinquents, the original gap between them and the control group being widened still more.

It is thus clear that, with the passage of the years from puberty to adulthood, the mental condition of the delinquents as a group had worsened appreciably more than that of the control group of the original nondelinquents.

Notes

1. *Unraveling Juvenile Delinquency*, p. 181.
2. *Unraveling*, p. 239.
3. The difficulties of diagnosis in the field of mental abnormality or aberration, especially as concerns neuroticism and psychopathic personality, must of course not be overlooked. It should be further stressed that the assessments for the follow-up periods were based on records and interviews.

VII Academic Education and Vocational Training

INTRODUCTORY

It will be helpful to review the educational activities and achievements of the delinquents and the nondelinquents, as determined in *Unraveling Juvenile Delinquency* and presented in the early chapters of the present work, so that we may bear in mind, as we examine the later situation, how the two groups fared with the passage of time and their growth into adulthood.

It will be recalled that, despite the original matching of the two sets of boys by age and general intelligence (among other yardsticks), and despite the similarity of the two groups in the age at which they entered the first grade, the delinquents turned out to be definitely more retarded than the boys in the control group. As previously noted, this finding is no doubt partly accounted for by the greater mobility of the delinquents' families and the consequent numerous changes of schools. But this does not completely account for the excessive repetition of grades and the marked backwardness of the delinquents in terms of achievement in relation to age level and grade placement.

To a much greater extent than the control group, the delinquent boys expressed hatred of school, resentment of its restrictions, lack of interest in school work. On the other hand, the few nondelinquents who disliked school did so because they found it difficult to learn and because they felt intellectually inferior.

It will be recalled, further, that when first interviewed, fewer delinquents than nondelinquents expressed definite preferences for certain subjects in the curriculum, although about half of each group markedly disliked some subjects. In equal incidence the delinquents and nondelinquents preferred manual training and disliked verbal disciplines; however, there was a more prevalent distaste among the delinquents not only for subjects requiring strict logical reasoning and persistency of effort but also for those dependent upon good memory. Although the delinquents showed less ability than the control group in reading and arithmetic, the differences between them were not so great in this respect as has sometimes been supposed. The delinquents, however, were somewhat more uneven in their school accomplishment as determined by their achievement in reading and arithmetic tests.

It will be recalled further that the school attainment of the delinquents was far below that of the control group, even less than might be expected in the light of their achievement as measured by the Stanford tests in reading and arithmetic.[1] This would seem to indicate a greater degree of maladaptation to the regimen of a school.

This deficiency is confirmed by the fact that a markedly higher proportion of the delinquent group than of the control group expressed a desire to leave school at once, while a much higher percentage of the nondelinquents planned to go on to high school, trade school, or beyond.

In vocational ambitions, likewise, the delinquents were different from the control group, a higher proportion of the former expressing impractical, childish notions about what they wanted to do in life, or inclining to adventurous occupations and to work requiring little training instead of to trades and more intellectual pursuits.

Unraveling also produced evidence of excessive incidence among the delinquents of various types of misconduct in school, both in point of seriousness and of persistency of misbehavior, especially truancy. This was the first and most frequent manifestation of revolt against the restrictive atmosphere of school among the delinquents who misbehaved in one way or another. Moreover, the various indications of antisocial inclination occurred at a much earlier age among the delinquents than among the very small group of nondelinquents who misbehaved in school. This is a fact which suggests, among other indications, the relative deep-rootedness of the emotional and behavioral difficulties of the delinquents.

But while *Unraveling* established beyond reasonable doubt that the traits, impulses, and behavior involved in the school situation are also found in that form of maladaptation to society's codes known as "delinquency," this chapter is not concerned with the subsequent criminalism of the two groups under comparison,[2] but only with their academic education and vocational training during the years beyond grammar school. Meanwhile, it is abundantly clear that despite the matching of the delinquents and the control group by general intelligence the delinquents were substantially inferior to the control group of nondelinquents in school achievement and related areas.

TABLE VII-1. AGE FIRST LEFT SCHOOL AS DETERMINED
DURING FIRST FOLLOW-UP INVESTIGATION

| | Delinquents | | Nondelinquents | |
	No.	%	No.	%
Less than 16 Years	273	62.3	54	12.2
16 Years	150	34.3	175	39.7
17 Years or Over	15	3.4	212	48.1
Total	438	100.0	441	100.0

$$\chi^2 = 319.55; P < .01$$

ACADEMIC EDUCATION

In considering educational achievement during adulthood, it should
be pointed out that the tracing of the men in the matter of schooling
was conducted only until the age of 25. It was considered that if a
person had not taken advantage of academic and vocational training
opportunities by the time he was 25, there was little likelihood of his
doing so thereafter.

Table VII-1 shows that among the delinquents the excessive proportion of three-fifths (62.3%) dropped out of school before the early age
of 16, while among the nondelinquents the incidence was only an eighth.
At the other end of the scale, only 3.4% of the delinquents, in marked
contrast to the high proportion of 48.1% of the control group, continued their schooling beyond the 17th birthday. The significance of
this finding for the subsequent careers of the two sets of youths demonstrates the need for great improvement in school regimes, curricula,
and teacher personality and training to reduce the proportion of drop-
outs from school who, as we shall see, become in a sense drop-outs
from other areas of life that call for training and foresight.

Table VII-2 shows that some of the youths did have second thoughts
about education, almost three-fifths of the delinquent group, compared

TABLE VII-2. AGE AT FINAL ACADEMIC ATTAINMENT
AS DETERMINED DURING FIRST FOLLOW-UP INVESTIGATION

| | Delinquents | | Nondelinquents | |
	No.	%	No.	%
Less than 16 Years	258	59.2	51	11.9
16 Years	152	34.8	158	36.7
17 Years or Over	26	6.0	221	51.4
Total	436	100.0	430	100.0

$$\chi^2 = 292.73; P < .01$$

TABLE VII-3.   ATTITUDE TOWARD FURTHER ACADEMIC STUDIES
AT END OF FIRST FOLLOW-UP PERIOD

| | Delinquents | | Nondelinquents | |
	No.	%	No.	%
Uninterested or Vague	407	95.1	341	78.9
Some Interest	14	3.3	48	11.1
Eager	7	1.6	43	10.0
Total	428	100.0	432	100.0

$$\chi^2 = 50.37; \; P < .01$$

to only an eighth of the control group, attaining their final academic
achievement by their 16th birthday; and only 6.0% of the delinquents
(compared to 3.4% in the previous assessment) and 51.4% of the
nondelinquents (compared to the earlier figure of 48.1%) did not close
the books permanently until after their 17th birthday.

Table VII-3 shows that, when questioned at the close of the first
follow-up period regarding their attitude toward further academic
study, 95.1% of the delinquents compared to 78.9% of the nondelinquents were either not interested, or expressed only vague, unreflective opinions. At the same time, far fewer of the former (1.6%) than
of the latter (10.0%) were eager to pursue further academic studies.

Variations in the major reason for stopping school reflect, as have
so many other indices, fundamental differences in character and cir-
cumstance between the delinquents and the nondelinquents. Table
VII-4 shows that there is some difference between the two groups in the

TABLE VII-4.   MAJOR REASON FOR STOPPING SCHOOL
AS DETERMINED DURING FIRST FOLLOW-UP INVESTIGATION

| | Delinquents | | Nondelinquents | |
	No.	%	No.	%
Own Volition	199	45.4	239	54.2
Committed to Correctional Institution	172	39.3	0	0.0
Earnings Needed	40	9.1	124	28.1
Induction or Enlistment in Armed Forces	10	2.3	67	15.2
Other Reasons	17	3.9	11	2.5
Total	438	100.0	441	100.0

$$\chi^2 = 262.15; \; P < .01$$

incidence of those who left of their own volition and simply from the motive of release from school obligations (45.4% vs. 54.2%); but, as could be expected, leaving school because of the *force majeure* of commitment to a correctional institution until beyond the school-age limit of 16 was the lot of 39.3% of the delinquents and not a single one of the nondelinquents. As another sign of superiority of the control group, a tenth of the delinquents (9.1%) quit school because their earnings were needed at home, compared to three-tenths of the nondelinquent group (28.1%). Here is an indication that it is not poverty per se that is crucial, but the manner of coping with it. Finally, leaving school because of induction or enlistment in the Armed Forces occurred among 2.3% of the delinquents and 15.2% of the control group.[3]

Before concluding this section on the subsequent academic schooling of the delinquents and the control group, it is informative to indicate the exact degree of academic achievement of the two groups at the close of the initial follow-up to age 25. Considering only categories which involve substantial numbers, Table VII-5 shows that 18.1% of the delinquents, as compared with 4.8% of the control group, had not, by

TABLE VII-5. EDUCATIONAL ATTAINMENT AT END OF FIRST FOLLOW-UP PERIOD

	Delinquents		Nondelinquents	
	No.	%	No.	%
Now in School	2	0.5	11	2.5
Special Classes; 6th Grade or Less	79	18.1	21	4.8
Grade 7 or 8 (did not graduate)	151	34.6	38	8.6
Completed Grade School	24	5.5	19	4.3
Grade 9 or 10	152	34.9	146	33.1
Grade 11 or 12 (did not graduate)	17	3.9	55	12.5
Graduated from High School	7	1.6	95	21.5
Entered Vocational School	2	0.5	8	1.8
Graduated from Vocational School	0	0.0	25	5.7
Entered College	1	0.2	16	3.6
Graduated from College	1	0.2	7	1.6
Total	436	100.0	441	100.0

$$\chi^2 = 250.42; \; P < .01$$

the close of the first follow-up period, shown an accomplishment beyond the sixth grade, and some even lower. An additional third of the delinquents (34.6%) compared to less than a tenth of the nondelinquents (8.6%) had not even completed the eighth grade satisfactorily; and another third of each of the two groups (34.9% and 33.1%) had achieved a ninth- or tenth-grade education. A striking difference between the delinquents and nondelinquents is the fact that graduation from high school (and in some cases further study) was achieved by only 2.5% of the delinquents in marked contrast to 34.2% of the nondelinquents.

Thus it is clear by the record of the later years that the earlier forecast, when the two groups were originally studied, has been essentially borne out so far as academic achievement is concerned.

SPECIAL VOCATIONAL AND PROFESSIONAL TRAINING

While it could perhaps not be expected that our two groups would strive to improve their academic status on reaching adulthood, it seems reasonable to hope that they would make a serious effort to acquire or improve their income-producing skills and vocations. This matter was looked into during the course of the initial follow-up period.

Table VII-6 shows that two-fifths of the delinquents (42.5%), compared to two-thirds of the nondelinquents (66.4%), had in fact acquired some special skill, trade, vocation, or profession by the close of the initial follow-up period. Here, again, the relative inadequacy of the delinquents of the original sample is manifest.

Table VII-7 shows that, of those who had acquired some special skills, 19.9% of the delinquents held skilled jobs (or better) at the end of the first follow-up period, in contrast to 35.8% of the nondelinquents.

Considering the total occupational picture, it may again be concluded that the relative inadequacy of the delinquents, noted originally in their

TABLE VII-6. SPECIAL SKILLS, TRADES, VOCATIONS, AND PROFESSIONS ACQUIRED DURING FIRST FOLLOW-UP PERIOD

	Delinquents		Nondelinquents	
	No.	%	No.	%
None	252	57.5	148	33.6
Some	186	42.5	293	66.4
Total	438	100.0	441	100.0

$$\chi^2 = 50.93; P < .01$$

TABLE VII-7.   HIGHEST SKILLS, TRADES, VOCATIONS, AND
PROFESSIONS ATTAINED DURING FIRST FOLLOW-UP PERIOD

	Delinquents		Nondelinquents	
	No.	%	No.	%
Semi-Skilled Job	149	80.1	188	64.2
Skilled Job	17	9.1	71	24.2
Armed Forces	11	5.9	13	4.4
Own Business	5	2.7	8	2.7
Semi-Professional	3	1.6	6	2.1
Professional	1	0.6	7	2.4
Total	186	100.0	293	100.0

$$\chi^2 = 21.16; \ P < .01$$

behavior when taken on for study in connection with *Unraveling*, is demonstrated to have persisted with the passage of time and the development of the youths into men.

Table VII-8 gives some indication of the extent to which special skills were acquired through the initiative of the youths themselves. Thus, while an eighth of the delinquents with special skills had gotten them through voluntary formal schooling (including correspondence courses), this was true of the much more substantial proportion of 44.9% of the nondelinquent group. Training in special skills was obtained in the Armed Forces by a fifth of the delinquents compared to a third of the control group. The acquisition of skills in correctional institutions was limited to 14.6% of the 185 delinquents involved. Most frequent was on-the-job training: 64.3 of the delinquents, com-

TABLE VII-8.   HOW SPECIAL SKILLS ACQUIRED
DURING FIRST FOLLOW-UP PERIOD

	Delinquents		Nondelinquents		
	No.	%	No.	%	P
Through Formal Schooling[a]	23	12.4	131	44.9	< .01
Armed Forces	42	22.7	93	31.8	< .05
Correctional Institution	27	14.6	0	0.0	< .01
On-the-Job Training	119	64.3	157	53.7	< .05
No. of Cases[b]	185	100.0	292	100.0	—

[a] Including correspondence courses.
[b] This is a multiple-category table; that is, an individual can be included more than once, and therefore the percentages will not add to 100.0.

TABLE VII-9.   UTILIZATION OF SPECIAL SKILLS
DURING FIRST FOLLOW-UP PERIOD

	Delinquents		Nondelinquents	
	No.	%	No.	%
None	16	9.8	18	6.8
Partial	55	33.7	61	23.0
Full	92	56.5	186	70.2
Total	163	100.0	265	100.0

$$\chi^2 = 8.38; \; P < .02$$

pared to 53.8% of the nondelinquents, having acquired industrial skills in this practical apprenticeship way.

As to the extent of actual use of the skills acquired, a tenth of the delinquents on whom reliable information was available were not employing their skills, and the same is true of 6.8% of the nonde-linquents, as seen in Table VII-9. However, fully employing the train-ing they had acquired were 56.5% of the delinquents, in contrast to 70.2% of the control group. Again, therefore, it must be concluded that on the whole the delinquent group presents a less favorable aspect than the nondelinquent group.

The majority of the delinquents, comprising almost twice the pro-portion of the nondelinquents (79.4% vs. 47.8%), were found to be either not interested at all in improving their skills and occupations or expressed only vague ideas concerning them (Table VII-10). But, as a further sign of the many qualitative differences between the delin-quents and the youths of the control group that were noted at the begin-ning and continued during subsequent years, a marked difference was found between the two sets of subjects with respect to ambition to improve skills and occupations: only 7.4% of the original delinquent

TABLE VII-10.   ATTITUDE TOWARD FURTHER
SPECIALIZED TRAINING AT END OF FIRST FOLLOW-UP PERIOD

	Delinquents		Nondelinquents	
	No.	%	No.	%
Uninterested or Vague	332	79.4	203	47.8
Some Interest	55	13.2	116	27.3
Eager	31	7.4	106	24.9
Total	418	100.0	425	100.0

$$\chi^2 = 93.87; \; P < .01$$

group evinced a genuine eagerness for further specialized training, as compared with 24.9% of the nondelinquents.

SUMMARY

The following major points emerge from the foregoing analyses of the educational and vocational achievements of the two sets of men under comparison.

In respect to *academic education,* some two-thirds of the delinquents, compared to only an eighth of the control group, dropped out of school before their 16th birthday; and only a few delinquents, compared to about half of the control group, continued their schooling to the age of 17 or over. Although large percentages of both groups showed little interest in further formal study (over nine-tenths of the delinquents and three-fourths of the nondelinquents), more of the nondelinquents than delinquents were eager to continue their education.

Commitment to a correctional institution was the cause of leaving school among almost two-fifths of the delinquents; and three times as many nondelinquents as delinquents left school because their earnings were needed at home.

As had been found originally in *Unraveling,* academic achievement in subsequent years continued to be lower in the delinquent group than among the members of the control group.

As to *vocational training,* while fewer delinquents than nondelinquents had achieved some special skill, trade, or vocation by the end of the initial follow-up period, the number of either group who had acquired a profession or semiprofession was small. A much higher percentage of the nondelinquents than of the delinquents had achieved their skills on their own initiative, through formal schooling. More nondelinquents than delinquents received their training in the Armed Forces; but more of the latter than of the former benefited from on-the-job training. As to the extent of actual use of the skills acquired, here again the nondelinquents made a better record, in that a higher proportion of them than of the delinquents were fully utilizing their new skills.

Notes

1. See *Unraveling,* pp. 141-143.
2. See Chapter XIV.
3. In a small number of cases it was possible to determine with accuracy the major reason for resuming academic education during the first follow-up period. A strong desire to do so in recognition that they should not have abandoned their studies originally was found for 7 delinquents and 34 nondelinquents Resumption of study owing to special opportunities or pressures occurred for 13 delinquents and 42 nondelinquents.

VIII   Domestic Relations

INTRODUCTORY

So much of the destiny of families — particularly of the children involved — stems from the initial stages of the formation and development of the family group that it is important to examine the outstanding details of the domestic relations of the men we are comparing. It is difficult to strive successfully against a bad start on the marital venture; and the strains and tensions that surround unfortunately mated parents are bound to influence the emotional climate of the home and hence the personality and character of the children. These inferences were sufficiently supported in *Unraveling Juvenile Delinquency* with respect to the parents of our delinquents and nondelinquents; and they gain added force from the marital history of the youths themselves as they set up families of their own. Although we have not studied the children of these men (time and funds not permitting), we wanted nevertheless to learn something of the atmosphere of their marital households.

COURTSHIP AND MARRIAGE

The first indication of marital responsibility is derived from an analysis of the civil condition of the subjects at the close of each of the follow-up periods.

By the end of the first follow-up span (see Table VIII-1), almost half of the former juvenile offenders (46.6%) and of the nonoffenders (48.9%), were still single. But by the end of the second follow-up period, only a fifth of the delinquents (22.8%) and of the nonoffenders (19.2%) had not yet married. Already, by the end of the first follow-up period, 11.9% of the delinquents, but only 2.5% of the nondelinquents, had separated. These proportions increased to 16.2% among the delinquents and 7.3% among the nondelinquents by the time they had reached age 31.

TABLE VIII-1. CIVIL CONDITION OF SUBJECTS
AT END OF EACH FOLLOW-UP PERIOD

	First Follow-Up Period				Second Follow-Up Period			
	Delinquents		Non-delinquents		Delinquents		Non-delinquents	
	No.	%	No.	%	No.	%	No.	%
Single[a]	204	46.6	216	48.9	100	22.8	85	19.2
Married and Living with Wife[b]	182	41.5	215	48.6	267	61.0	325	73.5
Living Apart[c]	52	11.9	11	2.5	71	16.2	32	7.3
Total	438	100.0	442	100.0	438	100.0	442	100.0

$$\chi^2 = 29.73; P < .01 \qquad \chi^2 = 21.64; P < .01$$

[a] Includes one widower among the nondelinquents in second follow-up period. Ten delinquents and 11 nondelinquents who were single at the time of the first follow-up interview actually married shortly before their 25th birthday, but are treated as single throughout the first follow-up period.

[b] Includes those: temporarily separated due to Armed Forces, imprisonment, illness, nature of occupation; not legally married, but living with mate.

[c] Include those: living apart because of incompatibility; legally separated or separated with divorce due; divorced (nisi decree is final).

Table VIII-2 shows that by the time they were 31, one marriage had been entered into by 66.5% of the delinquents and 77.4% of the nondelinquents; while 10.8% of the delinquents and only 3.6% of the control group had contracted two or more marriages. Thus, the lesser stability of the marital ventures of the delinquents becomes apparent, though the difference between them and the control group is not very marked.

Considering the rather uncertain economic status and future of the youths — especially the delinquents — it is a sign of immaturity and

TABLE VIII-2. NUMBER OF MARRIAGES CONTRACTED
UP TO END OF SECOND FOLLOW-UP PERIOD[a]

	Delinquents		Nondelinquents	
	No.	%	No.	%
None	99	22.7	84	19.0
One	290	66.5	342	77.4
Two	44	10.1	16	3.6
Three	3	0.7	0	0.0
Total	436	100.0	442	100.0

$$\chi^2 = 21.55; P < .01$$

[a] Including common law marriages.

TABLE VIII-3.   AGE OF SUBJECTS AT FIRST MARRIAGE

	Delinquents		Nondelinquents	
	No.	%	No.	%
Less than 19 Years	25	7.4	13	3.6
19 or 20 Years	62	18.3	45	12.6
21 or 22 Years	95	28.1	103	28.8
23 or 24 years	61	18.1	76	21.2
25 Years or Older	95	28.1	121	33.8
Total	338	100.0	358	100.0

$$\chi^2 = 11.01; \; P < .05$$

lack of foresight that so many of them embarked on the marital venture when they were still very young (see Table VIII-3). Among the delinquents, 25.7% had married by their 21st birthday as contrasted with 16.2% of the nondelinquents; and almost three-tenths of both groups were 21 or 22 years of age. Of the delinquents, 46.2% were 23 or older when they first married, compared to 55.0% of the nondelinquents.

As is shown in Table VIII-4, the wives, too — especially of the delinquents — were relatively young when they married: 34.8% of those who married men originally classified as juvenile delinquents were less than 19 when they entered upon the responsibilities of marriage, in comparison with 24.1% of those who married men originally classified as nondelinquents. In the case of both the male and female spouses, the delinquent group thus tended to be younger at time of marriage than the control group.

More revealing than age at marriage is the length of the courtship preceding marriage (see Table VIII-5). While the period of courtship preceding the marriage that took place during the first follow-up period was a year or longer among 50.6% of the delinquent group, it was

TABLE VIII-4.   AGE OF WIVES AT MARRIAGES
CONTRACTED DURING FIRST FOLLOW-UP PERIOD

	Delinquents		Nondelinquents	
	No.	%	No.	%
Less than 19 Years	18	34.8	54	24.1
19–22 Years	96	41.7	109	47.7
22 Years or Over	54	23.5	61	27.2
Total	230	100.0	224	100.0

$$\chi^2 = 6.21; \; P < .05$$

TABLE VIII-5. LENGTH OF COURTSHIP FOR MARRIAGES
OCCURRING DURING FIRST FOLLOW-UP PERIOD

	Delinquents		Nondelinquents	
	No.	%	No.	%
Less than 6 Months	42	18.7	17	7.6
6–12 Months	69	30.7	38	17.0
12–18 Months	38	16.9	36	16.1
18–24 Months	17	7.5	12	5.3
24 Months or Over	59	26.2	121	54.0
Total	225	100.0	224	100.0

$$\chi^2 = 41.82; \ P < .01$$

that long among the substantially higher proportion of 75.4% of the control group. At the other extreme, the length of courtship was less than six months among 18.7% of the delinquents compared to only 7.6% of the control group. Here again, therefore, less planning — at least a partial index of less maturity — was displayed by the delinquent than by the nondelinquent group.

Despite the fact that the delinquent and the control groups sprang from an equally underprivileged segment of society, Table VIII-6 shows that a considerably higher proportion of the marriages of the delinquents were forced (31.4%) than of the marriages of the nondelinquents (11.9%).

We have had various evidences here and there of the character of the delinquent and nondelinquent subjects. What about the character of the wives? Thorough investigation of records and, in many instances, interviews with knowledgeable persons, revealed the picture delineated in Table VIII-7.

Half the girls (49.1%) married to the delinquents in the first follow-up span and 80.7% of those who became the wives of the nondelinquents were of good character as determined by the finding that

TABLE VIII-6. FORCED MARRIAGES
DURING FIRST FOLLOW-UP PERIOD

	Delinquents		Nondelinquents	
	No.	%	No.	%
No	153	68.6	192	88.1
Yes	70	31.4	26	11.9
Total	223	100.0	218	100.0

$$\chi^2 = 24.53; \ P < .01$$

TABLE VIII-7. CHARACTER OF WIVES WITH WHOM MARRIAGE
CONTRACTED DURING EACH FOLLOW-UP PERIOD

	First Follow-Up Period				Second Follow-Up Period			
	Delinquents		Non-delinquents		Delinquents		Non-delinquents	
	No.	%	No.	%	No.	%	No.	%
Good	111	49.1	180	80.7	64	45.7	114	79.1
Fair	76	33.6	36	16.2	47	33.6	25	17.4
Poor	39	17.3	7	3.1	29	20.7	5	3.5
Total	226	100.0	223	100.0	140	100.0	144	100.0

$\chi^2 = 52.90$; $P < .01$ $\qquad$ $\chi^2 = 37.67$; $P < .01$

they were not known to police or courts, did not have illegitimate
children, and were known to their neighbors to be reputable. Of the
marriages contracted in the second follow-up span, 45.7% of the delinquents' wives and 79.1% of the nondelinquents' wives were women
of good character. Thus, half the marriages contracted by the delinquents in each span were not to girls of acceptable character as contrasted with a fifth of the marriages of the nondelinquents in each age
span.

Were the marriages, on the whole, harmonious? Is there a contrast, also, between the delinquents and nondelinquents in this respect?

Let us first consider the facts of Table VIII-8 regarding the general
relationships between husband and wife during each of the follow-up
periods. Their association was considered good if they were living
together amicably without undue quarreling or tension and no thought
of separation. Such was the case in the first follow-up period among
57.6% of the marriages of the former delinquents as contrasted with
86.6% of the marriages of the nondelinquents.

TABLE VIII-8. RELATIONSHIP BETWEEN SUBJECTS AND WIVES
DURING EACH FOLLOW-UP PERIOD

	First Follow-Up Period				Second Follow-Up Period			
	Delinquents		Non-delinquents		Delinquents		Non-delinquents	
	No.	%	No.	%	No.	%	No.	%
Good	132	57.6	194	86.6	166	51.7	286	80.6
Fair	29	12.7	17	7.6	79	24.6	36	10.1
Poor	68	29.7	13	5.8	76	23.7	33	9.3
Total	229	100.0	224	100.0	321	100.0	355	100.0

$\chi^2 = 52.21$; $P < .01$ $\qquad$ $\chi^2 = 63.34$; $P < .01$

Viewing the marital relationships of the delinquents and nondelinquents in the second age-span, it is clear that half (48.3%) of the marriages of the former juvenile offenders, either continuing or newly contracted, were not successful: in 24.6% of the cases the spouses were not at all compatible although living under the same roof, and in 23.7%, separation had already occurred. This deterioration in marital relationships was manifest among only 19.4% of the nondelinquents (10.1%, incompatible; 9.3%, separated). Thus, although a slight worsening occurred in the relationships of the spouses during the second follow-up span, nevertheless, a considerably higher proportion of the marriages of the nondelinquents than of those entered into by the delinquents were reasonably successful.

Related to the foregoing are the attitudes and practices of the two sets of married men with respect to the assumption of their responsibilities to wife and children, as breadwinners and as participants in the family life. Here again, as demonstrated in Table VIII-9, there is a marked contrast between the husbands who in childhood had been classified as juvenile delinquents and those of the control group.

Viewing the men during the first follow-up period, almost half (46.3%) of the original delinquent group must be described as sometimes or always derelict in their marital responsibilities, in contrast with only 10.7% of the nondelinquent control group. As time went on there was very little change in the proportions among the delinquents and the nondelinquents who did not fully assume their marital responsibilities. Obviously, then, here is one more evidence of the relative inferiority in character and conduct of the men who, as boys, had been included in our sample of persistent delinquents.

TABLE VIII-9. ASSUMPTION OF MARITAL RESPONSIBILITIES DURING EACH FOLLOW-UP PERIOD

| | First Follow-Up Period | | | | Second Follow-Up Period | | | |
| | Delinquents | | Non-delinquents | | Delinquents | | Non-delinquents | |
	No.	%	No.	%	No.	%	No.	%
Assumed Responsibilities	123	53.7	200	89.3	163	50.3	292	84.1
Sometimes Neglected Responsibilities	59	25.8	19	8.5	109	33.6	43	12.4
Neglected Responsibilities	47	20.5	5	2.2	52	16.1	12	3.5
Total	229	100.0	224	100.0	324	100.0	347	100.0
	$\chi^2 = 72.73$; P $<$ .01				$\chi^2 = 89.56$; P $<$ .01			

TABLE VIII-10. WIVES' EMPLOYMENT DURING
SECOND FOLLOW-UP PERIOD

	Delinquents		Nondelinquents	
	No.	%	No.	%
Did Not Work	131	45.5	143	41.3
Worked Occasionally	69	23.9	43	12.4
Worked Steadily (part or full time)	50	17.4	61	17.7
Worked Until Child Born	38	13.2	99	28.6
Total	288	100.0	346	100.0

$$\chi^2 = 29.73; \; P < .01$$

Whether "working out" by a wife can be looked upon as a reflection of her need to assume some of the financial burdens of the family or an escape from the home into a more exciting environment, Table VIII-10 reveals that equal proportions of the wives of both groups of men actually did go out to work during the second follow-up period. It should be noted, however, that more of the wives of the nondelinquents than of the delinquents worked only until a child arrived, which might reflect a better understanding of their role as mothers.

From Table VIII-1 it was seen that, by the end of the second follow-up span, 77.2% of the delinquents and 80.8% of the nondelinquents were married, although some were no longer living with their wives. Among the married men, one-tenth did not have any children (own, step, adopted), while the proportions of those having one, two, or more children were about the same in both groups (see Table VIII-11).

TABE VIII-11. NUMBER OF CHILDREN AT END
OF SECOND FOLLOW-UP PERIOD [a]

	Delinquents		Nondelinquents	
	No.	%	No.	%
None	32	9.5	35	9.7
One	73	21.7	75	21.0
Two	82	24.4	105	29.3
Three	68	20.3	75	21.0
Four or More	81	24.1	68	19.0
Total	336	100.0	358	100.0

$$\chi^2 = 3.79; \; P < .50$$

[a] Includes illegitimate children of married men, but not those of single men.

TABLE VIII-12. LEGITIMACY OF CHILDREN
BORN DURING EACH FOLLOW-UP PERIOD

	First Follow-Up Period				Second Follow-Up Period			
	Delinquents		Non-delinquents		Delinquents		Non-delinquents	
	No.	%	No.	%	No.	%	No.	%
One or More Born Out of Wedlock	81	46.6	30	22.9	52	21.6	27	9.3
All Legitimate	93	53.4	101	77.1	189	78.4	263	90.7
Total	174	100.0	131	100.0	241	100.0	290	100.0
	$\chi^2 = 18.07$; P < .01				$\chi^2 = 15.65$; P < .01			

Thus, since there was little or no variation in the number of children in each group, the economic burden was about equal among them.

However, considerably more of the delinquents than of the nondelinquents fathered children out of wedlock (Table VIII-12). This obviously reflects a more casual attitude toward marriage and family responsibility among the former juvenile offenders.

The extent to which the children lived with their parents is shown in Table VIII-13, where it is seen that a considerably lower proportion of the children of the former juvenile delinquents were, at the end of each follow-up period, actually living with both their parents.

TABLE VIII-13. WHEREABOUTS OF CHILDREN[a]
AT END OF EACH FOLLOW-UP PERIOD

	First Follow-Up Period					Second Follow-Up Period				
	Delinquents		Non-delinquents		P	Delinquents		Non-delinquents		P
	No.	%	No.	%		No.	%	No.	%	
With Subject and Wife[b]	124	66.0	120	90.2	< .01	220	72.4	289	89.2	< .01
With Subject	0	0.0	2	1.5	< .10	4	1.3	6	1.8	< .60
With Wife[c]	44	23.4	5	3.8	< .01	78	25.6	31	9.6	< .01
Other[d]	20	10.6	6	4.5	< .05	27	8.9	10	3.1	< .01
No. of Cases[e]	188	100.0	133	100.0	—	304	100.0	324	100.0	—

[a] Includes own or adopted children, as well as step-children.

[b] Includes common-law wife.

[c] Includes unmarried mother.

[d] With relatives of husband or wife; in foster homes or institutions.

[e] The data for the second follow-up period are multiple-category; that is, an individual can be included more than once, and therefore, the percentages do not add to 100.0.

INTERPERSONAL RELATIONSHIPS

Among the steadying forces of character are the affectional relations between parents and children, as well as family cohesiveness. As Montaigne has somewhere observed, with more truth than hyperbole, "There is less trouble in governing a private family than a whole kingdom." The influences of parent-child relationships follow down from generation to generation; and it ought therefore to be illuminating to take a look at some of the more subtle yet powerful ties within the newly-established families.

It will be remembered that about four-fifths of both groups had already married by the end of the second follow-up period. Were the families established by these young men more or less stable than the families in which they had themselves been reared?

As children, only 16.0% of the delinquents, in contrast to 61.8% of the nondelinquents, were members of *cohesive* households, which means that there were strong emotional ties among the members, joint interests, pride in the home, and a strong "we" feeling in general. Table VIII-14 shows that, in the households they established, 50.9% of the families of the delinquents and 82.0% of the families of the nondelinquents could be described as cohesive during the second follow-up period. This represents a marked improvement in the delinquent group and continuing improvement among the nondelinquents. Of course it is to be borne in mind that these are as yet young families with very young children, and what the future holds for them beyond age 31, one can only surmise. Over a fifth of the families of the delinquents and less than a tenth of the families of the nondelinquents were already pulling apart (22.3% vs. 7.5%), while a quarter of the families of the delinquents and a tenth of the nondelinquents' families were very much on the brink, for there were already some evidences of incompatibility on the part of one or more of the members.

TABLE VIII-14. COHESIVENESS OF FAMILY UNITS
DURING SECOND FOLLOW-UP PERIOD

	Delinquents		Nondelinquents	
	No.	%	No.	%
Cohesive	160	50.9	282	82.0
Some Elements of Cohesiveness	84	26.8	36	10.5
Not Cohesive	70	22.3	26	7.5
Total	314	100.0	344	100.0

$$\chi^2 = 71.83; P < .01$$

SUMMARY

The foregoing analysis further establishes a divergence between the delinquents and the control group in respect to what is probably the most significant aspect of life — marital and family relationships. By all the indices, the delinquents, grown to manhood and having established their own families, come off second best. Thus, they have essentially redrawn the dismal picture of their own homes when they were children.

The inferiority of the marital and family situations of the delinquents when compared with the nondelinquents is shown in the higher incidence among the former of marital instability, as judged by the proportions of households in which the spouses were already living apart. It is shown further in the greater number of remarriages among the delinquents. It is also indicated in the excessive incidence among them of very early marriages, of marriages which came about after relatively brief periods of acquaintanceship and courtship, and of forced marriages.

Marked divergence between the marital ventures and family situation of the delinquents and of the control group is also demonstrated in the far lower proportion among the former of marriage to women who could by reasonable definition be classified as of relatively good character.

As time went on, the lesser effectiveness of the families established by the delinquents in contrast to those of the nondelinquents emerged in the lower incidence of close, warm, constructive relations between the spouses and between them and their children. A marked contrast was also seen between the delinquents and the control group in attitudes and practices involving assumption of marital responsibilities, a far lower percentage of the former having assumed such obligations.

While, on the whole, there was less divergence between the delinquent group and the control group in respect to the number of children, a higher proportion of the delinquents had fathered children out of wedlock.

Finally, there was a much lower incidence of cohesiveness within the families established by the delinquents than in those of the nondelinquents, this clearly echoing the situation which had been found to exist among the subjects in their own childhood homes. The gap between the family situation of the delinquents and the nondelinquents may widen as time goes on in these as yet relatively young families.

IX   Industrial History

INTRODUCTORY

In the introductory section of Chapter X, certain statements are made regarding the economic condition of the *parents* of the two groups of young adults whose divergent paths we are following into manhood. Here it is appropriate to point out that, in *Unraveling Juvenile Delinquency*, more of the fathers of the delinquents were classified as unskilled laborers, or worked as truck drivers and teamsters, while the two paternal groups were quite similar in the proportions who worked at skilled or semiskilled trades, the delinquents' fathers contributing 29.6% to that category and the nondelinquents' 30.2%.

Considering the reasons why the families in which the boys grew up had to resort to financial aid, it was indicated that while 45.5% of the breadwinners in the families from which the delinquents came were able but unwilling to assume financial responsibility, this was true of only 25.1% of the control group. Further, while inadequacy of income stemming from economic depression and seasonal unemployment existed among 38.9% of the delinquents' families, such legitimate cause of outside aid was present in 59.1% of the families of the nondelinquents.

It was also shown in *Unraveling* that, while the customary work habits of the delinquents' fathers were *good* in 37.6% of the cases, this figure compares with the markedly higher incidence of 71.1% for the fathers of the nondelinquents.

SKILL AND WORK HABITS

Before considering how such indications of the character and habits of the fathers of our two sets of subjects compare with the subjects' own industrial characteristics it is well to note the age at which the boys first began to work (see Table IX-1).

The most frequent age-span of first employment was at 15 or 16,

TABLE IX-1. AGE SUBJECTS FIRST BEGAN TO WORK
AS DETERMINED DURING FIRST FOLLOW-UP INVESTIGATION

	Delinquents		Nondelinquents	
	No.	%	No.	%
13–15 Years	11	2.5	1	0.2
15–17 Years	349	80.2	217	49.9
17–19 Years	66	15.2	145	33.3
19 Years or Over	9	2.1	72	16.6
Total	435	100.0	435	100.0

$$\chi^2 = 117.70; \; P < .01$$

eight out of ten delinquents having started to work in those early years compared to only five in ten of the nondelinquents.

Turning now to the matter of industrial skill, Table IX-2 presents the situation for the two follow-up periods.

During the first follow-up span, only 6.5% of the delinquents, in contrast to 20.5% of the nondelinquents, could be characterized as skilled workers. During the second period, the number of skilled workers had risen in both groups, but the nondelinquents made greater progress than the members of the delinquent group: 27.4% of the delinquents, in contrast to the substantially higher proportion of 56.5% of the nondelinquents, could be characterized as skilled workers. At the other extreme, 62.0% of the delinquents were unskilled workers during the first span and 42.1% during the second, while unskilled workers among the control group amounted to 38.6% during the first period and only 14.6% during the second.

Turning from industrial skill, Table VIII-3 is concerned with the work habits of the two groups.

Work habits were found to be good (these men were reliable, indus-

TABLE IX-2. HIGHEST DEGREE OF INDUSTRIAL SKILL
DURING EACH FOLLOW-UP PERIOD

	First Follow-Up Period				Second Follow-Up Period			
	Delinquents		Non-delinquents		Delinquents		Non-delinquents	
	No.	%	No.	%	No.	%	No.	%
Unskilled	268	62.0	167	38.6	174	42.1	64	14.6
Semiskilled	136	31.5	177	40.9	126	30.5	127	28.9
Skilled	28	6.5	89	20.5	113	27.4	248	56.5
Total	432	100.0	433	100.0	413	100.0	439	100.0

$$\chi^2 = 60.63; \; P < .01 \qquad \chi^2 = 100.63; \; P < .01$$

TABLE IX-3. WORK HABITS DURING EACH FOLLOW-UP PERIOD[a]

| | First Follow-Up Period | | | | Second Follow-Up Period | | | |
| | Delinquents | | Non-delinquents | | Delinquents | | Non-delinquents | |
	No.	%	No.	%	No.	%	No.	%
Good	147	35.2	341	79.3	131	31.9	336	76.5
Fair	113	27.0	69	16.0	129	31.4	83	18.9
Poor	158	37.8	20	4.7	151	36.7	20	4.6
Total	418	100.0	430	100.0	411	100.0	439	100.0

$$\chi^2 = 194.63; \ P < .01 \qquad \chi^2 = 199.64; \ P < .01$$

[a] Includes those in Armed Forces throughout.

trious, an asset to the employer) among a third of the delinquents in each follow-up span (35.2% and 31.9%) as compared with far higher proportions among the nondelinquents (79.3% and 76.5%). At the other extreme, the substantial amount of 37.8% of the delinquents, in sharp contrast to only 4.7% of the nondelinquents, were classifiable as poor workers during the first period, (they were unreliable, loafed, were lazy, dishonest, wayward, ambitionless, or preferred to support themselves and their dependents from illicit occupations); and 36.7% of the delinquents and only 4.6% of the control group were in the poor category during the second period.

It is revealing to note, incidentally, to what degree the industrial training given in the penocorrectional institutions in which many of the delinquents spent time was put to practical use once they were released. As we have pointed out in prior writings,[1] there is something fundamentally wrong in the failure to implement the transition from imprisonment to freedom. It is the height of folly and irony to claim that modern penal institutions have a correctional and rehabilitative aim, and yet to ignore the crucial significance of continuous, intelligent, and sympathetic aid to the *ex*-prisoner in the difficult and hazardous task of crossing the bridge between disciplined institutional life and self-propelling freedom. But let us look at the extent to which industrial training was in fact provided our delinquents by the institutions to which they were sentenced and the extent to which, when it was given, our group actually made use of this institutional training on the outside.

Table IX-4 shows, first and most strikingly, that the considerable proportion of 39.2% of the delinquents involved never received usable training in the various institutions in which they were imprisoned before age 25. This is bad enough; but worse, perhaps, is the fact that 80.9%

TABLE IX-4. INDUSTRIAL TRAINING PROVIDED BY
CORRECTIONAL INSTITUTIONS AS DETERMINED
DURING FIRST FOLLOW-UP INVESTIGATION

	Delinquents	
	No.	%
None	162	39.2
Some	251	60.8
Total	413	100.0

of those who were given training never used such training as they did
receive (see Table IX-5).

Whether they were or were not employing the skills more or less
acquired in the penocorrectional institutions, it is revealing to consider if the reasons for unemployment among the delinquents and
the members of the control group during the last three years of each
follow-up period reflected inadequacy on the part of the subjects.

Table IX-6 indicates that, during the initial follow-up period, only
a fifth of the unemployed men of the original delinquent group had

TABLE IX-5. USE OF INDUSTRIAL TRAINING PROVIDED BY
CORRECTIONAL INSTITUTIONS AS DETERMINED DURING
FIRST FOLLOW-UP INVESTIGATION

	Delinquents	
	No.	%
None	203	80.9
Some	48	19.1
Total	251	100.0

TABLE IX-6. REASON FOR UNEMPLOYMENT
OCCURRING DURING LAST THREE YEARS
OF EACH FOLLOW-UP PERIOD

	First Follow-Up Period				Second Follow-Up Period			
	Delinquents		Non-delinquents		Delinquents		Non-delinquents	
	No.	%	No.	%	No.	%	No.	%
Reasons Reflecting Inadequacy	44	77.2	12	36.4	143	55.6	30	24.4
Legitimate Reasons	13	22.8	21	63.6	114	44.4	93	75.6
Total	57	100.0	33	100.0	257	100.0	123	100.0
	$\chi^2 = 14.80$; P < .01				$\chi^2 = 32.77$; P < .01			

legitimate reasons for being out of work, in contrast to almost two-thirds of the unemployed nondelinquents. It also shows that during the second span (which included a period of general unemployment), 44.4% of the higher number of unemployed delinquents had legitimate cause for not being on the job, compared with 75.6% of the far lower number of unemployed nondelinquents. Although there is little doubt that ex-prisoners find it much more difficult to obtain jobs than do the general run of applicants, the above figures nevertheless record an excess during both periods of delinquents whose reasons for unemployment could not be regarded as legitimate.

Related to this finding is the evidence provided in Table IX-7, which reflects the length of employment on the most recent job during each of the check-up spans.

It will be seen that, among the delinquents, the high proportions of 59.1% during the first period and 38.9% during the second held their most recent job for less than a year, as contrasted with the much lower proportions among the nondelinquents of 39.0% in the first follow-up period and 18.3% in the second. Further, it is in the continuance of steady employment for periods longer than four years that the nondelinquents vary substantially from the delinquents. While lengthy employment at one job may reflect stability, it may also reflect lack of initiative or ambition, or a failure to recognize opportunities for advancement. Whatever the motivation, among the delinquents, 13.8% held the same jobs for four or more years during the first period and 27.8% during the second; among the nondelinquents, 24.6%, during the first span, and the high proportion of 52.8% during the second.

TABLE IX-7. LENGTH OF EMPLOYMENT ON MOST RECENT JOB DURING EACH FOLLOW-UP PERIOD

	First Follow-Up Period				Second Follow-Up Period			
	Delinquents		Non-delinquents		Delinquents		Non-delinquents	
	No.	%	No.	%	No.	%	No.	%
Less than One Year	235	59.1	162	39.0	144	38.9	79	18.6
1–2 Years	47	11.8	70	16.9	48	13.0	43	10.2
2–3 Years	30	7.5	44	10.6	41	11.1	36	8.5
3–4 Years	31	7.8	37	8.9	34	9.2	42	9.9
4 or More Years	55	13.8	102	24.6	103	27.8	224	52.8
Total	398	100.0	415	100.0	370	100.0	424	100.0

$\chi^2 = 34.85$; P $<$ .01 $\qquad$ $\chi^2 = 61.77$; P $<$ .01

TABLE IX-8. EFFORTS TO IMPROVE OCCUPATIONAL STATUS
DURING EACH FOLLOW-UP PERIOD

| | First Follow-Up Period | | | | Second Follow-Up Period | | | |
| | Delinquents | | Non-delinquents | | Delinquents | | Non-delinquents | |
	No.	%	No.	%	No.	%	No.	%
Little or No Effort	323	83.2	214	51.3	202	51.1	67	15.4
Tried to Please Employer	14	3.6	31	7.4	116	29.4	146	33.5
Organized Effort	51	13.2	172	41.3	77	19.5	223	51.1
Total	388	100.0	417	100.0	395	100.0	436	100.0

$\chi^2 = 93.27$; P $< .01$ $\chi^2 = 140.58$; P $< .01$

Information was obtained also on whether efforts were made to improve occupational status during each of the follow-up periods; and in this respect too the nondelinquents had a superior record. Table IX-8 shows that, during the first period, organized effort at occupational improvement could be noted for only 13.2% of the delinquents; within the second period, for 19.5%. In contrast, 41.3% of the nondelinquents made a concerted effort to improve their occupational status during the first follow-up period and 51.1%, during the second. But the fact which repeats the dismal contrasts between the two groups — begun when they were boys and continued through the early reaches of adulthood — is that the very high proportions of 83.2% of the delinquents during the first period, and 51.1% during the second, made little or no effort to improve their occupational status, as contrasted with 51.3% of the nondelinquents in the first follow-up period and only 15.4% in the second.

Table IX-9, dealing with the earnings of the two sets of subjects under comparison, shows that, at the end of the first follow-up period, 86.9%

TABLE IX-9. AMOUNT OF WEEKLY INCOME AT END OF
EACH FOLLOW-UP PERIOD

| | First Follow-Up Period | | | | Second Follow-Up Period | | | |
| | Delinquents | | Non-delinquents | | Delinquents | | Non-delinquents | |
	No.	%	No.	%	No.	%	No.	%
None	37	10.5	21	5.2	5	1.5	5	1.2
Less than $80	269	76.4	277	68.4	134	39.3	85	20.3
$80 or Over	46	13.1	107	26.4	202	59.2	329	78.5
Total	352	100.0	405	100.0	341	100.0	419	100.0

$\chi^2 = 25.25$; P $< .01$ $\chi^2 = 33.70$; P $< .01$

TABLE IX-10. TYPE OF DEPENDENTS AT END
OF EACH FOLLOW-UP PERIOD

| | First Follow-Up Period | | | | Second Follow-Up Period | | | |
| | Delinquents | | Non-delinquents | | Delinquents | | Non-delinquents | |
	No.	%	No.	%	No.	%	No.	%
Wife and Children (if any)	167	71.7	169	74.5	240	78.2	288	82.1
Children Only	26	11.2	6	2.6	58	18.9	44	12.5
Parents or Other Close Relatives	40	17.1	52	22.9	9	2.9	19	5.4
Total	233	100.0	227	100.0	307	100.0	351	100.0

$\chi^2 = 13.99$; P < .01 $\qquad$ $\chi^2 = 6.93$; P < .05

of the delinquents were earning less than $80 a week; at the close of the second, 40.8% were in that relatively low income class. This was true of 73.6% of the nondelinquents at the close of the first follow-up span and of only 21.5% at the end of the second period. It is clear, then, that the delinquents proved inferior to the nondelinquents in earning capacity.

It must be borne in mind that some of the two sets of persons whom we first encountered as boys now have dependents.

Of those with dependents, Table IX-10 shows that 71.7% of the delinquents and 74.5% of the nondelinquents had a wife and children at the end of the first period; while at the end of the second period, the proportions were 78.2% and 82.1%, respectively. Those having only children, amounted to 11.2% of the former and 2.6% of the latter during the first period, and 18.9% and 12.5%, respectively, during the second.

TABLE IX-11. CONTRIBUTION TO SUPPORT OF DEPENDENTS
AT END OF EACH FOLLOW-UP PERIOD

| | First Follow-Up Period | | | | Second Follow-Up Period | | | |
| | Delinquents | | Non-delinquents | | Delinquents | | Non-delinquents | |
	No.	%	No.	%	No.	%	No.	%
Fulfilled Obligations Entirely	148	64.6	216	95.2	203	68.8	315	90.3
Fulfilled Obligations Partially	38	16.6	5	2.2	50	17.0	23	6.6
Neglected Obligations	43	18.8	6	2.6	42	14.2	11	3.1
Total	229	100.0	227	100.0	295	100.0	349	100.0

$\chi^2 = 65.96$; P < .01 $\qquad$ $\chi^2 = 48.13$; P < .01

How did these adults meet their obligations to their dependents? Did they contribute to their financial support even if not assuming the total responsibility?

It is evident from Table IX-11 that the conduct of both the delinquents and the members of the control group in the matter of taking care of their dependents is quite commendable, though here, too, the nondelinquents established a superior record: for while two-thirds of the delinquents carried out their obligations, the incidence among the nondelinquents was over nine-tenths. Moreover, larger proportions of the delinquents than of the nondelinquents were entirely remiss in their duty to dependents (18.8% vs. 2.6% and 14.2% vs. 3.1%).

As a final datum in this chapter, it should be noted (see Table IX-12) that, while the proportions engaging in illicit occupations during the first follow-up period were relatively small in both groups, here again the original nondelinquents had a cleaner record than the delinquents.

TABLE IX-12. ILLICIT OCCUPATIONS DURING
FIRST FOLLOW-UP PERIOD

| | Delinquents | | Nondelinquents | |
	No.	%	No.	%
None	253	81.1	404	97.6
Some	59	18.9	10	2.4
Total	312	100.0	414	100.0
		$\chi^2 = 56.29$; $P < .01$		

SUMMARY

Many more of the delinquents than of the nondelinquents began to work at the early ages of 15 and 16.

During the first follow-up span, far fewer of the delinquents than of the control group were skilled workers; and, while the total of such workers increased greatly during the second period, the gap between the delinquents and nondelinquents in this category widened. Also, there were half as many good workers among the delinquents as among the nondelinquents.

Only a fifth of the delinquents who had received training in correctional institutions ever translated this training into legitimate occupations on the outside.

During the last three years of both follow-up spans, more delinquents than nondelinquents were unemployed, and far fewer of the delinquents than of the control group gave legitimate reasons for their lack of employment. The delinquents held their most recent jobs in each follow-up period for less time than the members of the control group.

While a fifth of the delinquents were found to be engaged in illicit occupations, only a handful of the original nondelinquents were so occupied.

In both check-up spans, there were many more individuals from the nondelinquent category than the delinquent who had made serious efforts to improve their occupational status.

At the close of each of the periods, fewer delinquents than non-delinquents were earning relatively high wages.

While both groups in large measure fulfilled their economic obligations to their own families, the nondelinquents had a better record; far more of the delinquents than of the nondelinquents were entirely remiss in meeting their family obligations.

The foregoing findings show that, as the two groups grew to manhood, the industrial record of the original delinquents was inferior to that of the control group.

Notes

1. See our various follow-up studies, especially *500 Criminal Careers* (New York: Alfred Knopf, 1930; New York: Kraus Reprint, 1965) ; and *Criminal Careers in Retrospect* (New York: The Commonwealth Fund, 1943; New York: Kraus Reprint, 1966).

X   Economic Conditions

INTRODUCTORY

In *Unraveling Juvenile Delinquency* several significant findings were presented reflecting the economic condition of the parental families of the delinquents compared with those of the nondelinquents. It was indicated that, although both groups of boys had been selected for the study from the same generally underprivileged slum areas of Greater Boston, investigation revealed differences in actual economic status in favor of the families from which the control group of nondelinquents derived. While similar proportions (42.4% and 42.8%) of the families were found to be sporadically dependent on outside relief agencies, and 20.0% of the delinquents' families compared to 41.0% of the nondelinquents' were in economically marginal circumstances, only 14.6% of the latter were usually in a state of dependency in contrast to the much higher proportion of 36.2% of the families from which the delinquents derived.

What, now, of the economic condition of the families established by our youths when they married?

ECONOMIC STATUS AT DIFFERENT PERIODS

Table X-1 indicates that only 7.3% of the delinquents and 8.7% of the control group could be categorized as in comfortable economic circumstances before age 25. This means that there were sufficient resources for themselves and their dependents for at least four months in the event of a sudden reduction of the usual weekly income. Only 5.9% of the delinquents compared to 12.6% of the control group were in such circumstances during the 25-31 age-span. The marginal group (living on daily earnings and accumulating little or nothing, resorting to temporary aid to supplement lower incomes during seasonal unemployment or illness of a breadwinner) was the largest, comprising 64.6% of the delinquents and 85.0% of the nondelinquents during the

77377

TABLE X-1. USUAL ECONOMIC CONDITIONS
DURING EACH FOLLOW-UP PERIOD

| | First Follow-Up Period | | | | Second Follow-Up Period | | | |
| | Delinquents | | Non-delinquents | | Delinquents | | Non-delinquents | |
	No.	%	No.	%	No.	%	No.	%
Comfortable	27	7.3	36	8.7	24	5.9	55	12.6
Marginal	239	64.6	352	85.0	223	55.1	336	76.7
Partially, Erratically, or Entirely Dependent	104	28.1	26	6.3	158	39.0	47	10.7
Total	370	100.0	414	100.0	405	100.0	438	100.0

$$\chi^2 = 67.44; P < .01 \qquad \chi^2 = 93.96; P < .01$$

first check-up span, and 55.1% of the former compared to 76.7% of the latter, during the second.

Although the economic circumstances of both groups had improved to the extent that fewer of them were dependent on outside help, the better economic lot of the nondelinquents is again strikingly demonstrated by the fact that, while 28.1% of the delinquents had to be categorized as partially, sporadically, or entirely dependent on outside aid during the first follow-up span, this extreme condition existed among only 6.3% of the nondelinquents; and, while 39.0% of the former had to be so classified during the second period, the much smaller incidence of 10.7% of the latter fell into this category.

COMPARISON WITH ECONOMIC STATUS OF PARENTAL HOME

Another evidence of the improved economic condition of both groups over their childhood homes is seen in Table X-2 where a case-by-case comparison is presented between the economic status in the earlier stage and in the first follow-up period. However, Table X-2 shows that

TABLE X-2. COMPARISON OF ECONOMIC CONDITIONS DURING
FIRST FOLLOW-UP PERIOD WITH ECONOMIC CONDITIONS
DURING CHILDHOOD

| | Delinquents | | Nondelinquents | |
	No.	%	No.	%
Better	203	55.0	222	55.1
Same	144	39.0	168	41.7
Worse	22	6.0	13	3.2
Total	369	100.0	403	100.0

$$\chi^2 = 3.52; P < .20$$

100

the degree of improvement was the same for both the delinquents and the nondelinquents, since a little over half the former group as well as of the latter managed to rise to somewhat better economic circumstances. Only the small proportions of 6.0% of the delinquents and 3.2% of the control group had to be categorized as in worse condition than they had been as children.

EVIDENCES OF ECONOMIC STATUS

The economic condition of the two groups is reflected in certain indices, among them the value of property accumulated (see Table X-3).

TABLE X-3. VALUE OF PROPERTY ACQUIRED DURING
FIRST FOLLOW-UP PERIOD

	Delinquents		Nondelinquents	
	No.	%	No.	%
None	329	78.7	262	60.1
Less than $1,000	57	13.6	103	23.6
$1,000–2,000	14	3.4	35	8.0
$2,000 and Over	18	4.3	36	8.3
Total	418	100.0	436	100.0

$$\chi^2 = 35.45; \ P < .01$$

It is seen that, while only 21.3% of the delinquents had accumulated any property (home, land, business, investments, savings) during the first check-up period, the higher proportion of 39.9% of the nondelinquents had acquired some property. The more comfortable status of the nondelinquents is further reflected in the finding that, while 7.7% of the delinquents owned property worth $1,000 or more, the more

TABLE X-4. BY WHOM INSURANCE PAID
DURING FIRST FOLLOW-UP PERIOD

	Delinquents		Nondelinquents	
	No.	%	No.	%
No Insurance	158	37.7	31	7.1
By Subject	131	31.3	222	51.2
Partially by Subject	17	4.1	34	7.8
By Parents or Wife	68	16.2	76	17.5
By Others	13	3.1	6	1.4
Armed Services Insurance	32	7.6	65	15.0
Total	419	100.0	434	100.0

$$\chi^2 = 128.48; \ P < .01$$

TABLE X-5. INDEBTEDNESS DURING
FIRST FOLLOW-UP PERIOD

	Delinquents		Nondelinquents	
	No.	%	No.	%
None	194	52.3	270	63.4
Some	177	47.7	156	36.6
Total	371	100.0	426	100.0

$$\chi^2 = 10.03; P < .01$$

substantial proportion of 16.3% of the nondelinquents had such possessions.

Another relevant index of economic achievement is the matter of life insurance. Table X-4 shows that during the 17-25 age-span only 62.3% of the delinquents, in contrast to 92.9% of the nondelinquents, were insured. Only half of each insured group paid the entire premium themselves. The others depended on help from their parents, wives, other relatives; and, in some instances, they had Armed Services insurance.

Still another index of economic status is the fact and amount of indebtedness.

Tables X-5 and X-6 show that while it was established in the first follow-up period that 47.7% of the delinquents, as contrasted with 36.6% of the nondelinquents, had debts — on furniture, food, board and lodging, clothing, a car, and so on — the debts, where they existed, amounted to $400 or more among 46.7% of the delinquents who owed money and among 58.1% of the nondelinquents.

It is difficult to comment on this situation in view of the growing habit of buying "on time" on the part of the public at large. It might be suggested that the delinquents were not regarded by lenders as good credit risks.

TABLE X-6. SIZE OF DEBTS DURING FIRST FOLLOW-UP PERIOD

	Delinquents		Nondelinquents	
	No.	%	No.	%
Less than $200	40	23.7	22	14.2
$200–400	50	29.6	43	27.7
$400 and Over	79	46.7	90	58.1
Total	169	100.0	155	100.0

$$\chi^2 = 5.88; P < .10$$

AID FROM SOCIAL WELFARE AGENCIES

Considering the disadvantaged economic status of the subjects involved, it is not surprising that, as had been the case with their own parental families, the two groups of young men we are now comparing had to lean on outside assistance. Table X-7 shows that 38.7% of the delinquents turned for some aid to one or more social service agencies for themselves and/or for their dependents during the first follow-up span, compared to the appreciably lower proportion of 13.4% of the nondelinquents. During the second period, 45.6% among the former and 17.2% among the latter received such aid.

TABLE X-7. SOCIAL SERVICES DURING
EACH FOLLOW-UP PERIOD

| | First Follow-Up Period | | | | Second Follow-Up Period | | | |
| | Delinquents | | Non-delinquents | | Delinquents | | Non-delinquents | |
	No.	%	No.	%	No.	%	No.	%
None	265	61.3	381	86.6	230	54.4	365	82.8
Some	167	38.7	59	13.4	193	45.6	76	17.2
Total	432	100.0	440	100.0	423	100.0	441	100.0
	$\chi^2 = 72.38$; P < .01				$\chi^2 = 81.17$; P < .01			

But the support given the men and/or their families was not limited to economic help, as is shown in Table X-8. It will be seen that in the 17–25 age-span, financial relief given to the men and/or their immediate families was more common among the delinquents than the non-

TABLE X-8. NATURE OF SOCIAL SERVICES
DURING EACH FOLLOW-UP PERIOD

| | First Follow-Up Period | | | | | Second Follow-Up Period | | | | |
| | Delinquents | | Non-delinquents | | P | Delinquents | | Non-delinquents | | P |
	No.	%	No.	%		No.	%	No.	%	
Financial Relief	104	62.3	24	40.7	< .01	136	70.5	39	51.3	< .01
Family Welfare	56	33.5	22	37.3	< .70	77	39.9	39	51.3	< .10
Physical Health	54	32.3	28	47.5	< .05	82	42.5	22	28.9	< .05
Mental Health	24	14.4	8	13.6	< .90	39	20.2	25	32.9	< .05
Child Welfare	17	10.2	3	5.1	< .30	48	24.9	20	26.3	< .90
Vocational/Industrial	13	7.8	5	8.5	< .90	13	6.7	2	2.6	< .20
No. of Cases [a]	167	100.0	59	100.0	—	193	100.0	76	100.0	—

[a] This is a multiple-category table; that is, an individual can be included more than once, and therefore the percentages do not add to 100.0.

TABLE X-9. NUMBER OF DEPENDENTS
AT END OF EACH FOLLOW-UP PERIOD

	First Follow-Up Period				Second Follow-Up Period			
	Delinquents		Non-delinquents		Delinquents		Non-delinquents	
	No.	%	No.	%	No.	%	No.	%
None	204	46.6	214	48.4	124	28.6	91	20.6
One	69	15.7	80	18.1	50	11.5	53	12.0
Two	80	18.3	91	20.6	64	14.8	75	17.0
Three	56	12.8	45	10.2	70	16.2	97	21.9
Four or More	29	6.6	12	2.7	125	28.9	126	28.5
Total[a]	438	100.0	442	100.0	433	100.0	442	100.0

$$\chi^2 = 9.99; P < .05 \qquad \chi^2 = 10.29; P < .05$$

[a] Five men were confined for the major part of the second period, and therefore their status regarding number of dependents was considered "inapplicable."

delinquents (62.3% vs. 40.7%); and while the percentage of such aid increased in both groups during the 25–31 age-span (which involved some years of general economic depression), again, more of the delinquents and/or their families had outside financial help (70.5% vs. 51.3%). The excess of economic aid to the delinquents and their families as contrasted with the nondelinquents becomes more meaningful when we note in Table X-9 that there was, among the delinquents, essentially no excess of dependents. As regards other welfare services, there is no very substantial difference between the delinquents and nondelinquents within each follow-up period.

ECONOMIC TRENDS DURING FOLLOW-UP PERIODS

There remains now only to take note of the ups and downs in economic status among the two groups with the passage of the years. It is seen from Table X-10 that, during the last three years of the first follow-up period, the economic conditions of 84.8% of the delinquents remained static as contrasted with 71.8% of the nondelinquents. They showed improvement among 11.1% of the delinquents and among a higher proportion (27.9%) of the nondelinquents.

In the last three years of the second follow-up span, the economic circumstances of 59.6% of the delinquents and 37.0% of the nondelinquents had not changed; but conditions had improved among 35.7% of the delinquents and 60.0% of the nondelinquents. It would seem that there was more purposefulness among the nondelinquents in pulling themselves out of their earlier circumstances of poverty.

A final piece of evidence of the lesser capacity of the delinquents to

TABLE X-10. TREND IN ECONOMIC CONDITIONS
DURING LAST THREE YEARS OF EACH FOLLOW-UP PERIOD

| | First Follow-Up Period | | | | Second Follow-Up Period | | | |
| | Delinquents | | Non-delinquents | | Delinquents | | Non-delinquents | |
	No.	%	No.	%	No.	%	No.	%
Same	298	84.4	278	71.8	229	59.6	161	37.0
Better	39	11.1	108	27.9	137	35.7	261	60.0
Worse	16	4.5	1	0.3	18	4.7	13	3.0
Total	353	100.0	387	100.0	384	100.0	435	100.0

$$\chi^2 = 44.84; P < .01 \qquad \chi^2 = 48.31; P < .01$$

improve their economic status is afforded by comparison of the extent
of self-support among the two sets of young men at the close of each
check-up span (Table X-11).

During both follow-up periods, about three-fourths of the delinquents, compared to nine-tenths of the nondelinquents, were getting
along on the earnings of the subject and/or his spouse. A notable finding, however, is that, while 10.5% of the delinquents in the first follow-

TABLE X-11. EXTENT OF SELF-SUPPORT
AT END OF EACH FOLLOW-UP PERIOD

| | First Follow-Up Period | | | | Second Follow-Up Period | | | |
| | Delinquents | | Non-delinquents | | Delinquents | | Non-delinquents | |
	No.	%	No.	%	No.	%	No.	%
Earnings of Self and/or Wife	282	73.6	392	89.3	278	75.1	393	90.8
Partly by Earnings and Partly by Family and/or Public or Private Agencies	15	3.9	4	0.9	26	7.0	9	2.1
Partly by Unemployment or Disability Compensation	8	2.1	18	4.1	25	6.8	14	3.2
Entirely by Unemployment or Disability Compensation	16	4.2	18	4.1	10	2.7	10	2.3
Entirely by Family and Public or Private Agencies	22	5.7	7	1.6	12	3.3	6	1.4
Partly on Illegitimate Income	40	10.5	0	0.0	19	5.1	1	0.2
Total	383	100.0	439	100.0	370	100.0	433	100.0

$$\chi^2 = 72.56; P < .01 \qquad \chi^2 = 44.58; P < .01$$

up span, and 5.1% in the second, supported themselves partly through illegitimate income, not a single nondelinquent did so during the first period and only one during the second.

SUMMARY

Both groups were found to be in improved economic circumstances as young adults, in comparison with the more financially depressed conditions of the parental home. The upward movement was toward "marginality," an economic level that only occasionally required outside aid — in other words, a bare subsistence level. Only a handful of both groups had pulled themselves up to the achievement of "comfort," and even this was on a minimal level in most instances.

Although the burden of dependents was essentially equal, a higher proportion of the families of the delinquents than of the nondelinquents sought various forms of outside aid — largely economic — from social welfare agencies. Substantial proportions of both groups received assistance in connection with physical health needs; and, while the incidence of mental health aid did not vary among the delinquents and nondelinquents during the first period, it was greater among the *non*delinquents during the second. (It will be recalled that in their boyhood a higher proportion of them had been diagnosed as neurotics.)

While, over the years, not much property was accumulated by either group, the nondelinquents did have somewhat more than the delinquents, especially during the second follow-up span. Also, a greater proportion of the nondelinquents than of the delinquents had the foresight to carry life insurance, this being partially due to the insistence of relatives and to the fact that the nondelinquents had twice the proportion of government insurance from the Armed Services.

As to the extent of full self-support at the close of each check-up span, this was much more common among the nondelinquents than among the delinquents.

From the foregoing evidence it is again seen that for the most part the men who were originally classified as delinquents rendered a less favorable account of themselves than did those originally comprising the nondelinquent group.

XI Interests, Leisure, Companions, Church Attendance

INTRODUCTORY

In *Unraveling Juvenile Delinquency*, information about how the delinquent and nondelinquent boys used their hours of leisure was gathered and collated from several sources: interviews with their parents (usually the mother; sometimes also with older brothers and sisters); questioning of the boys' most recent teachers; and examination of the records of welfare agencies, settlement houses, boys' clubs, and other recreational centers. One classification of the data was along the lines of recreational preferences; and two characteristics stood out as differentiating the delinquents from the nondelinquents: a substantially higher incidence of boys among the former group whose activities reflected a thirst for adventure, and a far lower proportion of those who engaged in competitive activities. Another difference among the youths was the substantial excess in the percentage of delinquents who attended motion picture theaters as often as three or more times a week.

Regarding the companionships of the two sets of boys, the delinquents were much more inclined to membership in gangs while the nondelinquents avoided gangs almost entirely, preferring a few intimates who, like themselves, were largely nondelinquents.

As to supervised recreation in boys' clubs, settlement houses, and other such places of planned amusement, the delinquents showed far less initiative than the boys in the control group in seeking such outlets, and they attended such places less frequently and less spontaneously. In fact, almost twice as many delinquents as nondelinquents expressed a marked dislike for types of recreation in which there was adult supervision.

While a modification of these and similar findings is to be expected in looking into the spare-time activities of the boys grown to manhood, it may well be that the inclinations expressed early in life are in large measure followed in adulthood. Most of the findings about leisure-time interests were obtained at the end of the first follow-up period and were gained from interviews with the men and/or close members of their families, as well as from social agency records.

LEISURE TIME AT HOME

At the outset it is of value to learn the extent to which the young adults under discussion spent any leisure time at home instead of in saloons, poolrooms, and other such places.

TABLE XI-1. AMOUNT OF LEISURE TIME SPENT IN HOME DURING FIRST FOLLOW-UP PERIOD

| | Delinquents | | Nondelinquents | |
	No.	%	No.	%
Little or None	118	33.1	34	8.3
Some	182	51.0	314	76.8
All or Almost All	57	15.9	61	14.9
Total	357	100.0	409	100.0
		$\chi^2 = 78.51$; P < .01		

Table XI-1 shows that during the first follow-up period, only 15.9% of the delinquents and 14.9% of the nondelinquents spent all or most of their leisure time in the home of which they were a part. At the other extreme, 33.1% of the former and only 8.3% of the latter devoted little or none of their spare time to activities in the home.

It was clear, in *Unraveling*, that the homes of the delinquent boys were so unattractive as to tend to have an expulsive effect, the boys preferring the streets for their leisure-time activities. What was the situation later, when they were men?

Table XI-2 shows that 36.1% of the homes of the original delinquents were definitely classifiable as poor (overcrowded, unclean, generally unattractive), this comparing with only 8.6% among the

TABLE XI-2. SUITABILITY OF HOME FOR LEISURE TIME ACTIVITY DURING FIRST FOLLOW-UP PERIOD

| | Delinquents | | Nondelinquents | |
	No.	%	No.	%
Poor	128	36.1	35	8.6
Fair	114	32.1	111	27.4
Good	113	31.8	259	64.0
Total	355	100.0	405	100.0
		$\chi^2 = 107.56$; P < .01		

TABLE XI-3.   FAMILY GROUP RECREATION
DURING FIRST FOLLOW-UP PERIOD

	Delinquents		Nondelinquents	
	No.	%	No.	%
None	134	39.8	51	12.8
Slight	64	19.0	68	17.1
Customary	139	41.2	279	70.1
Total	337	100.0	398	100.0

$$\chi^2 = 79.74; P < .01$$

control group. At the other extreme, while 31.8% of the delinquents'
homes could be rated as *good* in this respect, double the proportion
(64.0%) of the homes of the nondelinquents fell into this favorable
category. Thus, considerably more of the households of both sets of
young adults could be rated as suitable for leisure-time activities than
were their childhood homes, the proportion of nondelinquents' homes
now adequate for such use being, however, substantially higher (64.0%
during the first follow-up period compared to 13.8% at the time of the
Unraveling Juvenile Delinquency investigation).

One of the important influences and indications of family solidarity
and mutual affection between the members is the extent to which they
share recreational activities. Table XI-3 shows that 39.8% of the
families of which the delinquents were a part had no such united family
enjoyment of leisure during the first follow-up span, this comparing

TABLE XI-4.   NATURE OF LEISURE ACTIVITIES AT HOME
DURING FIRST FOLLOW-UP PERIOD

	Delinquents		Nondelinquents		
	No.	%	No.	%	P
Radio and/or TV	223	93.3	348	93.0	< .90
Newspapers, Books, Magazines	193	80.7	320	85.6	< .20
Home Improvement	102	42.7	214	57.2	< .01
Playing with Children	69	28.9	100	26.7	< .60
Hobbies	31	13.0	92	24.6	< .01
Entertaining	18	7.5	46	12.3	< .10
Studying	16	6.7	74	19.8	< .01
Card Playing	5	2.1	6	1.6	< .70
Other	1	0.4	4	1.1	< .40
No. of Cases[a]	239	100.0	374	100.0	—

[a] This is a multiple-category table; that is, an individual can be included more than once,
and therefore the percentages do not add to 100.0.

with only 12.8% among the nondelinquents. At the other extreme, family group recreations were customary among 41.2% of the households of which the delinquents were a part, compared to 70.1% among the control group.

In what ways did the young men, delinquents and nondelinquents, spend their leisure hours at home?

Comparing the nature of leisure-time activities at home among the young men who, during the first follow-up period, actually did pass some of their spare time under the home roof, it is interesting to note from Table XI-4 that, expectably, over nine-tenths of both groups engaged in the familiar family pastimes of radio listening and television viewing. Some four-fifths of both groups devoted part of their leisure time to reading newspapers, magazines, or books; about a fourth of each group who returned home for leisure spent some of it in playing with their children or the children of relatives or neighbors. The differences between the delinquents and nondelinquents — outside of the fact that, as seen in Table XI-1, a higher proportion of the former spent little or no time at home — are evidenced in the findings that a lower proportion of the delinquents than of the nondelinquents (42.7% vs. 57.2%) passed some time in making home improvements; fewer delinquents than nondelinquents (13.0% vs. 24.6%) had constructive hobbies (such as stamp collecting, photography, playing musical instruments, painting, carpentry); and fewer (6.7% vs. 19.8%) carried on home studies (usually correspondence courses).

It is evident from the analysis up to this point that in the various aspects of use of leisure the path of the boys who had originally been included in the delinquent group is less straight and less bright than that of the young men who comprised the sample of nondelinquents in *Unraveling*.

OTHER PLACES OF RECREATION

Where, and in what activities, did our delinquent and nondelinquent youths spend their leisure time apart from the home during their early adult years?

Table XI-5 provides an indirect index of how the wide differences in original endowment and in early childhood standard-setting and habit formation, as recorded in *Unraveling*, influenced the conduct of our subjects as young adults. Thus, while 50.7% of the delinquents frequented taverns, barrooms, and nightclubs, only 18.4% of the nondelinquents were habitués of such places; and while 19.1% of the delinquents spent much time in hanging around street corners and

TABLE XI-5. OTHER PLACES OF RECREATION
DURING FIRST FOLLOW-UP PERIOD

	Delinquents		Nondelinquents		
	No.	%	No.	%	P
Cafes, Taverns, Barrooms, Night Clubs	183	50.7	72	18.4	< .01
At Homes of Friends or Relatives	147	40.7	281	71.9	< .01
Pool Rooms, Bowling Alleys	128	35.5	162	41.4	< .10
Dance Halls, Roller Skating Rinks	78	21.6	136	34.8	< .01
Street Corners, Corner Stores	69	19.1	37	9.5	< .01
Bookie Joints, Gambling Places, Penny Arcades	44	12.2	11	2.8	< .01
Race Tracks	18	5.0	14	3.6	< .40
Place of Employment	5	1.4	6	1.5	< .90
Educational Organizations	2	0.5	3	0.8	< .70
No. of Cases [a]	361	100.0	391	100.0	—

[a] This is a multiple-category table; that is, an individual can be included more than once, and therefore the percentages do not add to 100.0.

neighborhood stores where youths of similar inclination were accustomed to gather, only 9.5% of the nondelinquents did so. Again, while 12.2% of the former wasted much time (and money perhaps) in "bookie joints," gambling places, and penny arcades, only 2.8% of the latter did so. On the other hand, the frequenting of poolrooms, bowling alleys, dance halls, and roller-skating rinks was more numerous among the nondelinquents than the delinquents. Perhaps the most revealing finding is that, while 71.9% of the nondelinquents spent much of their leisure time in the homes of relatives or friends, the substantially lower proportion of 40.7% of the delinquents did so.

COMPANIONS

It should be recalled that the companions of the juvenile delinquents were largely of questionable character, 98.4% of the boys having one or more disreputable playmates; but this was so among only 7.4% of the nondelinquents. What changes were evident by the end of the first follow-up span?

Table XI-6 shows that the proportion of the delinquent group having some disreputable companions was reduced to 78.1% and that in the nondelinquent group it increased to 24.6%. (The latter rise will become clearer when we present the behavioral picture of the nondelinquents who became delinquent.) Table XI-6 also shows that, during the first follow-up period, the majority of both groups were neither

TABLE XI-6. TYPE OF COMPANIONS
DURING FIRST FOLLOW-UP PERIOD

	Delinquents		Nondelinquents	
	No.	%	No.	%
No Companions or a Few Friends	285	73.3	346	82.2
Gang or Crowd	104	26.7	75	17.8
Total	389	100.0	421	100.0
$\chi^2 = 9.35$; P $<$ .01				
Some Disreputable	299	78.1	103	24.6
Reputable	84	21.9	315	75.4
Total	383	100.0	418	100.0
$\chi^2 = 228.20$; P $<$ .01				

members of gangs nor of crowds but were attached to a few friends (delinquents, 73.3%; nondelinquents, 82.2%).

READING PRACTICES DURING FIRST FOLLOW-UP PERIOD

A major source of ideation and suggestion is reading matter. Considering the general socioeconomic class from which both the delinquents and the control group came, it might be expected that their reading materials would be quite similar. But this did not prove to be so.

As regards newspapers, Table XI-7 shows that while 49.5% of the delinquents read only tabloids, this was true of but 27.2% of the control group. There was also a divergence between the former juvenile delinquents and the control group of nonoffenders in the frequency of reading of newspapers (see Table XI-8), only 48.4% of the delinquents being daily readers as contrasted with the substantially greater proportion of 71.2% of the nondelinquents.

TABLE XI-7. TYPE OF NEWSPAPERS READ
DURING FIRST FOLLOW-UP PERIOD

	Delinquents		Nondelinquents	
	No.	%	No.	%
Tabloids Only	187	49.5	116	27.2
Tabloids and Nontabloids	182	48.1	310	72.6
None	9	2.4	1	0.2
Total	378	100.0	427	100.0
$\chi^2 = 53.54$; P $<$ .01				

TABLE XI-8.   FREQUENCY OF NEWSPAPER READING
DURING FIRST FOLLOW-UP PERIOD

	Delinquents		Nondelinquents	
	No.	%	No.	%
Daily	186	48.4	309	71.2
Not Daily	198	51.6	125	28.8
Total	384	100.0	434	100.0

$$\chi^2 = 44.17; P < .01$$

Table XI-9 shows a small — but statistically significant — divergence in the proportions of the two groups who were magazine readers (delinquents, 85.8%; nondelinquents, 94.0%).

However, as shown in Table XI-10, regularity of periodical reading did differ more markedly between the two groups, 23.6% of the delinquents compared to 43.4% of the nondelinquents being steady readers.

There is, moreover, a difference in the types of periodicals customarily read by the two groups, although, as is shown in Table XI-11, the patterns do not fall into clean-cut divergencies of taste reflective of differences in fundamental attitudes. What is perhaps the most revealing contrast in reading tastes is that 47.2% of the delinquents often read

TABLE XI-9.   MAGAZINE READING
DURING FIRST FOLLOW-UP PERIOD

	Delinquents		Nondelinquents	
	No.	%	No.	%
Some	339	85.8	408	94.0
None	56	14.2	26	6.0
Total	395	100.0	434	100.0

$$\chi^2 = 15.55; P < .01$$

TABLE XI-10.   FREQUENCY OF MAGAZINE READING
DURING FIRST FOLLOW-UP PERIOD

	Delinquents		Nondelinquents	
	No.	%	No.	%
Occasionally	224	66.1	204	50.0
Frequently	35	10.3	27	6.6
Regularly	80	23.6	177	43.4
Total	339	100.0	408	100.0

$$\chi^2 = 32.47; P < .01$$

TABLE XI-11. TYPE OF MAGAZINE READING
DURING FIRST FOLLOW-UP PERIOD

| | Delinquents | | Nondelinquents | | |
	No.	%	No.	%	P
Comics	160	47.2	82	20.1	< .01
Pictorial	118	34.8	199	48.8	< .01
News	68	20.0	129	31.6	< .01
Semiprofessional or Religious	26	7.7	74	18.2	< .01
Pulp	25	7.4	18	4.4	< .10
Fiction	25	7.4	67	16.4	< .01
Sports	20	5.9	40	9.8	< .10
Trade or Professional	6	1.8	36	8.8	< .01
Anything Available	3	0.9	2	0.5	< .60
No. of Cases[a]	339	100.0	408	100.0	—

[a] This is a multiple-category table; that is, an individual can be included more than once, and therefore the percentages do not add to 100.0.

"comics," while only 20.1% of the control group did so. While 34.8% of these delinquents were in the habit of reading pictorial magazines, this was true of 48.8% of the control group; and, while 20.0% of the delinquents read news periodicals, 31.6% of the control group did so. Furthermore, only 7.7% of the former read semiprofessional or religious journals, while the higher proportion of 18.2% of the nondelinquents found interest in such publications.

Although it might be expected that there was relatively little reading of books by the men comprising the two samples under comparison, such reading in fact turned out to be quite considerable, even before the avalanche of paperbacks. This fact is brought out in Table XI-12, from which it is also evident that the proportion of even occasional book readers was much lower among the delinquents than among the nondelinquents. And, expectedly, a lower proportion of the book-reading

TABLE XI-12. BOOK READING DURING FIRST FOLLOW-UP PERIOD

| | Delinquents | | Nondelinquents | |
	No.	%	No.	%
None	232	59.9	139	32.2
Some	155	40.1	293	67.8
Total	387	100.0	432	100.0

$$\chi^2 = 63.53; P < .01$$

TABLE XI-13. FREQUENCY OF BOOK READING
DURING FIRST FOLLOW-UP PERIOD

	Delinquents		Nondelinquents	
	No.	%	No.	%
Occasionally	86	56.6	148	50.7
Frequently	26	17.1	28	9.6
Regularly	40	26.3	116	39.7
Total	152	100.0	292	100.0

$$\chi^2 = 10.12_1 \text{ P} < .01$$

delinquents than of the control group read regularly, as shown in Table XI-13.

Finally, Table XI-14 shows some differences, also, in the types of books usually read. Thus, 31.6% of the delinquents who read books were interested in educational or religious books or books dealing with hobbies, in contrast with 41.3% of the nondelinquents; while 28.4% of the former liked to read books dealing with detectives, crimes, mysteries, this was true of only 16.7% of the nondelinquents; and while 12.9% of the book-reading delinquents read general fiction, 22.5% of the control group did so.

TABLE XI-14. TYPE OF BOOKS READ
DURING FIRST FOLLOW-UP PERIOD

	Delinquents		Nondelinquents		
	No.	%	No.	%	P
Educational, Religious, Hobby	49	31.6	121	41.3	< .05
Detective and Crime Fiction, Mysteries	44	28.4	49	16.7	< .01
Western Fiction	27	17.4	32	10.9	< .10
General Fiction	20	12.9	66	22.5	< .02
Adventure Fiction	19	12.3	31	10.6	< .60
Anything Available	9	5.8	9	3.1	< .20
Biography or Nonfiction	7	4.5	24	8.2	< .20
Romantic Fiction	6	3.9	3	1.0	< .05
Travel, Sports	3	1.9	10	3.4	< .40
No. of Cases[a]	155	100.0	293	100.0	—

[a] This is a multiple-category table; that is, an individual can be included more than once, and therefore the percentages do not add to 100.0.

ATTENDANCE AT MOVIES; BURLESQUE SHOWS

It will be recalled that there was excessive movie attendance among the delinquent boys when their use of leisure was originally investi-

TABLE XI-15.   FREQUENCY OF MOVIE ATTENDANCE
DURING FIRST FOLLOW-UP PERIOD

	Delinquents		Nondelinquents	
	No.	%	No.	%
None	3	0.8	3	0.7
Less than Once a Week	106	27.1	169	39.2
Once a Week	171	43.7	210	48.7
Twice a Week	65	16.6	31	7.2
Three or More Times a week	44	11.3	17	4.0
Erratic	2	0.5	1	0.2
Total	391	100.0	431	100.0

$$\chi^2 = 40.89; P < .01$$

gated. As time went on, the divergence between them and the control group, though somewhat less marked than originally, still reflected a greater tendency among the delinquents to spend considerable time in the make-believe world of motion pictures and vicarious adventure. As shown in Table XI-15, both groups were movie-goers, but 27.9% of the delinquents, as compared with 11.2% of the control group, went to the movies at least twice a week.

There was very little difference, in general, in the type of movie preferred, except that a somewhat higher proportion of the delinquents expressed a preference for comedies, as is shown in Table XI-16.

TABLE XI-16.   TYPE OF MOVIES PREFERRED
DURING FIRST FOLLOW-UP PERIOD

	Delinquents		Nondelinquents		P
	No.	%	No.	%	
Indiscriminate	152	38.6	166	38.7	< .99
Crime, Detective, Adventure, Mystery, War, Westerns	137	34.8	143	33.3	< .70
Musicals	108	27.4	113	26.3	< .80
Comedies	73	18.5	48	11.2	< .01
Drama	17	4.3	35	8.2	< .05
News, Sports	12	3.0	6	1.4	< .20
Romance	2	0.5	6	1.4	< .20
Cartoons	0	0.0	1	0.2	< .40
Documentary	1	0.3	0	0.0	< .30
Total	394	100.0	429	100.0	—

TABLE XI-17.   ATTENDANCE AT BURLESQUE SHOWS
DURING FIRST FOLLOW-UP PERIOD

	Delinquents		Nondelinquents	
	No.	%	No.	%
None	179	52.6	277	70.3
Some	161	47.4	117	29.7
Total	340	100.0	394	100.0

$\chi^2 = 24.19$; $P < .01$

Perhaps one suggestive sidelight is furnished by the extent to which the two sets of young men attended burlesque shows. Table XI-17 reveals that, while 47.4% of the delinquents attended such performances from time to time, only 29.7% of the nondelinquents frequented burlesque shows.

CIVIC INTERESTS AND CLUB MEMBERSHIP

Is there a difference between the former juvenile delinquents of *Unraveling* and the control group of nondelinquents in the extent of their interest in community affairs as young adults? Were they concerned with the betterment of their neighborhoods? Did they take part in any formal activities in this regard? Were they aware of their duties as citizens? Did they belong to civic organizations, political clubs, neighborhood improvement societies?

Table XI-18 reveals that, while both the delinquents and the members of the control group were largely deficient in interest in civic affairs, there was nevertheless a substantial difference in favor of the nondelinquents: thus, only 2.0% of the delinquents expressed a genuine interest in their community, as compared with 10.6% of the nondelinquents; and, while only 2.5% of the former indicated a slight interest in civic activities, 22.7% of the nondelinquents did. Some of these

TABLE XI-18.   INTEREST IN CIVIC AFFAIRS
DURING FIRST FOLLOW-UP PERIOD

	Delinquents		Nondelinquents	
	No.	%	No.	%
None	376	95.5	282	66.7
Slight	10	2.5	96	22.7
Active	8	2.0	45	10.6
Total	394	100.0	423	100.0

$\chi^2 = 108.15$; $P < .01$

TABLE XI-19.   ATTENDANCE AT CLUBS
DURING FIRST FOLLOW-UP PERIOD

| | Delinquents | | Nondelinquents | |
	No.	%	No.	%
None	333	86.0	312	74.3
Some	54	14.0	108	25.7
Total	387	100.0	420	100.0

$$\chi^2 = 17.36; \text{P} < .01$$

interests were stimulated by local veterans' organizations and some by local politicians who were able to capture the attention of these young men.

It will be recalled that, during the investigation of our subjects — as boys — in connection with *Unraveling*, the delinquent group was excessively averse to supervised recreation, such as settlement houses and boys' clubs. As will be seen in Table XI-19, in the 17–25 age-span this tendency persisted: for, while 14.0% of the delinquents attended various types of clubs, 25.7% of the control group did so.

What kinds of clubs for adults did the men of the two groups join? While the actual number of club members is small and half as many delinquents as nondelinquents became members, Table XI-20 shows that, among those who did join, a higher proportion of the delinquents than of the control group belonged to veterans' organizations; a lower proportion was attracted to recreational and to athletic clubs.

TABLE XI-20.   NATURE OF CLUBS ATTENDED
DURING FIRST FOLLOW-UP PERIOD

| | Delinquents | | Nondelinquents | | |
	No.	%	No.	%	P
Veterans Organizations	26	48.1	32	29.6	< .05
Recreational Clubs	12	22.2	43	39.8	< .05
Fraternal Orders	4	7.4	10	9.3	< .70
Religious Clubs	4	7.4	6	5.6	< .70
Political Clubs	3	5.6	1	0.9	< .10
Community Clubs with Civic Improvement Programs	2	3.7	3	2.8	< .80
Athletic Clubs	2	3.7	13	12.0	< .10
Other	3	5.6	6	5.6	—
No. of Cases [a]	54	100.0	108	100.0	—

[a] This is a multiple-category table; that is, an individual can be included more than once, and therefore the percentages do not add to 100.0.

CHURCH ATTENDANCE

It is generally accepted, even in this age of burgeoning skepticism and agnosticism, that religion is one of the most potent moral forces in society, the church constantly reminding parishioners of the conduct norms and standards set down in the Bible, and attendance at religious ceremonies reinforcing such reminders. What was the situation in respect to religious observances in the two groups under comparison?

From Table XI-21 the fact is established that while 40.8% of the delinquents attended church less frequently in young adulthood than in boyhood, only 17.4% of the nondelinquents were now less frequent church attendants.

Table XI-22 reflects a falling-off in church attendance both among the former juvenile delinquents and the nondelinquents. In their boyhood, only 6.5% of the delinquents and 4.2% of the nondelinquents did not attend church at all. During the last three years of the second follow-up period, 43.0% of the delinquents, in contrast to only 11.4% of the nondelinquents, did not attend church.

Much of the influence of religion for good is brought about indirectly through church societies. In not taking advantage of such fellowship,

TABLE XI-21. CHANGE IN FREQUENCY OF CHURCH ATTENDANCE DURING FIRST FOLLOW-UP PERIOD

| | Delinquents | | Nondelinquents | |
	No.	%	No.	%
Less Frequently	163	40.8	75	17.4
No Change	220	55.0	331	76.8
More Frequently	17	4.2	25	5.8
Total	400	100.0	431	100.0

$$\chi^2 = 55.35; P < .01$$

TABLE XI-22. CHURCH ATTENDANCE DURING LAST THREE YEARS OF SECOND FOLLOW-UP PERIOD

| | Delinquents | | Nondelinquents | |
	No.	%	No.	%
None	157	43.0	48	11.4
Occasional	171	46.9	177	42.0
Regular	37	10.1	196	46.6
Total	365	100.0	421	100.0

$$\chi^2 = 163.39; P < .01$$

TABLE XI-23.   ATTENDANCE AT CHURCH SOCIETIES
DURING LAST THREE YEARS OF FIRST FOLLOW-UP PERIOD

	Delinquents		Nondelinquents	
	No.	%	No.	%
None	385	97.0	340	81.0
Concerned with Religion Only	10	2.5	61	14.5
Concerned with Social or Civic Activities	2	0.5	19	4.5
Total	397	100.0	420	100.0

$$\chi^2 = 52.56;\ P < .01$$

both groups were to a great extent remiss; but, as shown in Table XI-23, the delinquents were more neglectful in this respect than the nondelinquents: only 3.0% of the delinquents ever attended church societies, as compared with 19.0% of the nondelinquents.

SUMMARY

More of the delinquents than of the nondelinquents spent most of their leisure time away from home. Part of this appeared to stem from the lesser suitability of the homes of the delinquents for recreational activities. Although a lower proportion of the delinquents participated in family group recreations, it is to be especially noted that a considerable improvement over their childhood situation occurred in both sets of adults.

Although many of the delinquents and nondelinquents had only a few friends, a much higher proportion of the delinquents' companions were criminals or otherwise disreputable than was the case among the nondelinquents.

The reading interests of the delinquents were found to be narrower than those of the nondelinquents, even their newspaper reading being more confined to tabloids. The apparently greater need for vicarious enjoyment among the delinquents is evident in the much higher proportion among them who attended movies excessively and frequented burlesque shows. Neither the delinquents nor nondelinquents were great "joiners" in adulthood, the delinquents even less so than the nondelinquents.

As to the religious interests of the delinquents and nondelinquents, there was a decline in church attendance among both groups — more so among the former. The delinquents were less regular church attenders and a smaller proportion of them joined church societies.

On the whole, then, there is again presented a contrast between the two groups grown to manhood, and once more it indicates that the delinquents function less effectively than the nondelinquents.

XII Ambitions, Frustrations, Maturation

INTRODUCTORY

During the course of the years most persons expect to make progress; to fulfill, at least partially, the ambitions of earlier stages, to remain on a relatively even keel despite the expectable frustrations with which an inscrutable fate presents them; in a word, to grow and mature. It is important to see whether the relative deficiency of the delinquent group, already noted in many ways, is reflected also in respect to ambitions, frustrations, and maturity. We are not concerned with assigning blame; nor are we too concerned, at this point, with trying to find reasons for the facts about to be presented. We are reminded of Samuel Butler's observation that "life is a matter about which we are lost if we reason either too much or too little." But facts are facts; and since we have a few unusual facts to present on certain aspects of the lives of our two groups of men, we sketch them in to add to the contrasting pictures of the delinquents and the nondelinquents already presented.

CONTENTMENT WITH POSITION IN LIFE

First, how do the two groups compare in their reflections regarding their lot in life, as expressed at the end of the first follow-up period when they were 25 years of age? Since our conclusions are based on statements made to the interviewers by the subjects, they do not have the precision of most of the other data contained in this study; but they are not altogether impressionistic.

The first question we were interested in was whether the men were on the whole content with their lot or whether they were clearly unhappy about one or another aspect of their lives — home, domestic situation, job, income, neighborhood, health. Did the delinquents differ significantly in this respect from the members of the control group?

Perhaps it is not unusual that, as will be seen in Table XII-1, very few of the delinquents or nondelinquents expressed satisfaction with

TABLE XII-1. CONTENTMENT WITH LOT IN LIFE
AT END OF FIRST FOLLOW-UP PERIOD

	Delinquents		Nondelinquents	
	No.	%	No.	%
Discontented	190	51.3	87	20.2
Fairly Contented	159	43.0	319	74.2
Contented	21	5.7	24	5.6
Total	370	100.0	430	100.0

$$\chi^2 = 88.06; P < .01$$

their circumstances or had no strivings for change (5.7% of the delinquents and 5.6% of the nondelinquents). Discontent with one or another aspect of life, but not with all, may be considered natural. Who among us does not experience this? But discontent with all aspects of life begins to border on the pathological, and this was found to characterize half (51.3%) of the delinquents but only a fifth (20.2%) of the nondelinquents. It is of course impossible to state with assurance that this pessimistic attitude reflects inferior adaptability on the part of the delinquents. If one reviews their wide-ranging disadvantages when compared with the control group, including the handicaps which burdened them both in childhood and adulthood, one might find reasons why the delinquents as a group are less satisfied with what life had brought them. One wonders whether the delinquents would agree with Benjamin Franklin's wise summing up: "Were it offered to my choice, I should have no objection to a repetition of the same life from its beginning, only asking the advantages authors have in a second edition to correct some faults of the first." Or perhaps their attitude comes closer to that of Mr. Justice Oliver Wendell Holmes: "On the whole I am on the side of the unregenerate who affirm the worth of life as an end in itself as against the saints who deny it."

But let us turn from such speculations to more facts.

ECONOMIC AND OCCUPATIONAL AMBITIONS

What aspirations did the two sets of men express regarding their material progress? Table XII-2 shows that, among the delinquents, 20.6% had no particular economic ambitions; among the nondelinquents, only 4.7% had no such specific ambitions.

What was the nature of the economic aspirations which they did have? Table XII-3 shows that, among the delinquents who expressed some economic ambitions, 40.2% desired a more adequate income,

TABLE XII-2.   ECONOMIC AMBITIONS
AT END OF FIRST FOLLOW-UP PERIOD

	Delinquents		Nondelinquents	
	No.	%	No.	%
Some	281	79.4	407	95.3
None	73	20.6	20	4.7
Total	354	100.0	427	100.0

$$\chi^2 = 46.88; P < .01$$

TABLE XII-3.   NATURE OF ECONOMIC AMBITIONS
AT END OF FIRST FOLLOW-UP PERIOD

	Delinquents		Nondelinquents	
	No.	%	No.	%
Modest but Steady Income	116	41.3	163	40.0
More Adequate Income	113	40.2	218	53.6
Make Lots of Money	52	18.5	26	6.4
Total	281	100.0	407	100.0

$$\chi^2 = 27.74; P < .01$$

this comparing with 53.6% of the nondelinquents. Among the former, 18.5% expressed the ambition "to make lots of money," in contrast with only 6.4% of the control group. Among the delinquents as well as the nondelinquents, however, equal proportions (two-fifths) looked forward to a modest but steady income.

Assessment of the various aims of the two groups shows in Table XII-4 that the economic ambitions of 68.0% of the delinquents and 87.2% of the nondelinquents could be regarded as reasonably realistic and achievable within the circumstances by which the men were surrounded and the strength of their urge for betterment of their status.

TABLE XII-4.   REALISM OF ECONOMIC AIMS
AT END OF FIRST FOLLOW-UP PERIOD

	Delinquents		Nondelinquents	
	No.	%	No.	%
Realistic	191	68.0	355	87.2
Unrealistic	90	32.0	52	12.8
Total	281	100.0	407	100.0

$$\chi^2 = 37.61; P < .01$$

TABLE XII-5. OCCUPATIONAL AMBITIONS
AT END OF FIRST FOLLOW-UP PERIOD

| | Delinquents | | Nondelinquents | |
	No.	%	No.	%
Some	260	70.1	391	91.6
None	111	29.9	36	8.4
Total	371	100.0	427	100.0

$$\chi^2 = 61.00; P < .01$$

What, now, of their occupational ambitions, as expressed at the end of the first follow-up period (see Table XII-5), when they were still young enough to strive for advancement?

Of the delinquents, 29.9%, compared with only 8.4% of the nondelinquents, expressed no ambition to improve their occupational status. But this leaves substantial percentages among both groups — though lower among the delinquents — who did have aspirations to better their employment status.

What, specifically, were their occupational aspirations? Table XII-6 shows that, of those expressing such ambitions, only 5.1% of the delinquents, compared with 11.0% of the control group, aimed at achieving professional or semiprofessional status. Equal proportions among the two groups (26.5% and 24.3%) wanted to become skilled or unskilled workers, and equal proportions (16.9%) wanted to have their own business. Among the delinquents, 15.0% — and in the control group, 4.6% — expressed the modest aim of having steady work.

TABLE XII-6. NATURE OF OCCUPATIONAL AMBITIONS
AT END OF FIRST FOLLOW-UP PERIOD

| | Delinquents | | Nondelinquents | |
	No.	%	No.	%
Continue to Advance	71	27.3	118	30.2
Become Skilled or Semiskilled Worker	69	26.5	95	24.3
Own Business	44	16.9	66	16.9
Have Steady Work	39	15.0	18	4.6
Become Civil Service Worker	24	9.2	51	13.0
Become Semiprofessional	10	3.9	25	6.4
Become Professional	3	1.2	18	4.6
Total	260	100.0	391	100.0

$$\chi^2 = 29.66; P < .01$$

TABLE XII-7. REALISM OF OCCUPATIONAL AIMS
AT END OF FIRST FOLLOW-UP PERIOD

| | Delinquents | | Nondelinquents | |
	No.	%	No.	%
Realistic	162	62.3	325	83.1
Unrealistic	98	37.7	66	16.9
Total	260	100.0	391	100.0

$$\chi^2 = 35.89; P < .01$$

Finally, and in general terms, 27.3% of the former and 30.2% of the latter simply looked forward to a continued advance in occupation.

How realistic were the occupational ambitions of the delinquents and nondelinquents, judging by their ability and circumstances to carry them through? Were they merely dreaming dreams or were there substantial reasons to think that they could actually follow through? Discussion with the men reflected a lack of realism among 37.7% of the delinquents compared to only 16.9% of the nondelinquents (Table XII-7) in their ambition to improve their position as workers — in terms of greater skill, steadier work, opportunity for advancement, civil service status, a business of their own, a vocation or profession.

EDUCATIONAL AMBITIONS

Turning now to the educational aspirations of the former juvenile delinquents and the nondelinquent control group, Table XII-8 shows that only 15.2% of the delinquents, as compared with 43.7% of the nondelinquents interviewed, expressed a desire for more schooling — professional or vocational.

As to the nature of these educational aims, Table XII-9 shows that, of those expressing some educational ambitions, only 8.8% of the few delinquents involved were eager to continue their academic schooling, compared to 27.7% of the larger number of nondelinquents.

TABLE XII-8. EDUCATIONAL AMBITIONS
AT END OF FIRST FOLLOW-UP PERIOD

| | Delinquents | | Nondelinquents | |
	No.	%	No.	%
None or Vague	317	84.8	237	56.3
Some	57	15.2	184	43.7
Total	374	100.0	421	100.0

$$\chi^2 = 75.98; P < .01$$

TABLE XII-9. NATURE OF EDUCATIONAL AMBITIONS
AT END OF FIRST FOLLOW-UP PERIOD

| | Delinquents | | Nondelinquents | |
	No.	%	No.	%
Courses to Advance Work Status	52	91.2	133	72.3
Continue Academic Schooling	5	8.8	51	27.7
Total	57	100.0	184	100.0

$$\chi^2 = 8.75; \ P < .01$$

FAMILY AMBITIONS

We consider next the aspirations to improve their family status among the two sets of men under comparison (both married and single).

Inquiry at the end of the first follow-up period — when 53.4% of the delinquents and 51.1% of the nondelinquents were (or had been) married — revealed that about half the delinquents (46.8%), in contrast with 29.7% of the nondelinquents, had not clearly defined their thoughts or ideals for their present or future families (see Table XII-10).

Of those expressing some ambitions relating to family life, Table XII-11 indicates that two-fifths of the delinquents and half of the nondelinquents wanted homes in better neighborhoods; a third of each group expressed a desire to own their homes; and a tenth of each expressed a desire for better equipped homes, or for roomier ones. A third of the delinquents and half the nondelinquents looked forward to having children, or to having more children. Very few of either group (9.6% of the delinquents and 3.4% of the nondelinquents) expressed any ambition to provide opportunities (educational, social, economic) for their children that would be better than those which they themselves

TABLE XII-10. FAMILY AMBITIONS
AT END OF FIRST FOLLOW-UP PERIOD

| | Delinquents | | Nondelinquents | |
	No.	%	No.	%
Some	197	53.2	298	70.3
None	173	46.8	126	29.7
Total	370	100.0	424	100.0

$$\chi^2 = 24.44; \ P < .01$$

TABLE XII-11. NATURE OF FAMILY AMBITIONS
AT END OF FIRST FOLLOW-UP PERIOD

| | Delinquents | | Nondelinquents | | |
	No.	%	No.	%	P
Home in Better Area	86	43.7	153	51.3	< .10
Own Home	65	33.0	109	36.6	< .50
Better Equipped or Larger Home	21	10.7	26	8.7	< .50
To Marry or Remarry	65	33.0	90	30.2	< .60
To Have Children or More Children	63	32.0	153	51.3	< .01
Provide Better Opportunity for Children	19	9.6	10	3.4	< .01
No. of Cases [a]	197	100.0	298	100.0	—

[a] This is a multiple-category table; that is, an individual can be included more than once, and therefore the percentages do not add to 100.0.

had had. Their children were, of course, as yet very small so that the time was perhaps not ripe even to express hopes for them.

On the whole, the ambitions for the family expressed by these young men were essentially realistic although here again the delinquents were less realistic than the nondelinquents (see Table XII-12).

EVIDENCES OF MATURATION

By the close of the second follow-up span, when the men were in their early thirties, there was sufficient evidence to permit a judgment of their maturity.

It is at this stage that the innate nature and early childhood conditioning told differing stories of the two groups: for, as can be seen in Table XII-13, while 44.7% of the delinquents had to be classified, on the basis of interviews and conduct, as immature — that is, as psychologically childish or infantile — this was true of only 8.0% of the nondelinquents. At the other extreme (and not now considering cases with some elements of maturity), only 28.0% of the delinquents, compared

TABLE XII-12. REALISM OF FAMILY AMBITIONS
AT END OF FIRST FOLLOW-UP PERIOD

| | Delinquents | | Nondelinquents | |
	No.	%	No.	%
Realistic	165	82.5	283	95.0
Unrealistic	35	17.5	15	5.0
Total	200	100.0	298	100.0
		$\chi^2 = 20.60$; P < .01		

TABLE XII-13. MATURITY AT END
OF SECOND FOLLOW-UP PERIOD

	Delinquents		Nondelinquents	
	No.	%	No.	%
Immature[a]	188	44.7	35	8.0
Some Elements of Maturity[b]	115	27.3	107	24.3
Mature	118	28.0	298	67.7
Total	421	100.0	440	100.0

$$\chi^2 = 182.81; P < .01$$

[a] Infantile or childish, unrealistic, undependable, irresponsible in all aspects of life — marriage, family relations, work, use of leisure, and so on.
[b] Responsible in some aspects of life, not in all.

with the very considerable proportion of 67.7% of the members of the control group, could definitely be characterized as *mature adults*.

It must be borne in mind that when these men were classified on the basis of conversations with them and others, as well as on evidences of their conduct as derived in intensive field inquiries, they were already 31 years of age. We wish simply to note the significant fact that in only a fourth of the delinquent group whose lives we began to study in *Unraveling,* when they were boys of an average age of $14\frac{1}{2}$ (many much younger), could it now be concluded that we were dealing with normally mature adults, that is, persons of a psychosocial development commensurate with their years. By striking contrast, this degree of maturation was found in two-thirds of the men whom, originally, we had classified as nondelinquent boys.

SUMMARY

A higher proportion of the delinquents than of the nondelinquents were, as adults, discontented with their lot in life, this variance being possibly due to differences in adaptability. Nevertheless, considerable proportions of the two groups of men had some ambitions, although the incidence was higher among the nondelinquents. While substantial percentages of the two sets of men wanted a more adequate income, or at least a modest but steady one, the ambitions of a higher proportion of the delinquents than of the control group were unrealistic. A smaller percentage of the former than of the latter aimed at becoming professionals or semiprofessionals; but, considering the sociocultural level from which both groups derived, their occupational ambitions were not on the whole very high or very different.

However, a marked divergence was found in their educational ambitions, a substantially greater percentage of the nondelinquents than of the delinquents being inclined toward further education.

The variance of the two groups is further illustrated in the finding that a higher proportion of the men of the control group than of the delinquents expressed aspirations to improve their family status, especially in respect to better homes in more wholesome neighborhoods, and in a desire to have children. Also, it was found that the ambitions of the men for their families were realistic among a lower proportion of the delinquents than of the control group.

The most striking variance between the two sets of men might have been foretold when they were examined psychiatrically and psychologically as children and when the early parent-child relationships were revealed in connection with *Unraveling.* Judging by the evidence in their early thirties, almost half of the delinquents had to be classified as emotionally childish or infantile — that is, of a maturity not commensurate with their age — in contrast with less than a tenth of the nondelinquents.

Once again certain divergences between the delinquents and the control group have emerged with the passage of the years.

XIII Military Experience

INTRODUCTORY

Many of our men performed military duty in one or another of the Armed Services. The military history of most of the 500 delinquents and 500 nondelinquents of *Unraveling Juvenile Delinquency* was studied only up to their 25th birthdays. The network of information sources necessary to accomplish this is touched upon briefly in Chapter IV. The time-spans involved covered such military action as the last year or two of World War II and the stationing of American Army units in Japan and West Germany (1944-45); the commitment of U. S. forces to aid the Republic of Korea in repelling the North Korean invaders, and the protection of Taiwan by the United States Navy (1950-53); and the sending of the Fleet to the Near East (1957). This is not to say that our young men served in any particular one of the above-mentioned military missions but only that during the follow-up period there was a demand for soldiers and naval personnel in which many of our subjects were involved.

It should be noted here that the data reported on in this chapter are based on larger samples of men than were included elsewhere in this book. As can be seen from Table XIII-1, it was possible to determine

TABLE XIII-1. SERVICE IN ARMED FORCES UP TO 25TH BIRTHDAY

| | Delinquents | | Nondelinquents | |
	No.	%	No.	%
Some	299	62.7	373	79.0
None	178	37.3	99	21.0
Total[a]	477	100.0	472	100.0

$$\chi^2 = 30.66; P < .01$$

[a] Five delinquents were deceased, and information was not available for 18 delinquents and 28 nondelinquents.

TABLE XIII-2. BRANCH OF SERVICE

	Delinquents		Nondelinquents	
	No.	%	No.	%
Army Only	187	62.5	227	60.9
Navy Only	101	33.8	140	37.5
Both Army and Navy	11	3.7	6	1.6
Total	299	100.0	373	100.0

$$\chi^2 = 3.53; P < .20$$

for 477 delinquents and 472 nondelinquents whether or not they had served in any branch of the Armed Forces prior to their 25th birthdays; and that 62.7% of the former and 79.0% of the latter had spent some time in such service.

NATURE OF MILITARY SERVICE

As regards the respective branches of these services, there appears to be no great variation in incidence among the two groups of men (see Table XIII-2).

Table XIII-3 shows marked variation between the delinquents and the control group in the reasons for which deferment from military duty was granted. Higher percentages of the delinquents were deferred for psychiatric causes (36.8%) and moral unfitness (28.2%), but there is an excess in the nondelinquent group of deferments for reasons of physical health.

Although information as to intelligence levels was available for relatively few of the two sets of men tested for military service, there is

TABLE XIII-3. REASONS FOR DEFERMENTS

	Delinquents		Nondelinquents		
	No.	%	No.	%	P
Psychiatric Causes	64	36.8	8	8.3	< .01
Moral Unfitness	49	28.2	3	3.1	< .01
Physical Causes	21	12.1	34	35.4	< .01
Occupational	15	8.6	14	14.6	< .20
Dependency	10	5.7	9	9.4	< .30
Mental Deficiency	7	4.0	7	7.3	< .30
Unknown	22	12.6	24	25.0	< .01
No. of Cases[a]	174	100.0	96	100.0	—

[a] Four delinquents and three nondelinquents served in the Armed Forces after their 25th birthday. This is a multiple-category table; that is, an individual can be included more than once, and therefore the percentages do not add to 100.0.

TABLE XIII-4. GENERAL CLASSIFICATION TEST SCORES

| | Army | | | | Navy | | | |
| | Delinquents | | Non-delinquents | | Delinquents | | Non-delinquents | |
	No.	%	No.	%	No.	%	No.	%
Below Average	29	49.1	19	24.4	24	42.9	27	27.8
Average	25	42.4	42	53.8	20	35.7	51	52.6
Above Average	5	8.5	17	21.8	12	21.4	19	19.6
Total	59	100.0	70	100.0	56	100.0	97	100.0

$$\chi^2 = 10.50; P < .01 \qquad\qquad \chi^2 = 4.64; P < .20$$

evidence (Table XIII-4) that an excess of below-average scores was attained by the delinquents in both the Army (49.1% vs. 24.4%) and Navy (42.9% vs. 27.8%).

From Table XIII-5 it will be observed that there was some difference between the delinquents and nondelinquents regarding the method of entrance into the Army. If entry via enlistment and voluntary induction are combined, it becomes evident that an excess of the delinquents sought Army service (71.2% vs. 58.0%), but the groups seemed equally willing to join the Navy (92.9% vs. 89.7%).

Table XIII-6 indicates that some two-thirds (68.2%) of the delinquents were 18 or younger when they first entered the Army, as contrasted with 44.2% of the nondelinquents. As to first entry into the Navy, here, too, a significantly higher proportion of delinquents than of nondelinquents were already in the Navy at 18 or younger (94.6% vs. 72.6%). One reason for these differences is probably not the generally greater eagerness of the delinquents to serve their country, but rather, we suggest, to satisfy a longing for adventure and perhaps even as a means of avoiding or delaying the responsibilities of civilian life.

TABLE XIII-5. METHOD OF FIRST ENTERING SERVICE

| | Army | | | | Navy | | | |
| | Delinquents | | Non-delinquents | | Delinquents | | Non-delinquents | |
	No.	%	No.	%	No.	%	No.	%
Enlistment	122	61.6	126	54.1	100	89.3	128	87.7
Voluntary Induction	19	9.6	9	3.9	4	3.6	3	2.0
Induction	57	28.8	98	42.0	8	7.1	15	10.3
Total	198	100.0	233	100.0	112	100.0	146	100.0

$$\chi^2 = 11.73; P < .01 \qquad\qquad \chi^2 = 1.24; P < .40$$

TABLE XIII-6.   AGE AT FIRST ENLISTMENT OR INDUCTION

	Army				Navy			
	Delinquents		Non-delinquents		Delinquents		Non-delinquents	
	No.	%	No.	%	No.	%	No.	%
Less than 17 Years	14	7.1	10	4.3	4	3.6	1	0.7
17 Years	45	22.7	42	18.0	79	70.5	67	45.9
18 Years	76	38.4	51	21.9	23	20.5	38	26.0
10, 20, 21 Years	30	15.1	92	39.5	5	4.5	32	21.9
22 Years and Over	33	16.7	38	16.3	1	0.9	8	5.5
Total	198	100.0	233	100.0	112	100.0	146	100.0
	$\chi^2 = 34.94$; P $<$ .01				$\chi^2 = 27.62$; P $<$ .01			

Despite the earlier entry of the delinquents into both the Army and the Navy, Table XIII-7 shows an excess among the delinquents of those spending less than a year in either service. This suggests that the delinquents, although apparently eager to enter the Armed Forces, did not perform as well as the nondelinquents; also, that some delinquents were discharged early from service when their youthful misbehavior was belatedly discovered.

Reflecting the lesser capacity or lack of real interest on the part of the delinquents to advance themselves in the services is the finding about the highest ratings achieved during their military careers. In this connection, the highest rating attained is some indication of intelligence, attention to duty, and qualities of leadership displayed. Table XIII-8 shows how the two sets of men fared in this respect. The lesser attainments of the delinquents in the Army are evidenced by the finding that only 8.7% of them achieved the status of sergeant or higher, while 25.5% of the nondelinquents did so. In the Navy, also, the delin-

TABLE XIII-7.   LENGTH OF SERVICE IN ARMED FORCES
UP TO 25TH BIRTHDAY

	Army				Navy			
	Delinquents		Non-delinquents		Delinquents		Non-delinquents	
	No.	%	No.	%	No.	%	No.	%
Less than 12 Months	56	28.3	18	7.7	25	22.3	12	8.2
12–24 Months	54	27.3	91	39.1	25	22.3	42	28.8
24–36 Months	35	17.7	49	21.0	24	21.4	28	19.2
36–48 Months	29	14.6	37	15.9	17	15.2	36	24.6
48 Months or More	24	12.1	38	16.3	21	18.8	28	19.2
Total	198	100.0	233	100.0	112	100.0	146	100.0
	$\chi^2 = 32.78$; P $<$ .01				$\chi^2 = 12.75$; P $<$ .05			

TABLE XIII-8. HIGHEST RATING ACHIEVED
IN ARMED FORCES

	Army			
	Delinquents		Nondelinquents	
	No.	%	No.	%
Private	70	40.2	21	10.9
PFC	58	33.3	59	30.7
Corporal	31	17.8	63	32.9
Sergeant (all types)	14	8.1	48	25.0
Commissioned Officer	1	0.6	1	0.5
Total	174	100.0	192	100.0

$$\chi^2 = 55.19; P < .01$$

	Navy			
	Delinquents		Nondelinquents	
	No.	%	No.	%
Apprentice Seaman	18	16.5	9	6.3
Seaman, 2nd Class	37	34.0	30	20.8
Seaman, 1st Class	30	27.5	51	35.4
Petty Officer	24	22.0	53	36.8
Lt. (Jr. Grade)	0	0.0	1	0.7
Total	109	100.0	144	100.0

$$\chi^2 = 16.56; P < .01$$

quents revealed a lesser capacity than the nondelinquents, reflected
in the lower proportion of 22.0% who became petty officers of one
type or another, as contrasted with 37.5% of the nondelinquents who
managed to achieve at least this status.

What, now, of the conduct of the two groups of men in the Armed
Forces?

BEHAVIOR IN ARMED FORCES

Table XIII-9 sets forth their conduct in each of the military services,

TABLE XIII-9. CONDUCT IN ARMED FORCES

	Army				Navy			
	Delinquents		Non-delinquents		Delinquents		Non-delinquents	
	No.	%	No.	%	No.	%	No.	%
Never Brought Up on Charges	67	39.9	182	87.5	32	28.6	101	69.6
Brought Up on Charges	101	60.1	26	12.5	80	71.4	44	30.4
Total	168	100.0	208	100.0	112	100.0	145	100.0

$$\chi^2 = 94.24; P < .01 \qquad \chi^2 = 42.71; P < .01$$

TABLE XIII-10. NUMBER OF TIMES
BROUGHT UP ON CHARGES IN ARMED SERVICES

	Army				Navy			
	Delinquents		Non-delinquents		Delinquents		Non-delinquents	
	No.	%	No.	%	No.	%	No.	%
One	30	29.7	18	69.2	22	27.5	19	43.2
Two	31	30.7	3	11.5	23	28.7	17	38.6
Three	14	13.9	2	7.7	11	12.5	2	4.6
Four	5	4.9	2	7.7	10	13.8	3	6.8
Five or More	21	20.8	1	3.9	14	17.5	3	6.8
Total	101	100.0	26	100.0	80	100.0	44	100.0

$\chi^2 = 15.70$; $P < .01$ $\qquad$ $\chi^2 = 8.50$; $P < .10$

showing at a glance the poorer behavior record of the former juvenile delinquents. While only 39.9% of the former delinquents were never brought up on charges in the Army, this clean record was established by the much higher proportion of 87.5% of the nondelinquents; and while somewhat less than three tenths (28.6%) of the delinquents enjoyed immunity from charges for offenses in the Navy, this was true of 69.6% of the control group.

The picture is filled in by the number of times the two sets of men were brought up on charges (Table III-10). It may be assumed that being charged once could involve error or prejudice on the part of the military authorities, but this is a more remote possibility when more than a single charge is involved. Of those who were brought up on charges, no fewer than 70.3% of the delinquents, in sharp contrast to 30.8% of the nondelinquents, had charges filed against them two or more times while in the Army; 72.5% of the offender delinquents, in contrast to 56.8% of the offenders in the control group, were charged more than once in the Navy. If the very extreme of the table — five or more charges — is examined, it is again evident that the lawful adjustment to military rules of the men who as boys were delinquents was far poorer than that of the nondelinquents: 20.8% vs. 3.9% in the Army; and 17.5% vs. 6.8% in the Navy. Thus, there is reflected a continuing behavioral divergence as adults of the two sets of human beings whom we first encountered as boys.

In Table XIII-11, the nature of the offenses with which the men were charged suggests that the same difficulty in adjusting satisfactorily to the discipline of parents and teachers and the demands of behavioral codes — which was originally noted in *Unraveling* — persisted in the

TABLE XIII-11. NATURE OF OFFENSES FOR WHICH
BROUGHT UP ON CHARGES IN ARMED SERVICES

	Army				Navy			
	Delinquents		Non-delinquents		Delinquents		Non-delinquents	
	No.	%	No.	%	No.	%	No.	%
Desertion or AWOL	227	81.1	27	65.8	132	53.4	48	49.5
Conviction by Civil Court	19	6.8	4	9.8	6	2.4	1	1.0
Larceny	6	2.1	1	2.4	14	5.7	4	4.1
Disobedience of Orders, Insubordination	5	1.8	4	9.8	47	19.0	18	18.6
Drunkenness	4	1.4	0	0.0	7	2.8	1	1.0
Fraudulent Enlistment	2	0.7	0	0.0	2	0.8	0	0.0
Resisting and/or Breaking Arrest	1	0.4	0	0.0	10	4.1	2	2.1
Other	16	5.7	5	12.2	29	11.8	23	23.7
Total No. of Offenses[a]	280	100.0	41	100.0	247	100.0	97	100.0

$$\chi^2 = 12.94; P < .10 \qquad\qquad \chi^2 = 10.34; P < .20$$

[a] For which it was possible to determine nature of offense.

former juvenile delinquents when they were faced with the demands of adult life.

In the Army, the great majority of offenses for both groups consisted of being absent without leave; there was, however, a substantially higher proportion among the delinquents than in the control group. Out of the 280 offenses committed by the former while in the Army, 81.1% were related to being absent without leave, compared to 65.8% of the small number of 41 offenses committed by the nondelinquents. This recalls the fact that in *Unraveling* it was shown that a much higher proportion of the young delinquents than of the boys of the control group were reported — in the course of interviews regarding their developmental history — to have been extremely restless children, unable to sit still, always wanting to be "on the go." However, while in the Navy, too, absence without leave was the most common offense, there the incidence was proportionately similar — 53.4% of the 247 offenses committed by the former delinquents and 49.5% of the 97 offenses committed by the control group.

The dispositions of the charges for which the men of the two groups were tried in the military services are shown in Table XIII-12.

Regarding offenses in the Army, 56.8% of the charges involving delinquents resulted in confinement, compared to 40.0% of the small

TABLE XIII-12. NATURE OF DISPOSITIONS OF OFFENSES
FOR WHICH BROUGHT UP ON CHARGES

	Army				Navy			
	Delinquents		Non-delinquents		Delinquents		Non-delinquents	
	No.	%	No.	%	No.	%	No.	%
Confinement	142	56.8	12	40.0	71	29.4	25	23.8
Discharge	46	18.4	7	23.4	29	12.0	4	3.8
Reduction in Grade	25	10.0	9	30.0	23	9.5	13	12.4
Forfeiture of Pay	23	9.2	0	0.0	48	19.8	21	20.0
Restriction and Extra Duty	7	2.8	1	3.3	48	19.8	37	35.2
All Other	7	2.8	1	3.3	23	9.5	5	4.8
Total No. of Offenses[a]	250	100.0	30	100.0	242	100.0	105	100.0
	$\chi^2 = 13.36$; P $< .05$				$\chi^2 = 15.68$; P $< .01$			

[a] For which it was possible to determine nature of disposition.

number of offenses involving members of the control group. Among
the former, 46 of the offenses resulted in discharge from the Army,
compared with only 7 cases among the nondelinquents; 25 of the
charges involving the former juvenile delinquents resulted in reduction
in grade, compared to 9 such cases in the control group; and while 23
of the charges against the former juvenile delinquents resulted in for-
feiture of pay, there were no such cases among the nondelinquents.

In the Navy, 29.4% of the charges against the former juvenile delinquents resulted in confinement, as compared with 23.8% of the
charges against the nondelinquent group. Forty-eight of the charges
against the delinquent group versus 37 of the nondelinquent resulted in
restriction to quarters and the imposition of extra duties. Dismissal
from the Navy was the consequence for 29 cases of the charges against
the delinquents and 4 cases of the nondelinquents. Although Table
XIII-12 speaks for itself, it should be stressed that a much higher proportion of the former juvenile delinquents than of the nondelinquents
were brought up on charges in both the Army and Navy.

On the whole, then, the misbehavior of the men who as boys were in
the delinquency category was both more frequent and more serious in
the Armed Services than that of the control group — a situation which,
unfortunately, might well have been foretold early in life.

NATURE OF DISCHARGES FROM SERVICE

This record can now be rounded out by considering the character of
the discharges given by the Armed Services to our delinquents and nondelinquents (Table XIII-13).

TABLE XIII-13. CHARACTER OF DISCHARGES FROM SERVICE[a]

	Army				Navy			
	Delinquents		Non-delinquents		Delinquents		Non-delinquents	
	No.	%	No.	%	No.	%	No.	%
Honorable	144	69.9	221	96.1	95	74.2	154	96.9
Dishonorable	62	30.1	9	3.9	33	25.8	5	3.1
Total No. of Discharges	206	100.0	230	100.0	128	100.0	159	100.0

$$\chi^2 = 54.63; \; P < .01 \qquad\qquad \chi^2 = 31.63; \; P < .01$$

[a] For each period served.

Out of 206 army discharges among the delinquents (including one for each period served), 30.1% were dishonorable — this compared to 3.9% for the nondelinquents. As regards exit from the Navy, 25.8% of the discharges were dishonorable in the case of the former delinquents, and 3.1% among the nondelinquents. Here, again, the contrast is emphasized between the group of men who in the original study had been classified as delinquents and those who comprised the nondelinquent group.

Further light is thrown on the behavior record of the two groups by Table XIII-14, which provides the reasons for discharges from the Army and the Navy.

Among the delinquents in the Army, 60.6% of the discharges were for normal reasons, this comparing with 88.8% for the nondelinquents. It is interesting to note that 57.8% of the nondelinquents' discharges occurred at the expiration of their enlistment period, while this was so of only 20.2% of the discharges among the delinquents. For the delinquents in the Navy, 57.4% of the discharges were for normal reasons, compared to 88.8% for the nondelinquents, with over 48.8% of these discharges occurring at the end of the enlistment period among the control group, compared to only 24.8% of the delinquents' discharges.

Considering the psychiatric and other medical reasons for discharge from the Armed Services, although the number of cases involved is small, it remains a fact that 13.3% occurred for these reasons among the delinquents in the Army, compared to 7.8% among the nondelinquents. In the Navy, 17.8% of the delinquents' discharges, compared to only 8.1% of the nondelinquents, were for psychiatric and other medical indications.

Finally, 26.1% of the Army discharges of the delinquents were for reasons of misconduct or fraudulent enlistment — this proportion in

TABLE XIII-14. REASONS FOR DISCHARGE FROM SERVICE

	Army				Navy			
	Delinquents		Non-delinquents		Delinquents		Non-delinquents	
	No.	%	No.	%	No.	%	No.	%
NORMAL								
Demobilization	59	29.1	61	26.3	36	28.0	61	38.1
Expiration of Enlistment	41	20.2	134	57.8	32	24.8	78	48.8
To Re-enlist	6	2.9	7	3.0	3	2.3	1	0.6
Other	17	8.4	4	1.7	3	2.3	2	1.3
Subtotal	123	60.6	206	88.8	74	57.4	142	88.8
PSYCHIATRIC AND MEDICAL								
Psychiatric	24	11.8	9	3.9	20	15.5	5	3.1
Medical	3	1.5	9	3.9	3	2.3	8	5.0
Subtotal	27	13.3	18	7.8	23	17.8	13	8.1
MISCONDUCT								
Sentence General Court Martial	16	7.9	5	2.1	22	17.0	4	2.5
Conviction by a Civil Court	13	6.4	2	0.9	5	3.9	1	0.6
Fraudulent Enlistment	14	6.9	0	0.0	3	2.3	0	0.0
Other Misconduct	10	4.9	1	0.4	2	1.6	0	0.0
Subtotal	53	26.1	8	3.4	32	24.8	5	3.1
Total No. of Discharges	203	100.0	232	100.0	129	100.0	160	100.0

$$\chi^2 = 101.13; \ P < .01 \qquad \chi^2 = 55.56; \ P < .01$$

contrast to only 3.4% for the control group. In the Navy, 24.8% of the separations for the delinquents were due to misconduct or fraudulent enlistment, compared with only 3.1% among the nondelinquents.

SUMMARY

At the threshold of their military service, a higher proportion of the delinquents than of the control group was deferred for psychiatric reasons or moral unfitness; and a higher proportion of the delinquents did not score so well on intelligence tests given in the Army and Navy.

Although a lower proportion of the delinquents than of the nondelinquents actually served in the Armed Forces, a higher proportion of the delinquents entered the Army voluntarily; both groups were equally eager to serve in the Navy. The delinquents sought Army or Navy service at an earlier age than the nondelinquents, probably in part to satisfy their more adventuresome inclinations. However, the length of service of the delinquents was shorter, and their performance in the Armed Forces was far less satisfactory. As might be anticipated, the behavior of the delinquents in the services was not as acceptable as that of the nondelinquents and resulted in a far higher proportion of dishonorable discharges from both services.

All in all, the pattern of divergence between the delinquents and nondelinquents already described in previous chapters continued in the Armed Services.

XIV   Delinquency in Childhood; Criminality in Adulthood

INTRODUCTORY

We come now to the goal toward which in a sense all the preceding analyses have been tending: namely, the later criminalism or non-criminalism of the delinquents and nondelinquents of *Unraveling Juvenile Delinquency* whose careers in adulthood have been traced. The preceding chapters, in addition to their intrinsic interest in shedding light on the kind of persons being considered, were necessary because antisocial conduct is not a sharply insulated phenomenon separate and apart from the nature and training of the human being involved; nor can criminality be considered apart from the conduct of offenders and nonoffenders in other avenues of self-expression — the home, the workshop, places of leisure.

NONDELINQUENTS WHO BECAME DELINQUENTS

At the end of Chapter IV, which dealt with the aims and techniques of the follow-up inquiries to age 31, we made a statement concerning the reliability of the original control group of nondelinquents. We there indicated that 37 of the nondelinquents were found, on retrospective inquiry, to have appeared in court as juveniles — that is, before they reached age 17, the limit of juvenile court jurisdiction in Massachusetts.

However, 62 of the boys, originally included in the nondelinquent group because they had committed no delinquencies up to the juvenile court age-limit, were later found to have committed offenses at ages beyond this limit, having been hailed into criminal courts for adults, and receiving sentences of varying degrees of severity. Of these original nondelinquents, 46 were first convicted during the 17-25 age-span. These initial crimes during adolescence were in many instances clearly associated with excessive drinking. Among the other offenses were abuse of a female child, breaking and entering, larceny, assault with a dangerous weapon. One conviction not related to drinking was for lewdness, another was related to drug addiction, and several of the young men were brought into court during the 17-25 age-span for disturbing the peace.

Sixteen among the 62 men who as boys had been nondelinquent were first convicted during the 25-31 age-span. Most of these first convictions were for drunkenness (or closely related offenses), as well as violation of license laws, gaming, offenses against the family, adultery. Only three of these belated first offenders appeared in court for serious crimes: one for armed robbery, one for violation of postal laws, one for larceny.

Why certain persons first become delinquent during adolescence or later is not a matter for discussion in the present volume. We may, in a subsequent publication, present a more detailed analysis of the boys originally included among the nondelinquent control group who did not show initial evidences of antisocial conduct until late adolescence or early adulthood.

FREQUENCY OF ARRESTS OF DELINQUENTS

All further analyses in this chapter and the following one are limited to the criminal behavior of the men who, as boys, made up the *delinquent* group in *Unraveling*. We shall, in all relevant instances, make comparisons between their status prior to age 17, between ages 17 and 25, and between ages 25 and 31. It is possible to compare their criminal records in all three age-spans because, in the course of the follow-up

TABLE XIV-1. FREQUENCY OF ARRESTS DURING THREE AGE-SPANS

	Prior to 17th Birthday		Between 17th and 25th Birthdays		Between 25th and 31st Birthdays	
	No.	%	No.	%	No.	%
None	0	0.0	84	19.2	170	39.3
One Arrest in Period	16	3.6	53	12.1	84	19.4
One in 6 Months	181	41.3	72	16.5	42	9.7
One in 12 Months	154	35.2	76	17.3	46	10.6
One in 24 Months	82	18.8	74	16.9	43	9.9
One in 24 or More Months	5	1.1	79	18.0	48	11.1
Total	438	100.0	438	100.0	433 [a]	100.0

$$\chi^2 = 468.24; P < .01$$

[a] Five men were confined in correctional institutions throughout the entire six-year period and therefore had no court appearances.

inquiries, we completed the criminal history to the 17th birthday of all the juvenile delinquents included in *Unraveling* who, when we first encountered them, had ranged in age between 9 and 16 and averaged 14½ years.

First, as to their frequency of arrest, Table XIV-1 shows that prior to the 17th birthday, two-fifths of the group had been arrested as often as once in six months; another third as often as once in twelve months; and a fifth of the group had been placed under arrest as frequently as once in only 12 or more months. Between the 17th and 25th birthdays, 19.2% of the young men were not arrested at all; 12.1% experienced a single arrest; 16.5% averaged one arrest for every six months they were in the community (that is, not in penal institutions); 17.3% averaged one arrest in 12 months. Between the 25th and 31st birthdays, however, the situation changed markedly; many of the former juvenile offenders had turned the corner of antisocial behavior, as was reflected in a diminution of arrest frequency. As many as two-fifths (39.3%) of the group had no arrests whatsoever; another fifth (19.4%) experienced only one arrest during the entire time they were in the community; 9.7% were still being arrested as often as once in six months; 10.6%, an average of once in 12 months; 21.0% had only one arrest in 24 months, or less. While some element of increased skill in avoiding arrest may be involved in this, the diminution in contacts with the police is due essentially to a reduction in criminal conduct.

GRAVITY OF OFFENSES FOR WHICH ARRESTED

Classification of crimes in terms of relative seriousness is beset with inherent complications. In recent years attempts have been made to bring some order into the process of judgment by those engaged in reporting on crime, so that a relatively uniform index, comparable among various jurisdictions, can be established.[1] The list of offenses we use here is a simple one, based on many years of experience in investigation. As to the relative gravity of offenses, we believe that crimes should be listed according to maximum punishment possible under the penal law and the minimum punishment required, since this reflects the sociopolitical judgment of the legislative representatives of the people regarding the respective harmfulness of the offenses to society. But legislation in the various states varies with regard to the seriousness of the different acts as reflected in the punishments provided. Further, many and varied offenses have similar statutory minimum and maximum punishment limits, whether they be crimes against the person or against property. Thus, a choice of relative gravity must still be made between them.

We have felt that a simple classification which is perhaps more real-istic than legalistic is desirable, since it derives from reflection upon the varying degrees of individual danger and social harm typically or usually resulting from the different offenses. This is, of course, imme-diately open to differences of opinion. Nevertheless, reasonable agree-ment is possible when one reflects on the ramifications and consequences of various crimes. Receiving stolen goods, for example, may have serious social consequences beyond any single act of receiving in that it may entice many youths to steal, burglarize, or rob in the knowledge that they can readily convert their loot into cash and that the criminal receiver will not ordinarily betray them. Again, certain offenses against the integrity of the family may ultimately have far more serious consequences in the lives of several persons and in the welfare of society than result from such a crime as embezzlement; yet offenses involving domestic relations are usually not listed among really serious crimes. Abuse of a female child may in the long run have more grave conse-quences than a single act of robbery.

Thus, it is impossible altogether to avoid differences of opinion in the classification; nevertheless, considering the various offenses as a whole, one may arrive at a reasonable ordering in terms of their gravity or seriousness in the general run of cases. This is essentially what legislatures do piecemeal (and therefore not very satisfactorily); it is what groups of scholars do in assigning varied punishments for differ-ent crimes while drafting a new penal code; and this is what we have attempted to do, relying on long experience.

Such an approach may have some weaknesses from the point of view of comparability with penal code provisions in other jurisdic-tions, but it suits the aims of the present research. We have in general retained the original classification of offenses presented in *500 Crim-inal Careers.*[2] Some minor modifications were made to take account of the crimes committed by the boys — grown to manhood — whose careers we present in the present work. In Table XIV-2 we have classi-fied the offenses along the lines indicated in Appendix C.

Prior to the 17th birthday, our men were of course boys charged with "juvenile delinquency"; but they were so designated on the basis of the offenses listed in Table XIV-2, the great majority of which, had they been committed beyond age 16, would have been chargeable as crimes. As to *serious* crimes against the person, one boy was arrested for felonious homicide; and 3.0% of the boys, for grave sex offenses. Among serious property offenses, 7.8% of the boys were apprehended for robbery and 1.8% for arson. While the very considerable pro-

TABLE XIV-2. NATURE OF ALL OFFENSES FOR WHICH ARRESTED DURING THREE AGE-SPANS[a]

	Prior to 17th Birthday		Between 17th and 25th Birthdays		Between 25th and 31st Birthdays		
	No.	%	No.	%	No.	%	P
SERIOUS							
Homicide	1	0.2	7	2.0	8	3.0	< .01
Violent and/or Pathologic Sex Offenses	13	3.0	21	5.9	8	3.0	< .10
Robbery	34	7.8	100	28.2	56	21.3	< .01
Arson	8	1.8	3	0.8	3	1.1	< .50
Extortion	0	0.0	0	0.0	2	0.8	< .05
Burglary	300	68.5	172	48.6	74	28.1	< .01
Larceny	377	86.1	225	63.5	87	33.1	< .01
Perjury	0	0.0	1	0.3	1	0.4	< .50
Receiving Stolen Goods	14	3.2	20	5.6	11	4.2	< .30
Other Theft Offenses	7	1.6	10	2.8	13	4.9	< .05
Abduction or Kidnaping	1	0.2	2	0.6	5	1.9	< .05
Selling Narcotics	0	0.0	1	0.3	1	0.4	< .50
Serious Violations of Motor Vehicle Laws	20	4.6	43	12.1	25	9.5	< .01
Escape or Rescue of Prisoner	3	0.7	16	4.5	14	5.3	< .01
MINOR							
Petty Larceny	110	25.1	59	16.7	10	3.8	< .01
Offenses Involving Domestic Relations	1	0.2	43	12.1	52	19.8	< .01
Simple Assault	29	6.6	71	20.1	28	10.7	< .01
Malicious Mischief	96	21.9	35	9.9	13	4.9	< .01
Offenses Involving Drugs or Drunkenness	9	2.1	154	43.5	124	47.2	< .01
Violation of Liquor Laws	0	0.0	1	0.3	1	0.4	< .50
Offenses vs. Public Order	79	18.0	101	28.5	39	14.8	< .01
Minor Sex Offenses	13	3.0	13	3.7	14	5.3	< .30
Violation of Technical Motor Vehicle Laws	46	10.5	109	30.8	52	19.8	< .01
Juvenile Offenses	135	30.8	6	1.7	1	0.4	< .01
Violation of Parole or Probation	348	79.5	93	26.3	61	23.2	< .01
No. of Cases[b]	438	100.0	354	100.0	263	100.0	—

[a] Listed in order of seriousness of offense.

[b] This is a multiple-category table; that is, an individual can be included more than once, and therefore the percentages do not add to 100.0.

portion of 68.5% had been arrested for burglary, no fewer than 86.1% of the juveniles had been taken into juvenile court for larceny (other than petty theft), and 3.2% of the boys for receiving stolen goods.

Turning now to the acts of a *less serious* nature for which the men were arrested as juveniles, 25.1% were taken into custody for petty larceny; 6.6%, for simple assault; 21.9%, for malicious mischief; and only 2.1%, for offenses involving drugs or drunkenness. In addition, 18.0% of the juveniles were arrested for various offenses against the public order; and 10.5%, for violations of technical motor vehicle laws. As to acts for which only juveniles are chargeable (truancy, stubborn child), 30.8% of the boys were arrested for such offenses, while violation of the conditions of probation or parole resulted in the arrest of 79.5% of the juveniles at one time or another prior to the 17th birthday.

Between the 17th and 25th birthdays, only 354 of the 438 young men whose offenses as juveniles have just been described, were arrested; and there were also changes in the proportions of the offenses for which the young men were brought into court. As concerns arrest for *serious* crimes in the 17-25 age-span: although only 2.0% of the young men were arrested for homicide and 5.9% for serious sex offenses, no fewer than 28.2% were apprehended for robbery; and while being taken into police custody for burglary and larceny was less frequent than in the earlier age period, the substantial proportions of 48.6% were arrested for burglary and 63.5% for larceny. As to *less serious* offenses, 16.7% of the young men in the 17-25 age-span were arrested for petty larceny; 12.1%, for unlawful conduct involving domestic relations; 20.1%, for simple assault; and 9.9%, for malicious mischief. Almost half the young men (43.5%) were brought into court for offenses involving drugs or drunkenness (mostly drunkenness); 28.5%, for offenses against the public order; and a fourth of them (26.3%) were arrested for violating the conditions of their probation or parole.

Between the 25th and 31st birthdays, the total number of men arrested for various crimes fell to 263 among the 438 men under study. Regarding *serious crimes,* although only 3.0% of the men were arrested for homicide and 3.0% for grave sex offenses, 21.3% were apprehended for robbery, 28.1% for burglary, and 33.1% for larceny (exclusive of petty larceny). As to *less serious* offenses for which the men were arrested in the 25-31 age-span, an increasing proportion — 19.8% — were arrested for offenses involving domestic relations, largely explainable by the fact that so many more of them are now married. There was a slight increase in the proportion of men arrested for drunkenness and offenses involving drugs (mostly the former) as compared with the earlier age-span (47.2% vs. 43.5%). The proportion taken into custody for offenses against the public order declined from 28.5% in the 17-25 age-span to 14.8% of the men arrested during the 25-31 age-span. Police intervention for technical violations of motor vehicle laws dropped from 30.8% in the 17-25 age-span to 19.8% in the 25-31 age-span. Finally, in the 25-31 age-span, about a fourth of the young men (23.2%) were arrested for violation of probation or parole regulations; this is similar to the proportion apprehended for such violations in the 17-25 age-span, but it represents a marked drop from the 79.5% of the juveniles arrested for such violations before age 17.

COURT APPEARANCES, CONVICTIONS, DISPOSITIONS

Regarding the contacts of our offenders with courts, we consider first a comparison of the number of court appearances at the three age levels.[3]

It is evident from Table XIV-3 that prior to their 17th birthday our subjects had a considerable record of court appearances (either in the Boston Juvenile Court or in juvenile sessions of the various District

TABLE XIV-3. NUMBER OF COURT APPEARANCES
DURING THREE AGE-SPANS

	Prior to 17th Birthday		Between 17th and 25th Birthdays		Between 25th and 31st Birthdays	
	No.	%	No.	%	No.	%
None	0	0.0	84	19.2	170	39.3
One	16	3.6	52	11.9	85	19.6
Two	38	8.7	42	9.6	40	9.2
Three	82	18.7	43	9.8	36	8.3
Four	81	18.5	38	8.7	31	7.2
Five or Six	116	26.5	59	13.5	34	7.8
Seven or Eight	62	14.1	54	12.3	11	2.5
Nine or Ten	24	5.5	30	6.8	9	2.1
Eleven or Twelve	9	2.1	13	3.0	5	1.2
Thirteen or Over	10	2.3	23	5.2	12	2.8
Total	438	100.0	438	100.0	433[a]	100.0

$$\chi^2 = 377.79; P < .01$$

[a] Five men were confined in correctional institutions throughout the entire six-year period and therefore had no court appearances.

Courts of Boston). While 12.3% appeared only once or twice, 37.2% were brought into court three or four times; 26.5%, five or six times; and the substantial remainder of 24.0%, as often as seven or more times.

In the 17-25 age-span, 19.2% of the 438 young men had no court appearances, and 21.5% had made only one or two court appearances. However, 18.5% were prosecuted in criminal courts three or four times; 13.5%, five or six times; and the considerable proportion of 27.3%, no fewer than seven times.

Between the 25th and 31st birthdays, the number of court appearances markedly declined. Thus, the proportion appearing in court dropped from 100.0% before age 17, to 80.8% in the 17-25 age-span, to 60.7% in the 25-31 age-span. Not only were fewer men taken to court, but the number of court appearances fell, for now only 16.4% appeared in court five or more times, as compared to 40.8% in the 17-25 age-span, and 50.5% before age 17.

Of the men who appeared in court, 95.5% of those in the 17-25 age-span, and 84.4% of those in the 25-31 age-span, were convicted (see Table XIV-4).

In the period prior to the 17th birthday, 14.2% of the 438 boys involved were "convicted" once or twice as juvenile delinquents; 39.9% were found to be delinquent three or four times; and 45.9%, five or more times. During the period between the 17th and 25th birthdays, 37.0% had one or two convictions in a criminal court; 21.7%, three

TABLE XIV-4. NUMBER OF CONVICTIONS ARISING FROM COURT APPEARANCES DURING THREE AGE-SPANS

	Prior to 17th Birthday		Between 17th and 25th Birthdays		Between 25th and 31st Birthdays	
	No.	%	No.	%	No.	%
None	0	0.0	16	4.5	41	15.6
One	19	4.4	75	21.2	87	33.1
Two	43	9.8	56	15.8	41	15.6
Three	93	21.2	39	11.0	36	13.7
Four	82	18.7	38	10.7	16	6.1
Five	63	14.4	36	10.2	9	3.4
Six	57	13.0	28	7.9	8	3.0
Seven	31	7.1	25	7.1	6	2.3
Eight or More	50	11.4	41	11.6	19	7.2
Total	438	100.0	354	100.0	263	100.0

$$\chi^2 = 251.26; P < .01$$

TABLE XIV 5. NATURE OF DISPOSITIONS OF ARRESTS
DURING THREE AGE-SPANS

	Prior to 17th Birthday		Between 17th and 25th Birthdays		Between 25th and 31st Birthdays		
	No.	%	No.	%	No.	%	P
Dismissed	123	28.1	243	68.7	165	62.7	< .01
Nol-Prossed	7	1.6	16	4.5	2	0.8	< .01
Filed[a]	354	80.8	209	59.1	99	37.6	< .01
Fined	14	3.2	142	40.1	81	30.8	< .01
Probation	262	59.8	72	20.3	41	15.6	< .01
Suspended Sentence	313	71.5	161	45.5	89	33.8	< .01
Department of Child Guardianship	45	10.3	0	0.0	0	0.0	< .01
Nonpenal Institution	5	1.1	0	0.0	0	0.0	< .05
Correctional School	432	98.6	0	0.0	0	0.0	< .01
Jail	0	0.0	34	9.6	30	11.4	< .01
House of Correction or State Farm	10	2.3	147	41.5	69	26.2	< .01
Reformatory	34	7.8	124	35.0	7	2.7	< .01
Prison	0	0.0	70	19.8	52	19.8	< .01
No. of Cases[b]	438	100.0	354	100.0	263	100.0	—

[a] In the great majority of cases "filed" involves final disposition of the charge; very occasionally, a case may be tried later. In the above table "filed" involves a disposition after a plea or finding of guilty.

[b] This is a multiple-category table; that is, an individual can be included more than once, and therefore the percentages do not add to 100.0.

or four; and 36.8% were found guilty five or more times. During the years between the 25th and 31st birthdays, 48.7% had one or two convictions; 19.8%, three or four; and 15.9%, five or more.

Turning now to the disposition of the cases, Table XIV-5 indicates that complaints were dismissed against 28.1% of the juveniles, compared to 68.7% of the men during the 17-25 age-span and 62.7% during the 25-31 age period. Moreover, no fewer than four-fifths of the juveniles had one or more of the charges against them filed by the courts,[4] this comparing to 59.1% of the men in the criminal courts during the 17-25 age-span and 37.6% of those in the 25-31 age-span.

Considering the dispositions after conviction (following a finding of delinquency or a verdict of guilty), it is obvious that a fine was resorted to in far fewer juvenile court cases than in criminal courts for adults. As might be anticipated, there was much more frequent use of probation and suspended sentence at the juvenile level than in the criminal courts. There were of course no cases in the criminal courts which resulted in commitment to the Department of Child Guardianship, to a nonpenal institution, or to one of the correctional schools; but it is to be noted that correctional school commitment constituted the major type of disposition for juveniles found delinquent. Sentence to house of correction was imposed on a small number of delinquents, compared to some two-fifths of the offenders so sentenced in the criminal courts during the 17-25 age-span, and a fourth of those sentenced during the 25-31 period. There were only 34 sentences to a reformatory in the case of juveniles, while 35.0% of the offenders in the 17-25 age-span received such sentences and 19.8% were committed to prisons; in the 25-31 age-span, the figures were 2.7% and 19.8%, respectively.

SUMMARY

The most striking finding of this chapter is the fact that, while the great majority of the original nondelinquent boys continued, as adults, on the straight and narrow path of law-abidingness, for the original delinquent boys the record was modified with the passage of time, particularly during the 25-31 age-span, where there was a substantial reduction in criminalism, especially of the more serious kind. While a fifth of the original delinquents turned out to be nonoffenders during the first follow-up span, the proportion rose to almost a half during the second period (see Table XIV-6).

Reduction in the commission of serious criminal acts with advancing years suggests the important role of *delayed maturation* in the abandonment of major crime. While such offenses diminished, however, lesser offenses — drunkenness, vagrancy, simple assault, offenses against the family (such as nonsupport and desertion) — increased. This is the correlative side of the increasing *integration* on the part of certain

TABLE XIV-6.   SERIOUSNESS OF CONDUCT
DURING EACH FOLLOW-UP PERIOD

	First Follow-Up Period		Second Follow-Up Period	
	No.	%	No.	%
Serious Offender	261	59.6	127	28.9
Persistent Minor Offender	11	2.5	16	3.7
Occasional Minor Offender	67	15.3	84	19.2
Nonoffender	99	22.6	211	48.2
Total	438	100.0	438	100.0

$$\chi^2 = 89.58; P < .01$$

offenders whose maturation had evidently been delayed. Some offenders never achieve adequate maturity, and as they grow older they tend to commit petty misdemeanors often associated with *disintegration* of organism and morale. We will have something to say about this in the concluding chapters.

Notes

1. Probably the most original and realistic effort has been that of Thorsten Sellin and Marvin E. Wolfgang, in *The Measurement of Delinquency* (New York: John Wiley, 1964). See especially pp. 1-70, 318, 334-349.

2. Appendix C, pp. 354-356.

3. It should be borne in mind that the three periods are not of equal length: the period to age 17 spanning about six years; the first follow-up period covering eight years; and the second follow-up period, six years.

4. The custom has grown up in juvenile courts of giving the child charged with delinquency a chance to prove his capacity to be law-abiding and then to file the charge so as to avoid giving him an official record of delinquency.

XV   Penocorrectional Experiences

INTRODUCTORY

In the prior chapter we compared the nature and disposition of the court appearances and convictions of the delinquents who are the subjects of this follow-up inquiry and summarized the changes in the gravity of their delinquent behavior with the passage of time. We turn now to a description of their correctional experiences (probation, commitment to penocorrectional institutions, parole).

NUMBER AND LENGTH OF CORRECTIONAL EXPERIENCES

Having convicted these men of various offenses, how did society, through its penocorrectional facilities, deal with them?

Table XV-1 shows that, in the years before their 17th birthday,

TABLE XV-1. NUMBER OF CORRECTIONAL EXPERIENCES
DURING THREE AGE-SPANS

	Prior to 17th Birthday		Between 17th and 25th Birthdays		Between 25th and 31st Birthdays	
	No.	%	No.	%	No.	%
None	0	0.0	8	1.8	39	15.2
One	1	0.2	111	25.5	66	25.7
Two	31	7.1	55	12.6	52	20.3
Three	69	15.8	56	12.9	28	10.9
Four	66	15.1	40	9.2	26	10.1
Five	58	13.2	32	7.4	21	8.2
Six	52	11.9	39	9.0	5	1.9
Seven	54	12.3	38	8.7	5	1.9
Eight	33	7.5	21	4.8	5	1.9
Nine or More	74	16.9	35	8.1	10	3.9
Total	438	100.0	435	100.0	257	100.0

$$\chi^2 = 329.51; P < .01$$

only one of the 438 delinquents under study had but a single correctional experience. Two or three periods of correction were imposed on 22.9% of the juvenile offenders; four or five, on 28.3%; and, as an indication that the corrective medicine employed was evidently not "curing" them, almost half the total number of 438 delinquents — the substantial proportion of 48.6% — were subjected to no fewer than six or more correctional experiences.

It will be recalled that 354 men were arrested and, of course, fewer convicted between the 17th and 25th birthdays. However, some young men were still serving sentences imposed prior to their 17th birthday. Actually, only 1.8% of the young-adult offenders underwent no correctional experiences; during the 17-25 age-span 25.5% had but a single such treatment; an additional 25.5% had two or three; 16.6%, four or five; and, though not so numerous as in the prior period, a substantial proportion of the group, 30.6%, were subjected to six or more penocorrectional experiences. Once again, therefore, society's remedies for the "cure" of crime were evidently not very effective.

How about the third period — between the 25th and 31st birthdays? Here, too, some men were still serving sentences imposed in the prior period. However, Table XV-1 shows that 15.2% of the men then involved had not a single penocorrectional experience during this age-span; 25.7% had one; 31.2% had two or three; 18.3% of the offenders had four or five penocorrectional encounters; but there was a substantial drop to only 9.6% in the proportion who had as many as six or more such experiences. In this statistic one begins to get a hint that it is not so much the efforts of the courts and the penocorrectional apparatus that bring about abandonment of criminality, as the benign, if belated, collaboration of Nature and Nurture, and that these forces operate *selectively* on individuals.

But perhaps the treatment experiences were too brief for the men to "learn by experience" that "crime does not pay." Let us therefore look next at Table XV-2, which deals with the length of penocorrectional control.

Prior to the 17th birthday, 2.5% of the juvenile delinquents spent less than 12 months under control of correctional officials, either as probationers, or in institutions, or on parole; 16.2% spent 12–24 months; 20.1%, 24–36 months; and three-fifths of the group (61.2%) were subjected to various types and techniques of penocorrectional manipulation for periods of 36 months or longer. Between the 17th and 25th birthdays, 10.8% of the young men who were undergoing penocorrectional treatment during these years were under control for less than

TABLE XV-2. LENGTH OF TIME FOR ALL
CORRECTIONAL EXPERIENCES DURING THREE AGE-SPANS

	Prior to 17th Birthday		Between 17th and 25th Birthdays		Between 25th and 31st Birthdays	
	No.	%	No.	%	No.	%
Less than 12 Months	11	2.5	46	10.8	44	20.2
12–24 Months	71	16.2	68	15.9	42	19.3
24–36 Months	88	20.1	61	14.3	31	14.2
36–48 Months	93	21.2	50	11.7	30	13.8
48–60 Months	70	16.0	55	12.9	26	11.9
60–72 Months	56	12.8	41	9.6	24	11.0
72 Months or More	49	11.2	106	24.8	21	9.6
Total	438	100.0	427	100.0	218	100.0

$$\chi^2 = 106.22; \ P < .01$$

12 months; 30.2%, for 12 to 36 months; and the substantial proportion of 59.0% for at least 36 months. Of the 218 men involved between the 25th and 31st birthdays, 20.2% were subjected to a total of less than 12 months of correctional treatment: 33.5% were under penocorrectional control for 12–36 months; and 46.3%, for 36 months or longer.

The foregoing analysis may suggest that perhaps many of the men were under intra- and/or extramural treatment for too long, rather than for too brief a time; but, on reflection, the fundamental question is raised as to whether a major inadequacy of correctional activities is at least partially attributable to an inherent weakness in sentencing practices. Courts are given much discretion in respect to whether the convict shall remain in the community or be sent to prison; in the choice of the type of penal or correctional facility to be employed in the individual case; and in the duration of imprisonment, although in this last respect their authority is subsequently modifiable by boards of parole. The whole situation suggests that *there is not enough planned and penetrating individualization of justice throughout.*

PROBATION AND PAROLE

One of the penocorrectional treatment facilities developed during the present century — for which there was much hope — is the supervision of offenders in the community instead of behind prison walls. As is well known, there are two types of such extramural treatment: probation, which is granted by the court in lieu of a sentence to an institution (with or without a suspended sentence of imprisonment); and parole,

TABLE XV-3. NUMBER OF EXTRAMURAL CORRECTIONAL
EXPERIENCES DURING THREE AGE-SPANS

	Prior to 17th Birthday		Between 17th and 25th Birthdays		Between 25th and 31st Birthdays	
	No.	%	No.	%	No.	%
None	1	0.2	15	3.4	81	31.5
One	31	7.1	158	36.3	102	39.7
Two	88	20.1	110	25.3	35	13.6
Three	102	23.3	65	14.9	19	7.4
Four	95	21.7	39	9.0	9	3.5
Five	60	13.7	23	5.3	2	0.8
Six or More	61	13.9	25	5.8	9	3.5
Total	438	100.0	435	100.0	257	100.0

$$\chi^2 = 458.14; P < .01$$

which is usually granted by an independent board after a period of incarceration. Table XV-3 sets out the total number of extramural corrective experiences — both probation and parole.

Prior to the 17th birthday, 7.1% of the 438 juvenile delinquents involved had but a single extramural supervisory experience. The substantial number of 43.4% underwent two or three such periods; 35.4%, four or five; and 13.9% had six or more varied periods and intensities of probation and/or parole. Between the 17th and 25th birthdays, 3.4% of the 435 young adult offenders then involved had no extramural experiences; 36.3% had only one period of supervision outside prison or jail; 40.2% had two or three such experiences; 14.3% had four or five; and 5.8%, six or more. Between the 25th and 31st birthdays, 31.5% of the 257 men then involved had no extramural experiences; 39.7% underwent only one; 21.0% had two or three; 4.3% had four or five; and the remainder (3.5%) had as many as six or more periods of correctional supervision outside institutions.

The length of time during which these youths and men were under extramural oversight is shown in Table XV-4, and it should be noted that the time-spans frequently represented a total of several periods of extramural supervision.

Prior to the 17th birthday, 19.4% of the juvenile delinquents placed on probation and/or parole were under extramural supervision for less than a total of 12 months. However, 26.8% of the juveniles experienced extramural oversight for a total of 12–24 months; 26.3%, for 24–36 months; and 27.5%, for at least 36 months. Between the 17th and 25th birthdays, 23.8% were under probation

TABLE XV-4. LENGTH OF TIME UNDER
EXTRAMURAL SUPERVISION DURING THREE AGE-SPANS

	Prior to 17th Birthday		Between 17th and 25th Birthdays		Between 25th and 31st Birthdays	
	No.	%	No.	%	No.	%
Less than 12 Months	85	19.4	100	23.8	62	35.2
12–24 Months	117	26.8	104	24.8	63	35.8
24–36 Months	115	26.3	105	25.0	30	17.0
36–48 Months	65	14.9	55	13.1	14	8.0
48 Months or More	55	12.6	56	13.3	7	4.0
Total	437	100.0	420	100.0	176	100.0

$\chi^2 = 38.38; P < .01$

and/or parole supervision for less than 12 months; 24.8%, for 12–24 months; 25.0% were under such control for 24–36 months; and 26.4% were given such oversight for at least 36 months. Between the 25th and 31st birthdays, 35.2% of the men undergoing extramural supervision were under control for less than 12 months; 35.8% for 12–24 months; 17.0% for 24–36 months; while the remaining 12.0% received extramural correctional supervision for at least 36 months.

It is to be noted that while the average length of time under oversight outside penocorrectional institutions was similar for the first two age-spans, it decreased in the later years among those for whom such supervision was prescribed. This may have been due in part to more frequent violations of the conditions of probation or parole in the younger age groups. Without detailed consideration of the psycholgic and behavioral tendencies of each offender, of his particular response to various aspects of extramural oversight, and of the quality of supervision and aid, it is impossible to determine the extent to which the length of the periods of oversight was appropriate. A distinction should be drawn, however, between probation, which is the extramural correctional and rehabilitative treatment of the individual offender at the court level, and parole oversight provided after the offender has served a term of incarceration.

PROBATIONARY OVERSIGHT

Distinguishing, then, between probation and parole, there are some especially interesting findings in Table XV-5, which notes the number of separate probation experiences for the men undergoing treatment during the three age-spans under consideration.

TABLE XV-5.   NUMBER OF PROBATION EXPERIENCES
DURING THREE AGE-SPANS

	Prior to 17th Birthday		Between 17th and 25th Birthdays		Between 25th and 31st Birthdays	
	No.	%	No.	%	No.	%
None	50	11.4	235	54.0	134	52.1
One	135	30.8	105	24.1	71	27.6
Two	144	32.9	46	10.6	27	10.5
Three	76	17.4	31	7.1	12	4.7
Four or More	33	7.5	18	4.2	13	5.1
Total	438	100.0	435	100.0	257	100.0

$$\chi^2 = 237.54; \; P < .01$$

First, as to the period prior to the 17th birthday, only 11.4% of the 438 juvenile delinquents involved received no pre-imprisonment supervisory attention in the community. To quote the familiar statement from the bench, the large majority of the delinquents were "given a chance on probation." Thus, 30.8% had one probation experience; 32.9%, two; 17.4%, three; while the remaining 7.5% were under extramural supervision at least four times. Between the 17th and 25th birthdays, the high proportion of 54.0% of the young adults undergoing treatment were never under probationary supervision; 24.1% had one period of probation; 10.6%, two; 7.1%, three; and 4.2%, four or more. (Not all of these were newly-imposed probations; some were on sentences given before age 17 and still continuing after the offenders' 17th birthday.) The proportions for the 25-31 age-span closely resembled those for the earlier period.

On the whole, then, probationary oversight was less frequently resorted to by the criminal courts than by the juvenile courts, a conclusion supported by the findings that while 88.6% of the youthful offenders were placed on probation at one time or another before age 17, 46.0% experienced probation in the 17–25 age-span, and 47.9% between ages 25 and 31.

What, now, about the length of time on probation?

Table XV-6 shows that, of the total number of delinquents who were placed on probation one or more times prior to the 17th birthday, 34.3% were under this form of extramural supervision for a total of less than six months, a span which it might reasonably be assumed was too brief to make an impression. (However, the brevity of probation is largely related to violation of probation rules followed by commitment.) There is little gain in this respect with reference to the additional

TABLE XV-6.   LENGTH OF TIME ON PROBATION
DURING THREE AGE-SPANS

	Prior to 17th Birthday		Between 17th and 25th Birthdays		Between 25th and 31st Birthdays	
	No.	%	No.	%	No.	%
Less than 6 Months	133	34.3	48	24.0	15	12.2
6–12 Months	83	21.4	45	22.5	28	22.8
12–18 Months	83	21.4	48	24.0	33	26.8
18–24 Months	41	10.6	14	7.0	11	8.9
24–30 Months	28	7.2	26	13.0	15	12.2
30–36 Months	15	3.8	7	3.5	6	4.9
36 Months or More	5	1.3	12	6.0	15	12.2
Total	388	100.0	200	100.0	123	100.0

$$\chi^2 = 52.99; P < .01$$

21.4% who were under probationary oversight for only 6–12 months. A like proportion were on probation for 12–18 months; 10.6% for 18–24 months; and the remaining 12.3%, for longer periods.

Between the 17th and 25th birthdays, 24.0% were on probation for less than six months; 22.5%, for 6–12 months; 24.0%; for 12–18 months; 7.0%, for 18–24 months; and the remaining 22.5%, for more extensive periods. During the period between the 25th and 31st birthdays, 12.2% of those undergoing probationary treatment were under this form of extramural oversight for less than six months; 22.8%, for 6–12 months; 26.8%, for 12–18 months; and 88.9%, for 18–24 months. The remaining 29.3% were under supervision in the community for longer periods.

It will be observed that with the passage from juvenile delinquency to adult criminality, there occurred a progressive decrease in the proportion of those under probationary oversight for less than six months, from 34.3% of the juveniles who were given probation, to 24.0% in the 17–25 age-span, to 12.2% in the 25–31 age-span.

Of special significance is the incidence of misconduct during probation which was considered so seriously violative of the conditions of probation as to call for surrender of the probationer to the court.

A striking fact confronts us at the outset in Table XV-7: of the 388 *juvenile probationers* involved, only 8.5% did not have to be surrendered to the court! Only half the group (50.7%) were surrendered once; 27.3% had to be returned to the court for reconsideration on two occasions; and the remaining 13.5%, on three or more occasions. Between the 17th and 25th birthdays, 42.0% of the lower num-

TABLE XV-7. NUMBER OF PROBATIONS ON WHICH SURRENDERED DURING THREE AGE-SPANS

	Prior to 17th Birthday		Between 17th and 25th Birthdays		Between 25th and 31st Birthdays	
	No.	%	No.	%	No.	%
None	33	8.5	84	42.0	67	54.5
One	197	50.7	67	33.5	27	21.9
Two	106	27.3	27	13.5	14	11.4
Three or More	52	13.5	22	11.0	15	12.2
Total	388	100.0	200	100.0	123	100.0

$$\chi^2 = 145.93; P < .01$$

ber of 200 adult probationers involved were never surrendered to the sentencing tribunal; 33.5% were brought before the court once for violation of the conditions of probation; 13.5%, twice; while 11.0% were surrendered three or more times. Between the 25th and 31st birthdays, the considerable proportion of 54.5% of 123 adult probationers were never brought back to court for violation of the conditions of their probation; 21.9% were surrendered once; 11.4%, twice; and the remaining 12.2%, three or more times.

It should not be overlooked that the number of surrenders to the sentencing court for reconsideration of the privilege of probation is partially dependent on the number of probation officers at the court's disposal and the intensity of their supervision. Nevertheless, on the evidence available, it is a fact that, with the passage of time, the proportion of surrenders of probationers diminished sharply.

PAROLE OVERSIGHT

Turning now to parole, which involves extramural supervision following a term of imprisonment, Table XV-8 presents some of the salient facts.

The table shows that during the period prior to the 17th birthday, 11.9% of the 438 juvenile delinquents had not been placed on parole, although most of them had been in correctional schools; 37.2% had one period on parole; 26.9% were twice released from correctional school on parole; and the remaining 24.0% experienced three or more separate periods of post-incarceration oversight in the community. Between the 17th and 25th birthdays, 6.9% of the young adult offenders had never been paroled; 55.4% had one period of parole oversight; 26.2%, two; and 11.5% had three or more such periods of extramural supervision following imprisonment. During the years between the

TABLE XV-8. NUMBER OF PAROLE EXPERIENCES
DURING THREE AGE-SPANS

	Prior to 17th Birthday		Between 17th and 25th Birthdays		Between 25th and 31st Birthdays	
	No.	%	No.	%	No.	%
None	52	11.9	30	6.9	178	69.3
One	163	37.2	241	55.4	62	24.1
Two	118	26.9	114	26.2	14	5.4
Three or more	105	24.0	50	11.5	3	1.2
Total	438	100.0	435	100.0	257	100.0

$$\chi^2 = 456.92; \; P < .01$$

25th and 31st birthdays, the considerable proportion of 69.3% of the 257 offenders then involved were given no post-institutional parole oversight; 24.1% had one parole period; 5.4%, two; and only 1.2% of the men had three periods of parole supervision after incarceration.

The length of time during which the boys and men were on parole is set out in Table XV-9.

Prior to the 17th birthday, 18.1% of the 386 boys involved had post-incarceration oversight for less than six months; 22.3% were under parole supervision for 6–12 months; 13.2%, for 12–18 months; 17.6%, for 18–24 months; and the remaining 28.8% were on parole for 24 or more months, 10.4% of them for at least 36 months. During the span between the 17th and 25th birthdays, 15.1% of the 405 ex-prisoners then involved were on parole for less than six months; 19.0%,

TABLE XV-9. LENGTH OF TIME ON PAROLE
DURING THREE AGE-SPANS

	Prior to 17th Birthday		Between 17th and 25th Birthdays		Between 25th and 31st Birthdays	
	No.	%	No.	%	No.	%
Less than 6 Months	70	18.1	61	15.1	25	31.6
6–12 Months	86	22.3	77	19.0	19	24.0
12–18 Months	51	13.2	63	15.6	17	21.5
18–24 Months	68	17.6	60	14.8	8	10.1
24–30 Months	40	10.4	47	11.6	4	5.1
30–36 Months	31	8.0	33	8.1	4	5.1
36 Months or More	40	10.4	64	15.8	2	2.6
Total	386	100.0	405	100.0	79	100.0

$$\chi^2 = 32.37; \; P < .01$$

for 6–12 months; 15.6% were supervised in the community for 12–18 months after imprisonment; 14.8%, for 18–24 months; and the substantial remainder of 35.5% for at least 24 months. Within the 25–31 age-span, 31.6% of the 79 men then involved were on parole for less than six months; 24.0%, for 6–12 months; 21.5% received post-institutional oversight for 12–18 months; 10.1%, for 18–24 months; and the remaining 12.8%, for 24 months or longer.

Apart from whatever deterrent effect there may be in the consciousness of the parolee that violation of the conditions of parole might, if discovered, result in his return to prison to serve the remainder of a sentence, it is difficult to assess what the relation is between the time spent under extramural supervision and the favorable or unfavorable long-term results of the experience. It seems reasonable, however, to conclude that the length of oversight of the offender in the community should not be governed so much by the particular offense involved as by the offender's attitude and behavior within and outside the institution.

In this connection, it is of some aid to examine the record of *revocations* of parole permits, bearing in mind that both the caseload of each parole officer and the nature of the conduct that comprised violation of the conditions of parole are involved. Table XV-10 deals with the number of revocations of parole permits because of violation of the terms of the privilege of spending part of the sentence at large in the community.

Prior to the 17th birthday, 36.8% of the 386 juvenile delinquents involved had no parole revocations and 27.7% more had only a single revocation. Of the total, 19.4% experienced two cancellations of the parole permit; 16.1%, three or more. During the period between the

TABLE XV-10. NUMBER OF PAROLES REVOKED
DURING THREE AGE-SPANS

	Prior to 17th Birthday		Between 17th and 25th Birthdays		Between 25th and 31st Birthdays	
	No.	%	No.	%	No.	%
None	142	36.8	246	60.8	38	48.1
One	107	27.7	100	24.7	33	41.8
Two	75	19.4	41	10.1	8	10.1
Three or More	62	16.1	18	4.4	0	0.0
Total	386	100.0	405	100.0	79	100.0

$$\chi^2 = 80.21; P < .01$$

17th and 25th birthdays, 60.8% of the 405 young-adult parolees involved had no revocations; 24.7% had one; 10.1% had two; and 4.4%, three or more. Within the 25–31 age-span, 48.1% of the 79 parolees involved had no revocations; 41.8% more had one; and 10.1% had two.

So much for probation and parole as experienced by the delinquents as juveniles and young adults.

INTRAMURAL PENOCORRECTIONAL EXPERIENCES

Let us next examine the *intramural* penocorrectional experiences of the offenders as boys and as adults. These refer to sentences to correctional schools, reformatories, jails, prisons. Table XV-11 indicates the number of institutional commitments.

Proceeding once more according to our tripartite division of the age-spans under consideration, 1.4% of the 438 juvenile delinquents involved never experienced incarceration for their antisocial acts prior to the 17th birthday, and 40.6% were sent to correctional institutions only once after a finding of delinquency; 24.0% experienced two incarcerations; 17.3%, three; 8.7%, four; while the remaining 8.0% of juvenile delinquents were imprisoned no fewer than five times. Between the 17th and 25th birthdays, 35.2% of the 435 young adult offenders involved were never imprisoned for their crimes but were supervised extramurally; 20.9% had only one period of incarceration; 15.2% were incarcerated twice; 9.9%, three times; 10.6% were committed four times; and the remaining 8.2% had no fewer than five or more imprisonments. During the span between the 25th and 31st birthdays, 38.5% of the 257 offenders then involved experienced no

TABLE XV-11. NUMBER OF INTRAMURAL CORRECTIONAL
EXPERIENCES DURING THREE AGE-SPANS

	Prior to 17th Birthday		Between 17th and 25th Birthdays		Between 25th and 31st Birthdays	
	No.	%	No.	%	No.	%
None	6	1.4	153	35.2	99	38.5
One	178	40.6	91	20.9	62	24.1
Two	105	24.0	66	15.2	50	19.5
Three	76	17.3	43	9.9	27	10.5
Four	38	8.7	46	10.6	13	5.0
Five or More	35	8.0	36	8.2	6	2.4
Total	438	100.0	435	100.0	257	100.0

$$\chi^2 = 212.19; P < .01$$

institutionalization for their crimes; 24.1% were incarcerated once; 19.5%, twice; 10.5%, three times; 5.0%, four times; and the remaining 2.4%, more than four times.

One more finding on this scroll of crime and punishment deals with the length of incarceration of the offenders as juvenile delinquents and as adult criminals (see Table XV-12).

It will be seen that, as juvenile delinquents, 41.7% of the 432 boys undergoing intramural supervision were incarcerated for a total of less than 12 months; 35.4% were held in correctional schools or reformatories for 12–24 months; 15.0%, for 24–36 months; 5.8%, for 36–48 months; and the remaining 2.1%, for longer periods. Between the 17th and 25th birthdays, 35.1% of the 282 young men then involved were incarcerated for a total period of less than 12 months; 15.2%, for 12–24 months; 11.3%, for 24–36 months; 9.6%, for 36–48 months; and 28.8%, for at least 48 months. During the period between the 25th and 31st birthdays, 37.3% of the 158 adult offenders in question were imprisoned for a period of less than 12 months; 12.7% were behind bars for 21–24 months; 12.0%, for 24–36 months; 14.6%, for 36–48 months; and 23.4%, for longer spans of time. Thus, the proportion of lengthy incarcerations (36 or more months) increased markedly following the juvenile years.

LEGAL STATUS AT CLOSE OF EACH PERIOD

Before summarizing and commenting on the findings regarding the incidence of probation, parole, and incarceration among the 438 juvenile offenders whose criminal careers were followed to age 31, it is of interest to describe their legal status at the end of each of the three periods under

TABLE XV-12. LENGTH OF INCARCERATION
DURING THREE AGE-SPANS

	Prior to 17th Birthday		Between 17th and 25th Birthdays		Between 25th and 31st Birthdays	
	No.	%	No.	%	No.	%
Less than 12 Months	180	41.7	99	35.1	59	37.3
12–24 Months	153	35.4	43	15.2	20	12.7
24–36 Months	65	15.0	32	11.3	19	12.0
36–48 Months	25	5.8	27	9.6	23	14.6
48 Months or More	9	2.1	81	28.8	37	23.4
Total	432	100.0	282	1000.0	158	100.0

$$\chi^2 = 147.78; P < .01$$

TABLE XV-13.   LEGAL STATUS AT END OF SPECIFIED PERIODS

	At Age 17		At Age 25		At Age 31	
	No.	%	No.	%	No.	%
In Community	17	3.9	295	67.4	335	76.8
On Probation	23	5.2	30	6.8	23	5.3
On Parole	254	58.0	12	2.7	6	1.4
In Correctional Institution	133	30.4	84	19.2	51	11.7
Fugitive from Justice	8	1.8	9	2.1	16	3.7
Awaiting Trial	3	0.7	8	1.8	5	1.1
Total	438	100.0	438	100.0	436[a]	100.0

$$\chi^2 = 764.63; \text{P} < .01$$

[a] Two men were in mental hospitals on their 31st birthdays.

consideration. (We are concerned now with all 438 men and not only with those who had been convicted.)

Table XV-13 shows that at the end of juvenile court jurisdiction — that is, up to the 17th birthday — only 3.9% of the 438 juvenile delinquents were living in the community without supervision. Only a small proportion (5.2%) were on probation; almost a third (30.4%) were in correctional schools; and over a half (58.0%) were on parole.

On their 25th and 31st birthdays, the proportion of young men *not* under legal restraint jumped from 3.9% at age 17, to 67.4% at 25, and to 76.8% at age 31. There was a consequent drop of offenders in institutions: from 30.4% at age 17, to 19.2% at age 25, and 11.7% at age 31. A marked drop occurred also in the proportion of men on parole: from 58.0% at age 17, to only 2.7% at age 25, and 1.4% at age 31.

SUMMARY AND COMMENT

It is difficult to assess the merits of the disposition of these offenders at various stages; to determine which of them should have been dealt with by probation alone, or by probation accompanied by a suspended sentence to a correctional institution; which should have been sent to institutions other than the ones to which the courts sentenced them; which of the sentences were too long and which too short; which allocation of the total sentence between incarceration and parole was wise and which not — all this in the light of what must be the ultimate rational aim of the entire system of criminal justice, that is, to protect society most effectively while safeguarding the legal and humanitarian rights of each offender. It is easy to be dogmatic about "the deterrent aim of punishment"; or why, in view of the heinous crime involved in a particular case, a sentence is too short, or the prison regime too comfortable; or about the need of combining the deterrent, morally educative, reformative, and rehabilitative aims of punishment. There has been far too much futile theorizing here, as well as in probing the etiology of delinquency and recidivism, and far too little of engaging in the difficult task of assembling, verifying, and organizing facts which might help to answer crucial questions.

One such fact is that with the passage of time there has been an appreciable diminution in recidivism among our original juvenile delinquents.

Another basic matter to be inferred from the evidence is that the efforts of the sociolegal apparatus to "reform" and "rehabilitate," or at least "deter," the offenders involved, do not seem on the whole to have done as much good as the operations of Mother Nature and Father Time. Only the "protection of society" through relatively brief periods of incarceration of the offenders, thus limiting the opportunity for the commission of further crimes, is a value achieved by the existing sociolegal techniques.

PART III "THE PAST IS PROLOGUE"

XVI   Theoretical Implications

INTRODUCTORY

In considerable detail and variety we have examined the past and present status of the two groups of human beings compared in this work. The descriptive analysis has indicated beyond reasonable doubt that, in all of life's activities considered in this inquiry, the men who as boys comprised our sample of juvenile delinquents have continued on a path markedly *divergent* from those who as juveniles had been included in the control group of nondelinquents. Continuing divergence, virtually always to the disadvantage of the delinquents, has been found during the long follow-up span to age 31 to exist not only in their crime records but in other significant areas of their life activity. It is revealed in the standard of academic education and vocational training ultimately achieved by the two sets of men; in their industrial record (in terms of skills, work habits, and illicit occupations); in their economic status (including the incidence of self-support, dependency, debts incurred); in the various aspects of their domestic relations (including differences in the number of illegitimate children, in attitudes and practices involving assumption of family responsibilities, in family attachments); in their use of leisure (including variance in family group recreations, out-of-home recreations, unwholesome habits); in their companionships (including adherence to antisocial gangs); in their neglect of religious duties; in their conduct in the Armed Forces (including incidence of deferments and discharges for psychiatric reasons and moral unfitness, and the number discharged following general court-martial); in their ambitions and aspirations; and in other respects. Since there is a summary at the end of each of the preceding chapters, it serves no useful purpose to repeat the findings in detail.

However, one aspect of the trend of consistent divergence between the delinquents and nondelinquents is worth special mention: the vari-

ance of the two groups has been shown to be most striking in the finding
that, while the majority of the boys originally included in the nondelinquent control group continued, down the years, to remain essentially
law-abiding, the great majority of those originally included in the delinquent group continued to commit all sorts of crimes in the 17–25
age-span. Beyond these years, the phenomenon of a drop-off in the
incidence of criminality, already noted in our other follow-up studies,[1]
suggests, as a provocative hypothesis deserving of special research by
physiologists and endocrinologists, the influence of a process of *delayed
maturation.*[2] We consider this in a later section of the present chapter.

Meanwhile, the fact should be emphasized that, while an appreciable
proportion of the original delinquents either abandoned crime altogether
or became petty nuisance offenders, it still remains true that three-fifths
of them were committing serious crimes during the 17–25 age-span and
three-tenths were doing so during the second follow-up period. Thus
their initial divergence from the nondelinquents in *Unraveling* continued
with the passage of time; for in the control group only a few became
serious offenders.

SIGNIFICANCE OF FINDINGS FOR ETIOLOGIC THEORY

The basic inference derived from the evidence of continuing and
marked divergence of the original delinquent group from the nonde-
liquent control group in many major aspects of life's activity is this:
that the *mass* impact of the external societal environment, or the general
culture, is less significant in generating delinquency and extending it
into criminal recidivism than are the biologic endowments of the individual and the parental influences of the formative years of early
childhood.

In other words, it is not poverty that basically accounts for the
original differences and continuing diversity of the two groups; for
both sets of juveniles were in circumstances of poverty to begin with.[3]
It is not lack of economic and sociocultural opportunity that basically
and largely accounts for their original and continued divergence; for
both groups were in this respect equally deprived. It is not residence
in a slum that is the fundamental cause of delinquency and recidivism;
for both groups lived in urban slums.[4]

In short, the generalized, unilateral, all-embracing "explanations"
of delinquency and recidivism do not adequately explain because they
do not *discriminate.* They do not distinguish between a differing response of various *individuals* to many of the potentially malign influences of the slum area, or "ghetto." The external, general culture with

which the unilateral theories deal, while reflecting remote influences indirectly involved in the background of both delinquents and nondelinquents, are not nearly so determinative of delinquency or nondelinquency as the quality of the parents and children and the under-the-roof culture of the home.[5]

In reflecting upon the mechanisms of etiology, one must conclude that the all-embracing *constants* in the general environmental situation can contribute relatively little to an understanding of any *individual's* maladjustment to the demands of ethical norms and legal codes. The malign influences of the slum somehow do *not* produce delinquency among the great majority of those who live in such potentially evil communities. Moreover, there are numerous delinquents who reside, not in slums but in "good" neighborhoods, in city or suburb; and the "affluent society" does not always produce happy, contented, and law-abiding children.[6] What has as yet not been adequately explored is the extent to which and in what respects parental affectional attitudes and disciplinary practices, family cohesiveness, and parental standards of ethics and behavior in *nonslum* regions vary as between families which contribute delinquent children and those which do not.

It goes without saying that a conclusion of the primary and prime importance of parent-child relations in the guidance and control of childhood and subsequent behavior in adolescence and young adulthood does not mean that general social programs for the reduction of poverty, improvement of slum areas, and extension of opportunity to millions of the disadvantaged and underprivileged are not needed. Strictly speaking, however, this is not the issue under discussion. The issue is rather: which influences are most frequently, potently, and selectively involved in generating delinquency in childhood.[7]

CAUSATION IN THE ANALYSIS OF DELINQUENCY

In connection with theories of delinquency causation,[8] the multidisciplinary evidence of our comparisons of delinquents with a control group of nondelinquents should be persuasive proof that, on the whole, boys having in their make-up and early home conditioning certain identifiable traits and factors which markedly differentiate delinquents from nondelinquents are very likely to turn out to be delinquents, and a substantial proportion of them are likely to continue their criminal behavior at least into adolescence and early adulthood. In this generalized sense of high probability of the origin and persistence of antisocial conduct in the presence of a syndrome of characteristics of person and *intimate milieu* that distinguishes delinquents from nondelinquents in the mass, a rough etiologic relationship has been established in *Unraveling Juvenile Delinquency* and has been confirmed in the present work with the passage of a substantial segment of time.

Thus it is clear that not all the traits and factors arrived at inductively and included in our general etiologic formulation will be found in all delinquents and not found at all in the nondelinquents. For example, the fact that twice as many delinquents as nondelinquents were originally found to be of the closely knit, muscular, energetic *mesomorphic* physique type does not mean that mesomorphy per se is inevitably related to delinquency. The very fact that 30% of the nondelinquents were also of such physique immediately contradicts any such notion. Again, such a trait as *defiance*, which one would naturally regard as closely related to delinquent behavioral tendencies, was found to exist in 50% of the delinquents; but 12% of the control group of nondelinquents were similarly characterized; and the very fact that half the delinquent group did not display this trait further reveals the inadequacy of conclusions about "causation" based on a single factor.

Even a small cluster of factors frequently involved in delinquent behavior may not, of itself, have sufficient potency in the light of the other influences involved to tip the scales in the case of boys who manage to remain nondelinquent. Thus, in any realistic sense, the cause of an effect is that *totality of conditions sufficient to produce it.* Persistent delinquency and continuing criminality are not the potential result of only one factor, or even a combination of factors, which markedly differentiates delinquents from nondelinquents, but of each of several varied combinations. Just as death, although always the same terminal event, may be the result of various preceding sequences or combinations of conditions, so the development of delinquency, or continuing criminality, may be the product of a variety of different internal and external conditions which are associated with maladapted behavior; and not all of them are indispensable to the result in any particular case. Despite the variety and complexity of etiologic involvements, however, certain combinations or syndromes of internal and external conditions tend to occur more *frequently* than others; and it is both etiologically significant and preventively and therapeutically useful to distinguish these most frequent syndromes of traits and factors. Such information is of value both in identifying *potential* delinquents at a very early age, when therapeutic-preventive intervention is likely to be most promising, and in focusing on the frequently occurring combinations of influences so that intervention can be pointed and realistic.

In emphasizing that our findings tend to confirm the view that delinquency involves both the biological make-up of the individual offender and his immediate forebears, and the family drama in which he and his parents play leading roles, especially during the first few years of life, we do not mean to ignore certain ideas which have been stressed by some sociologists. For example, we have in the past noted the influence of culture conflict in stimulating violation of social norms in some cases.[9] Again, we recognize the special influences that are involved in the recent rise of delinquency in middle-class and upper-class regions. But such influences — rapid social mobility, conflicts in values and standards, weakening of middle-class and upper-class value systems so that they no longer guide behavior as much as in the past — are two, three, or more stages removed from the immediately and intimately operative ones. For, as previously pointed out, the influences of the culture, and of exposure to rapid change from one subculture to another, are *selective*. Individuals react differently to the impact of cultural standards. That is why such general etiologic theories as the "delinquent subculture," or the working-class or middle-class subculture, or the "interstitial area," or the slum or "ghetto," or the process of "differential association" and other nondiscriminative, all-embracing general theories, do not adequately account for the operative facts in etiology.

Despite the many unwholesome and antisocial features of our culture — its excessive materialism, its stress on "success," its recent overwhelming assaults on values by various mass-communication media, its encouragement of the spread of "literature" of pornography and violence, the weakening hold of the church and formal religion — the majority of people are, in normal times, relatively law-abiding. In the research of which the present study is an extension (*Unraveling Juvenile Delinquency*), we had no difficulty in finding 500 *nondelinquent* boys living in underprivileged and high-delinquency areas of Greater Boston.

In other words, antisocial aspects of culture are only *potential* or *possible* causes of delinquency. Persons of varied innate natures and differing early parent–child relationships respond in different ways to those elements of the culture which they wish, or are impelled, to *introject*, some of them transforming such cultural elements into antisocial motives. Environment can play no role in conduct unless and until it is, as it were, emotionally absorbed, becoming a part of the motivating force for or against the taboos and demands of the prevailing culture, its values, and its norms. For this reason it is indispensable to study individuals as well as broad social dynamics. Whatever future research may yet disclose about the causes of delinquency in the affluent segment of our society, as regards delinquency among the underprivileged, the emphases suggested by our analyses in the present and in prior works are supported by the facts.

EMPHASIS ON PERSONAL VERSUS GROUP INFLUENCES

In recent years there has been a steadily increasing attack on what is referred to as "barren empiricism" in studies of the etiology of delinquency. There has been a correlative insistence that research into etiology must be "guided by a theory," as in the physical sciences; and it has been assumed that group, class, and cultural approaches are guided by a theory and are therefore more illuminative of etiologic relationships than the study of the traits and factors involving the individual and his intimate under-the-roof milieu. Insistence that theories which center on generalizations regarding group or cultural influences in society are *ipso facto* superior assumes without proof that such an approach is more explanatory and more revealing than the painstaking systematic comparison of delinquents and nondelinquents along many avenues of multidisciplinary exploration. Preoccupation with generalized theories in criminology has thus far yielded rather barren results.[10] The insulation of some sociologists from the discipline of biology has not helped the situation. Fortunately, there is evidence of a growing interest among social scientists in the relevancy of biological experiments and insights to the more penetrating understanding of social and societal problems. D. G. Glass, an authority in social psychology has recently said:

> Contemporary social scientists no longer adhere to a simplistic environmental determinism, just as contemporary biologists no longer embrace a genetic determinism. In both fields the importance of an interaction between the organism and his environment is recognized. Neither the genetic parameter nor the environmental parameter alone can account for more than a portion of behavioral variability.
>
> With the development of an interactional approach, a revitalized interest in the genetics of behavior has been witnessed.[11]

Organization of a recent conference sponsored by the Social Science Research Council's Committee on Biological Bases of Social Behavior (and by the Russell Sage Foundation and Rockefeller University) was "guided by the premise that recent advances in research on genetics portend serious social, ethical, and legal consequences in the not too distance future."[12] One of the speakers at the conference (William Thompson of Queen's University, Ontario, Canada) pointed out that behavioral genetic questions are relevant "particularly for patterns of social interaction and aggression. On the basis of a thorough review of animal experiments, he concluded that early in life the organism is capable of being altered in various ways, including changes in its temperament and attitude of social posture toward other members of its species. Later in development the shaping of behavior patterns becomes possible."[13]

Another speaker at the conference (Theodosius Dobzhansky of Rockefeller University) is cited by Glass:

> The stock argument of some psychologists and sociologists is that since educators and social workers cannot do anything about people's heredity they may as well forget it. In reality they can do a lot about it; if they recognize that the human natures are not uniform but multiform, they may take steps to provide conditions in which everybody, or as nearly everybody as possible, is able to do his best.[14]

The last observation puts one in mind of the suggestion for establishing various "therapeutic communities" or "family refuges," such as have been proposed by certain American clinicians and social workers.[15]

It is indeed encouraging that certain farsighted leaders of various disciplines concerned more or less directly with human behavior are beginning to abandon their "scholarly insularity" and are taking steps to develop a "unified biosocial science."[16] It is in this spirit that we have long urged the indispensability of a multifaceted approach to the problems of etiology, therapy, and preventive techniques in delinquency and crime. In our experience, search for one or another supposedly unifying theory to "explain" delinquency is not only vain in the present state of knowledge, but harmful to penetrating research. G. B. Vold has expressed it well:

> It is not to be expected that criminological theory will develop wholly adequate and acceptable explanations of criminal behavior until the whole group of "the behavior sciences" reaches a corresponding adequacy of theoretical explanation of human behavior in general. The criminal will continue to be a human being, and his behavior will be only in degree and in special ways different from that of the non-criminal. Hence, criminological theory and human behavior theory in general may be expected to make relatively parallel developments.[17]

In the meantime, it cannot seriously be contended that any unilateral theory of the etiology of delinquency, whether it is exclusively or almost exclusively sociologic or biologic, supplies the comprehensive and penetrating explanation that is needed. The research described in

Unraveling Juvenile Delinquency, and extended in the present work, does no more than bring together in relatively integrated fashion many individual and social variables that originally differentiated the delinquents from the nondelinquents and that, in many avenues of later activity, continue through the years of early adulthood to distinguish them. There are of course certain traits and factors in which, originally and later, no statistical variance between the delinquents and the nondelinquents was found; but these are not nearly so numerous as those which clearly set off the delinquents from the control group.[18]

MATURATION AND RECIDIVISM

The importance of biological inquiries into criminologic problems has been discussed. A special aspect of this is one already adverted to — that is, the relation of belated maturation to the abandonment of criminal activities or to change from aggressive, serious criminalism to commission of petty "nuisance" offenses. It was pointed out in Chapter XII that there is a significant difference in the percentages of the two sets of men judged as mature by the close of the second follow-up period. In several of our prior follow-up studies as well,[19] we came to the conclusion — after ruling out many factors possibly involved[20] — that a major explanation of persistent recidivism must be sought in the lack of maturity on the part of those who, having begun their delinquencies as boys, continued their criminal behavior into adolescence and early adulthood despite all efforts of legally organized society, with its police, prisons, and parole systems, to rehabilitate them. Those men who, in their late twenties or early thirties, did abandon criminality were persons who, after an apparently delayed maturation process, finally achieved enough integration and stability to make their intelligence and emotion effective in convincing them that crime does not lead to satisfaction.

Maturation is a complex process and concept. It embraces the development of a stage of physical, intellectual, and affective capacity and stability, and a sufficient degree of integration of all major constituents of temperament and personality to be adequate to the demands and restrictions of life in organized society. Common experience indicates that, as the average person passes through the various age-spans from childhood, through puberty, into adolescence and beyond, there are certain changes in his development and in the integration of his various physical, intellectual, affective, and volitional-inhibitory powers. Normally, when he reaches chronologic adulthood, the development and consolidation of his physical and mental powers make it easier for him to achieve a capacity for self-control and foresight; to postpone immediate desires for later, less hazardous, and more rewarding ones; to profit by experience; to develop perseverance, regard for the opinion of others, self-reliance, self-respect, and other such attributes useful in adaptation to life, to the demands of society and its values, norms, and religious and legal codes; and to avoid drifting into, or persisting in, crime and its frequent consequences of disgrace and punishment, often leading to a point of no return. However, individuals differ in their innate biological equipment and organization, and in their early conditioning at home and in school; so that development and integration of powers sufficient to lead to "maturity" are not always achieved at the normal age-spans.

It must of course be recognized that external circumstances which occur with the passage of time contribute to the maturation process. We are beginning a correlation of the findings regarding the maturity status of the delinquents and nondelinquents with data from *Unraveling* and from the follow-up inquiry. The results should illumine the findings concerning the role of both internal and external circumstances in reducing criminal behavior with advancing years.

A psychoanalytic approach to the delayed maturation concept might emphasize that, owing to "fixation" of the "libido" at childhood levels, a clinically recognized "infantilism," or immaturity of personality, not infrequently exists in persons who might otherwise attain a degree of maturity commensurate with persons of their own age. In fact, from many angles the conduct of numerous persistent criminals may be regarded as infantile: witness their impulsiveness; their lack of forethought or clumsy planning; their unrealistic ambitions; their inability to postpone immediate desires for distant goals; their incapacity or unwillingness to profit from numerous experiences of arrest and punishment; their inability to assume marital, familial, and industrial obligations appropriate to an adult age and responsibility; and other signs of immaturity which have been indicated in prior chapters.

In *Later Criminal Careers*,[21] a systematic comparison was presented which indicated that the years from about 25 to 35 are the most crucial in the lives of offenders, since it appears that it is during this age-span that the peak of a sifting-out process occurs, differentiating those who have matured normally from those who are unlikely to reach a stage of maturity sufficient to abandon antisocial conduct and who will either end their days as criminals in jails, or in almshouses, or on the streets. In *Juvenile Delinquents Grown Up*,[22] a comparison was presented of numerous traits and social factors in the make-up and background of the ultimately reformed, as opposed to those of the persistent criminals, originally investigated as boy delinquents, who had passed through the Boston Juvenile Court and had been examined by the Judge Baker Foundation.[23] That investigation confirmed the suggestion made in *Later Criminal Careers* that, during the years which brought the delinquent boys into early manhood, a differentiation occurred between those offenders whose delinquency was probably due more to adverse environmental and educational influences than to any organic weaknesses, and those whose continuing inability or reluctance to conform to the demands of a complex society was more nearly related to innate (though partly, also, to early-conditioned) abnormalities that set limits to the capacity to achieve a socially adequate degree of maturity and adaptability. The former, sooner or later — especially in their late twenties and early thirties — acquire the requisite degree of organic integration of their innate impulsive tendencies, affect, and intelligence; the latter hardly ever achieve a stage of maturity requisite to normal adaptation in our complex, largely urban, society and culture. Despite their arrival at a high chronologic age-level, they continue to be maladapted and to be criminalistic, either seriously or in terms of persistent petty offenses and habitual vices, until they are physically and mentally "burned out," as it were. Misbehavior due in large part (though not exclusively) to *un*integration gives way to misbehavior related to *dis*integration, until the organism runs down and finally stops.[24]

To the evidence of our prior studies involving other samples of delinquents and criminals, there is now added the proof of the situation over the years with regard to the boys who had comprised the experimental delinquent group of *Unraveling*. It will be recalled that, while the original nondelinquents largely continued to be law-abiding as they grew to adulthood, the picture was different for the original delinquent group. However, the portrait was not static, but improved at certain stages. Prior to the 17th birthday, 90.4% of the 438 boys were serious offenders; between the 17th and 25th birthdays — that is, during the first follow-up span — the proportion dropped markedly to 59.6%; but, most strikingly, between the 25th and 31st birthdays, it declined to 28.9%. Thus, it is reasonable to infer that, with the passage of time, long-delayed maturation has come to this group of men, and with this belated ripening and integration of the powers of affect, intelligence, and control, there has resulted a diminuation in the commission of serious crimes. As for petty offenses, it will be recalled that while there were relatively few *persistent minor* offenders, there has been a small rise in occasional petty offenders among the former delinquents from one age-span to another (9.6%, 15.3%, 19.2%).

Since there has been relatively little change in external social conditions in the regions inhabited by the delinquents, the improvement cannot be attributed to this. Thus, it seems imperative that, in addition to the study of societal-cultural influences in delinquency and recidivism, the aid of biochemists, physiologists, endocrinologists, and psychologists be enlisted to focus attention on the *erratic maturation* phenomenon. This may or may not be related to original constitutional variations in physique type or to other findings in *Unraveling Juvenile Delinquency* not yet drawn into the picture, such as disproportion-indexes in various anthropologic measurements of different segments of the body as to which the delinquents were compared with the nondelinquents,[25] and the striking differences between them in the pace of growth of the two sets of boys.[26] For reasons such as these, it is especially gratifying to note the recent insistence on collaboration between social scientists and biologists. The problem of *man-in-society* is much too complex to be left exclusively to the single disciplines of sociology, or psychiatry, or neurology, or biology, or biochemistry. We are certain that by systematic collaboration, meaningful advances can be made in the better understanding of delinquency and recidivism. This will mean delay in the development of theory, but the history of criminology has shown that the quest for some all-embracing, unifying theory to explain antisocial behavior has been a failure and has distracted attention from the urgent task of assembling more and more accurate, objective, and comprehensive facts, at all relevant levels.

The delay in theory construction and the imperfection of existing factual studies need not cause pessimism in experimenting with individual and social modes of prevention and therapy. It is useful to recall that in the field of medicine much good was accomplished on the basis of mere approximations to etiologic involvements. Until Edward Jenner's discovery of smallpox vaccine in 1798, smallpox took a heavy toll in disfiguration and death. Jenner's great contribution made it possible to control this disease, even though its specific etiology had not been definitely established. Similarly, the efficacy of quinine in treatment of fever was known to the Peruvian Indians for centuries before the significant connection between disease and cure was determined. Cinchona bark was introduced into Europe by the Jesuits in 1632. Soon thereafter it was used by Sydenham, enabling him to differentiate malarial from nonmalarial fevers on the basis of the therapeutic response to treatment with quinine. Yet the "cause" of malaria was not known until 1880, when the French army surgeon, Laveran, discovered and described the malarial parasites in the red blood cells. Thus, during a period of some two-and-a-half centuries, the treatment of malaria by cinchona bark and its derivatives was based exclusively upon empirical clinical evidence. To cite still another example, although the discovery by the Yellow Fever Commission of the United States Army that yellow fever is transmitted by a species of mosquito resulted in the virtual eradication of this disease, its exact etiologic agent was long unknown. The search for the real villain resulted in our day in the tragic death of the great Noguchi.

Bearing such precedents in mind, we do not hesitate, in a concluding chapter, to sketch some suggestions for prevention of delinquency gleaned from the major findings of *Unraveling* and from the present follow-up of the delinquents and nondelinquents, even though "specific causation" will long present many puzzles.

Notes

1. S. and E. T. Glueck, *Criminal Careers in Retrospect* (New York: The Commonwealth Fund, 1943; New York: Kraus Reprint, 1966) ; S. and E. T. Glueck, *Juvenile Delinquents Grown Up* (New York: The Commonwealth Fund, 1940; New York: Kraus Reprint, 1966).

2. For a recent informative article on abatement of criminality with age, see R. Boyer, B. M. Cormier, B. Grad, "Statistics on Criminal Processes," *The Canadian Journal of Corrections*, 8: 104-119 (1966).

3. Long ago, E. H. Sutherland, an outstanding sociologic criminologist, recognized this fact: "The thesis of this paper is that the conception and explanations of crime which have just been described are misleading and incorrect, that crime is in fact not closely correlated with poverty or with the psychopathic and sociopathic conditions associated with poverty." "White-Collar Criminality," in L. Wilson and W. L. Kolb, *Sociological Analysis* (New York: Harcourt, Brace, 1949), p. 788. He presents the general hypothesis of differential association and social disorganization to explain both white-collar criminality and lower class criminality.

4. See S. Glueck, "Ten Years of *Unraveling Juvenile Delinquency*," *The Journal of Criminal Law, Criminology and Police Science*, 51: 284-287 (September–October 1960).

5. The parents are not merely conveyors of the surrounding general culture, but also its selective filters and modifiers.

6. See, for example, the discerning analysis in "The Affluent Delinquent," by G. J. Pine, *Phi Delta Kappan*, December 1966.

7. In the most comprehensive "welfare state" in the world, Sweden, where there are no slums and where the people are "taken care of" from the cradle to the grave, there is a mounting rate of delinquency, illegitimacy, and alcoholism.

8. We are fully aware of the pitfalls in the concept of "cause." We have always emphasized that we use the term to mean a high statistical probability of etiology rather than an inevitable one-to-one cause-and-effect linkage in each case. For an excellent discussion of the by-no-means simple concept of "cause" in criminology, see Hermann Mannheim's masterly treatise, *Comparative Criminology* (Boston: Houghton Mifflin, 1965), pp. 5-12.

9. "Eleanor Glueck found that the social and economic conditions of these second generation children were not more unfavourable than those of their parents, and she concluded that their higher crime rate could, therefore, be due only to their more intense culture conflict." *Ibid.*, p. 540. The article referred to is "Culture Conflict and Delinquency," *Mental Hygiene*, 21:46-66 (January 1937).

10. G. B. Vold, *Theoretical Criminology* (New York: Oxford University Press, 1958) ; S. Glueck, "Theory and Fact in Criminology," *British Journal of Delinquency*, 7: 92-109 (October 1956).

11. "Genetics and Social Behavior," *Items*, 21:1 (March 1967). See also C. B. Jacobson and V. L. Magyar, "Toward a Better Tomorrow," *American Association of University Women Journal*, 60:74 (January 1967) : "Current knowledge of human genetics is permitting significant advances in medical, moral, and theological interpretations of genetic disease. The clinical management of congenital malformations, infertility, mental retardation, and developmental sexual abnormalities may in the next ten years undergo revolutionary changes, *if* this expanded scientific knowledge is paralleled by pragmatic innovations in the supporting medical and legal institutions of our society."

12. Glass, "Genetics and Social Behavior," p. 2.

13. *Ibid.*, p. 3.

14. *Ibid.*, p. 4.

15. See C. Downing Tait, Jr., M.D., and Emory F. Hodges, Jr., M.D., *Delinquents, Their Families, and the Community* (Springfield, Ill.: Charles C. Thomas, 1962), pp. 116-135. See also Gordon Shipman, "Probation and the Family." *Probation*, 23: 106-114 (1944-45).

16. Glass, "Genetics and Social Behavior," p. 5.

17. *Theoretical Criminology*, pp. 314-315.

18. The social significance of some of these "complacent" traits and factors in *Unraveling* is discussed in E. and S. Glueck, "Delinquents and Nondelinquents in Depressed Areas: Some Guidelines for Community Preventive Action," *Community Mental Health Journal*, 2: 213-218 (Fall 1966).

19. S. and E. Glueck, *Later Criminal Careers* (New York: The Commonwealth Fund, 1937; New York: Kraus Reprint, 1966) ; *Juvenile Delinquents Grown Up* (New York: The Commonwealth Fund, 1940; New York: Kraus Reprint, 1966) ; *Criminal Careers in Retrospect* (New York: The Commonwealth Fund, 1943; New York: Kraus Reprint, 1966) ; *After-Conduct of Discharged Offenders* (London: Macmillan, 1945; New York: Kraus Reprint, 1966).

20. As an illustration of the method used, see S. and E. Glueck, *After-Conduct of Discharged Offenders*, pp. 76ff.

21. Chapter x.

22. Pages 107ff.

23. Now known as the Judge Baker Guidance Center.

24. For a detailed discussion of our views on this complex matter, see *After-Conduct of Discharged Offenders*, chap. vii.

25. *Unraveling Juvenile Delinquency*, pp. 335-339. Dr. Carl C. Seltzer, a highly experienced anthropologist, who was responsible for the anthropometry, concluded: "The individual analysis of the disproportions shows clearly that in seven out of the ten indices *the frequency of disproportions is substantially lower in the delinquent group than in the non-delinquent group*. In one instance the delinquents are more disproportionate than the non-delinquents, and in the two remaining disproportions there are no significant differences between the two series." *Ibid.*, p. 339.

26. "At least as important as the matter of gross body *size* are the very interesting indications with regard to the *growth patterns* of the two juvenile groups." It appears that in the case of many of the measures here studied, the younger juvenile delinquents are smaller in average gross size than the nondelinquents until about the fourteenth year when the delinquents catch up to the nondelinquents, and finally in most instances surpass them as they grow older. In other words, *the delinquents exhibit a lag in physical growth until about the fourteenth year, after which time they begin to show slight superiorities in gross dimensions over the nondelinquents.*

"The really significant growth spurt of the delinquents takes place apparently between the thirteenth and fourteenth years. This is clearly indicated by the fact that in fifteen out of the sixteen measurements there is a greater difference in the delinquents than in the nondelinquents between the mean gross dimensions of the 13-year-old class and the 14-year-old group. It is thus evident from the data that the so-called 'adolescent growth spurt' takes place somewhat later among the delinquents than among the non-delinquents." *Ibid.*, pp. 316 and 317.

XVII Some Practical Implications

INTRODUCTORY

The evidence in this work calls for basic improvement in delinquency *prevention* and in crime *suppression.* Improvement in the suppression of crime is a different problem from that of early identification of potential juvenile delinquents followed by skillful intervention to divert the expectable antisocial career. While it has been demonstrated in the foregoing pages that, both in dealing with prospective and actual juvenile wrongdoers and in coping with experienced, mature criminals, society's efforts have not been very successful with the subjects of this book, it is not our aim here to discuss the weaknesses of the administration of police and prosecutory agencies, of sentencing practices, of correctional institutions and techniques, of probation and parole, or the crying need to improve the selection, training, and deployment of correctional personnel all down the line. These matters have recently been comprehensively dealt with by the President's two Crime Commissions.[1] The basic problems involved in the administration of criminal justice in the case of adult offenders have also been adequately gone into in prior crime surveys.[2] Moreover, by the time officials and institutions for adult offenders take hold of the crime problem, they are dealing, as has been amply demonstrated in the present book, largely with "finished products." The evidence clearly points to the crucial significance of preventing delinquency at a very early stage in life. Hence, this concluding chapter is devoted essentially to *fundamental delinquency prevention.*

Programs of delinquency prevention focused on prophylaxis — that is, on defending and protecting children from the malaise of antisocial maladjustment — may be divided roughly into three types, not ignoring the fact that there are no sharp lines of cleavage between them. The first of these circles of influence on behavior deals with very general, permeative socioeconomic forces that affect an entire culture and therefore exert an impact on both nondelinquents and delinquents, albeit selectively. Such all-embracing general welfare efforts at preventing antisocial conduct are only remotely and indirectly related, in certain instances, to the genesis and formation of undesirable attitudes, character, delinquency, and criminality. The second circle of crime-preventive strategies consists of programs and techniques which, though not organized chiefly and specifically to cope with the roots of maladjustment and delinquency, still have some natural, though incidental, relationship to the specific problem. The third and most intimate circle of preventive activity is made up of programs and techniques designed specifically to deal with the conditions for which reasonable evidence exists that they tend greatly to enhance the risk of children becoming delinquent.

In the past, European criminologists have generally recommended the first type of all-embracing attack on the weaknesses of the social order. They have couched their suggestions for crime prevention in very general terms. In more recent years, especially in the era of the much-publicized "Great Society" and the "War on Poverty," this has also been the favored approach of certain American criminologists. But while there can be little quarrel with the generalization that "every measure that helps to make the people physically, mentally, and economically healthier is a weapon in the struggle against the world of crime,"[3] or that the slums should be eliminated (if possible), such suggestions are aimed at sets of influences too remote from those specifically involved in the social evils of delinquency and crime to be especially relevant. The target-area they aim at is not made up of the conditions that greatly enhance the probability of delinquency, but rather of *all* unwholesome conditions of society; not specifically the predelinquent or potential delinquent, but *all* persons.[4]

As to the second circle of crime-preventive programs, although it is much closer to the operative mechanisms of the delinquency problem, it is still not specially designed to cope with it. As has been correctly pointed out, "Except for the police, children's courts, and reformatory institutions, public and private agencies are not organized primarily for the prevention of crime and delinquency. This function is considered to be an adjunct to or a by-product of their other related purposes. Direct services, designed mainly as crime preventives, are few; the indirect services are many."[5] The writer adds that, since such "fairly typical indirect preventive services" as wholesome recreational facilities, adequate housing, good schools, and the like "can contribute a vital and significant force in the lives of everyone," they have "justifiably had claimed for them the function of contributing to delinquency . . . prevention."[6] As we shall note, the types of agencies mentioned can be brought into play especially in coping with problems presented by delinquency-prone children. This illustrates the fact that sharp lines cannot be drawn between the three zones of crime-preventive effort noted, although the data of the present study suggest that it is desirable to bring into focus more well-defined areas of attack.

The third type of delinquency-preventive project is intended specifically to cope with the problems of *early discovery and timely treatment* of the situations and forces inside and outside the endangered child that are commonly found to be associated with proneness to delinquency.[7] Within the penumbra of such specific situations and forces there are to be found some of the influences of the wider penumbras of the second and first of the above-mentioned approaches. Nevertheless, the clues to fundamental prevention disclosed in this and prior volumes suggest more well-defined target areas at which to aim specific, relevant measures.

SPECIFIC TARGETS OF DELINQUENCY PREVENTION

1. *The predelinquent and the delinquent.*

The problems of delinquency and recidivism involve both biologic (genetic) and *intimate* social aspects (family life), though they are of course influenced indirectly by all-pervasive societal standards and practices in the moral, religious, economic, and legal areas.

As to genetic endowment, little can be done at this stage of human attitude and biological science.[8] But much can and should be done to improve family life and the guidance of children in home and school. In this connection, we reaffirm some ideas regarding measures for delinquency prevention that were set forth in various prior works; for the evidence of the present research amply confirms the basic facts and strengthens the inferences for prophylactic measures previously suggested.

First, let us recall some characteristics of delinquents which in varying measure (but with statistical validity) distinguish them from the control group of nondelinquents.

The greater incidence among delinquents of boys of the *mesomorphic* constitution,[9] and the traits frequently found associated with this muscular, well-knit, energetic physique type,[10] should suggest to all persons and agencies intimately concerned with the wholesome guidance of youth — teachers, community recreational and boys' club workers, police, as well as parents — that special allowance and provision should be made in all major channels of self-expression for the greater energy-output and corresponding traits and interests of mesomorphic boys. Other types also require special consideration; for example, the fragile, sensitive *ectomorph,* of whom the *non*delinquents had an excess (39.6% versus 14.4%). To supply legitimate outlets for different physique types is a challenge to the ingenuity of those who guide and supervise children.[11]

Turning next to certain outstanding traits of delinquents as derived from the Rorschach Test and psychiatric interviews, it will be recalled that many of these are of such a nature as to interfere with an acceptable taming of primitive impulses; they tend instead to facilitate uncontrolled, unthinking antisocial actions. Among these early stirrings of undesirable tendencies in many children are defiance of or ambivalence to authority, excessive feelings of hostility, extreme suspiciousness, a tendency to destructiveness, sadistic inclinations, marked impulsiveness with defective self-control, preponderance of a tendency to resolve emotional tensions and conflicts through an impetuous "acting out," deficiency in conscientiousness and in self-criticism, and other such symptoms of impending antisocial trouble if the child is not aided by sympathetic, understanding and patient adults.

Such traits, which on the whole, differentiate delinquents from nondelinquents, tell their own story as to why it is that, in the grim record of our maladjusted boys as delinquents and adolescent and young adult criminals, the efforts of juvenile and adult courts and attending services failed so often to change the course of habitual antisocial inclinations. Even at the juvenile court level, the officials were already often dealing with a finished product; for the character distortions were in many cases already well-formed and deep-rooted.[12]

Yet, even at the juvenile court stage, it is possible to improve matters by taking into account certain facts regarding those cases among a thousand juvenile delinquents studied in an earlier work whose behavioral outcomes, during a five-year span after the end of the period of prescribed treatment, were carefully investigated.[13] Thus it is possible to pick up, constructively, a substantial proportion of the total of delinquents brought into court, provided intelligent discrimination between individuals is used.

But *pre-court* recognition of serious emotional and characterical deviations, followed by timely treatment, is more likely to divert delinquent tendencies and has the advantage of involving more children. That is why there is great need for a considerable increase in the number of mental health clinics that will be available to school, vocational, and recreational experts, clergy and parents, at early signs of certain trait inclinations and behavioral trends that suggest deep-seated and developing emotional troubles.

2. *The family.*

Turning now to the family, it will be recalled that many crucial differences were found between the parents of the delinquents and those of the other boys. These include, for example, the more frequent intellectual and emotional abnormalities of the delinquents' grandparents under whose care the delinquents' parents had themselves been reared; the higher incidence of alcoholism and criminality in the families in which the delinquents' parents had grown up; the more extensive physical, intellectual, and emotional handicaps, as well as drunkenness, among the parents of the delinquents; the greater dependence of these parents on various relief agencies than of the parents of the nondelinquents.

Such facts demonstrate that society has the major task of breaking the vicious circle of character-damaging influences on children which are exerted by parents who are themselves the distorted personality and character products of adverse parental influences in the prior generation.[14] Some of this heritage is biological rather than social; the very persistence among our delinquents of socially undesirable and self-defeating behavior over the years, while the nondelinquent counterparts made progress and on the whole remained law-abiding, would suggest the probability of biological involvements. As pointed out, at the present stage little can be done with such aspects of the problem. But as to other aspects, much might be accomplished if sufficient, adequately staffed agencies were set up to give wide guidance to each generation of prospective parents and young spouses in the requisites of mental hygiene and of happy and wholesome family life. The program should also include some aspects of intelligent and tactful advice on family-planning.[15]

The task demands a tremendous multiplication of psychiatric, social, religious, and educational resources for improving the basic equipment of present and prospective parents for assumption of a wholesome, healthy, and satisfying marital role. There can be little doubt, in the light of the facts marshaled in the preceding pages, that it is almost futile to treat the child apart from the parents who contribute so much to make him what he is. Without concentration on *improvement of family life* and guidance of parents and prospective parents, dollars spent on housing projects, massive welfare services, recreational activities, and other well-intentioned services, though contributing to the solution of other societal problems, will however not play a definitive role in sweeping back the mounting tide of youthful maladjustment and delinquency *without preparation for marriage and child-rearing, and improvement of the emotional climate of family life.*

A striking experiment in the District of Columbia tends to demonstrate this: The Youth Council, which carried on a number of imaginative programs, "operated an extensive Maximum Benefits Project from 1954 through 1958 at the Taylor Elementary School. . . . A total of 179 children who had been behavior problems in school were referred to the project during its lifetime. Half of these were treated and half were maintained as a control group. . . . The project staff became quickly aware of the futility of trying to work with a child in a school setting unless something could be done to alter the home situation which was contributing to the child's problems. In February 1956 and February 1958 systematic surveys were made to determine each child's subsequent school behavior and academic performance. Teachers reported better behavior for the treated group in the 1956 survey, but the later survey in 1958 showed negligible differences between the treated and untreated groups. The treated ones actually had more court and police contacts than the untreated children. The rate of school misbehavior and police contact followed the predictability curve regardless of whether intervening treatment had been attempted. The project concluded that conventional child guidance techniques in a school setting are not effective; that standard services do not reach multiproblem families; that special services to schools without extensive family work are wasteful; that a child's home situation is the primary determining factor in his adjustment to the larger community; that delinquency-prone children can be identified at an early age, and that services must be developed to motivate and train adult family members to be better parents."[16]

It is strikingly obvious in our day that little progress can be made in the prevention of attitudes and practices involved in delinquency until *family life* is strengthened through a large-scale, pervasive, many-faceted, continuous program designed to bring to bear all the resources of mental hygiene, social work, education, and religious and ethical teaching upon this central issue. Many families — those of nondelinquents as well as of delinquents — would benefit from such a development. But here, as elsewhere, families shown to have delinquency-prone children need the guidance most.

It will be recalled that certain other unwholesome parent-child relationships, in addition to those already noted, were found strikingly to differentiate the domestic situation and home atmosphere of delinquents from those of nondelinquents. Far more of the homes of the former were physically or psychologically broken; far more of the mothers of the delinquents allowed their children to shift for themselves during leisure hours; far fewer of their fathers evinced sympathy and affection for the boy in question; and, while there was much more warmth on the part of the mothers generally, fewer of the delinquents' mothers had a healthy, affectionate relationship to the son. A far lower proportion of the delinquents, in turn, were warmly attached to the father and mother; a far lower percentage of the delinquents than of the control group accepted their fathers as desirable models for emulation; in far greater measure than the nondelinquents, the delinquents were convinced that neither parent was genuinely concerned with their welfare; and the disciplinary practices of the delinquents' parents were far less adequate than those of the control group.

All this represents a dynamic area of intrafamilial cross-currents which in large measure account for the persistent maladjustment of the boys who became delinquent and who ripened into adult criminals. A situation is presented which, though highly involved and complex, might be attacked by concentrating on a series of specific elements of the entire emotion-laden area. If, for example, there were community agencies to instruct parents patiently and sympathetically with regard to the emotional significance of various disciplinary practices and to demonstrate how behavior tendencies improve when discipline is both fair and firm and rooted in affection, they might gradually learn to adopt such practices with socializing effect on their children. Some headway might be made in rendering family life more hygienic and happy and thereby reducing children's behavioral maladjustments. Parents must be patiently and sympathetically taught simple elements of the dynamics of parent–child relationships; of the struggle the young child must go through in the process of adjusting his natural drives and their affective accompaniments in relation to mother, father, brothers and sisters; of the role of the father as the first "ego-ideal," or man-pattern; and, in general, of the great part played by early parent–child experiences in the crystallization of the child's basic personality and character traits which will be carried into adulthood and become ever more difficult to modify with the passage of time.

But additional specialized guidance is also called for prior to the establishment of the family. The differentiative traits and practices of the parents and of the sons themselves when they achieved manhood, lead to the conclusion that all the community's agencies for guiding young people in the proper selection of mates and in preparation for marital life — those specializing in family problems — need greatly to expand their personnel and enrich their techniques.

3. *The school.*

Thus far, our suggestions for fundamental prevention have derived in large measure from the characteristics which, on the whole, distinguish delinquents from nondelinquents, and from various pathologic conditions in the home. But in addition to the home, the *school* is the arena in which children learn ideals and standards of acceptable conduct. A great deal of time is spent in school and at very impressionable ages. Much more goes on in the classroom than the mere commerce in "readin', writin,' and 'rithmetic"; and what does transpire is of an essentially feeling-charged nature. The teacher cannot altogether rid herself of her own emotional problems through the channel of drilling students in the curriculum; and she may tend to work out her problems in anger-laden disciplinary practices. Nor do the pupils leave behind their emotional freight when they enter the classroom — their worries about parental anger, neglect, drunkenness, criminality.

The deep-rooted nature of the temperamental and characterial traits found to differentiate persistent delinquents from nondelinquents, and the extremely early age at which delinquents first manifest marked difficulties in adjustment as expressed in misconduct, should make one realize how essential it is for schools, particularly, to be equipped to discover *potential* delinquents before the trends of maladapted behavior become too fixed, and to distinguish among children already "acting up" the true delinquent from the pseudodelinquent. For the schools are in a strategic position to note such marked deviations and difficulties of adaptation at the age of five or six, or earlier, when children first enter. True prevention of delinquency involves *character prophylaxis* — that is, the testing of children early in life to detect malformations of character and personality and to cope with their influences at a stage when the twig can still be bent.[17] A *"preventive medicine"* of personality and character is as necessary as early medical examination and preventive treatment of physical disorders.

However, the difficulty of the task of early recognition and treatment of delinquency-endangered or delinquency-prone children and their uninformed parents — and a chief reason why so little is being accomplished in this vital area — involves the fact that when a child first begins to display signs of maladjustment it is very difficult to say whether these are true danger-signals of persistent delinquency in the offing or merely transient indications of a youngster's "trying his wings" and testing out the authoritative adults. Bits of maladapted and even delinquent behavior at this early age and stage are not necessarily prodromal of impending persistent delinquency.[18] It therefore becomes of prime importance to devise a method of *identifying* very early in life those children who are headed for trouble unless their indicated direction can be constructively diverted.

Is there a sufficiently reliable instrument for making this critically important distinction between the potentially delinquent child and the child who will probably soon outgrow his difficulties of adaptation?

Our study of a great many traits and factors distinguishing actual persistent delinquents from a control group of nondelinquents, the major thrust of which has been confirmed by the data of subsequent follow-up investigations, has made possible the construction of the necessary instrument. This device has been shown — on several occasions and with different samples of cases — to be reasonably effective in distinguishing boys with a high delinquency *potential* from those with a relatively low risk.[19] The predictive instrument was developed from certain potent distinguishing factors in the family background of the two sets of subjects contrasted.

Three "experience tables" were originally developed from the data in *Unraveling Juvenile Delinquency*: the first, the *social-factor* table, deals with factors in the parent-child relationships and with family cohesiveness; the second is based on certain *basic character traits* which were found markedly to differentiate the delinquents from the control group; the third is founded on highly distinguishing *traits obtained from psychiatric interviews* of the delinquents and the nondelinquents. Thus far, however, only the *social-factor table* (with necessary modifications because of the frequency of families without a father in the home) has been validated through its application to other young children in New York City and Washington, D.C., followed by careful checkups on degree of correspondence of the table's predictions with actual subsequent behavior.[20]

Probably one reason why the social prediction table has been found to have considerable potency in classifying youngsters into such categories is because the family factors involved are interrelated with many other factors and traits in parents and children that have been shown to increase or lower the chances of subsequent delinquency. The social prediction table demonstrates that maladaptive acts and antisocial influences involved in delinquency, though extremely numerous and complexly interrelated, can be potently represented by a handful of indices. This does not of course mean that only a small number of criminogenic influences are actually involved in the development of an antisocial character and career; it means, simply, that just a few factors, proven markedly to differentiate a large sample of true delinquents from a control sample of true nondelinquents, are enough for the purposes of prediction, though not sufficient for adequate understanding and therapy.

More recently, other predictive devices have been developed to take account of "the prejudice against this approach . . . among those who fear not only that the civil rights of children and parents may be infringed, but that the children erroneously identified as delinquents would be unnecessarily stigmatized."[21] These tables — one based on four behavioral manifestations in school, the other on five activities reflecting adventuresome interests — have not yet been tested on other samples. However, judging by the wide divergence between the delinquents and nondelinquents in respect to the data involved in the original table, and the fact that there is a high correlation of the placement of the delinquents and nondelinquents between the more recent tables and the earlier one, it can reasonably be expected that these later devices, if tested on other samples of cases, would also show great discriminative power in prediction.

In the meantime it may be observed that if we were to accept as sound the argument of those who oppose identification techniques to disclose the children who are especially vulnerable,[22] we should logically close all child guidance clinics, dismiss school counselors and visiting teachers, and sit back complacently (as, unfortunately, we too often have been doing) until the child has developed into a true persistent delinquent or gang-member and then bring him into court with the usual far-from-satisfactory results illustrated by the follow-up data in Chapters XIV and XV.

The choice presented to a community is whether its citizens prefer to let potentially delinquent children ripen into persistent offenders or to intervene preventively, in specific instances shown to involve high risk of delinquency, at a stage in development which gives the promise of changing their dangerous attitudes and behavior. This can be done through aiding the parents of such children to modify their damaging and nonaffectionate (or sometimes morbidly overprotective) attitudes and practices which have been demonstrated in many prior instances to be potent influences toward maladapted conduct. The follow-ups of the subjects of the present study, as well as our previous follow-up studies, have consistently shown the tragic role of *deep-rootedness* in rendering antisocial behavior impervious to the usual methods of "treatment" thus far provided by society.[23]

Unlike the skepticism regarding the value of predictive devices which has been voiced in some quarters, their use is commended in the *Report of the President's Commission on Crime in the District of Columbia.* In describing the experiments on early prevention of delinquency carried on under the Maximum Benefits Project operated by the District's Youth Council, the Commission states:

> The delinquency diagnosis and prediction phase of the project was considered the most encouraging. A refinement of the Glueck Prediction Tables, revised for the District to take into account the large number of fatherless children in the project, proved to be 100 percent accurate in predicting nondelinquency and 81 percent accurate in predicting delinquency. By 1965, 108 of the 134 (80 percent) in the high probability category had proved to be delinquent, although only 17 percent of the entire group were over 18.[24]

It should be recognized that in an enlightened educational system the school could function as the litmus paper of personality and character, reflecting early in the child's growth the acid test of his success or failure in his first attempts to cope with the problems of life posed by a restrictive society outside the home.

But what does the school system require to make it possible for it to carry on *beyond* the stage of early identification of the maladjusted child?

We have seen that delinquent boys largely possess certain temperamental and personality traits and special abilities and disabilities which distinguish them from the general run of nondelinquents. We have also seen that, because of the poor parent–child relationships predominating in delinquents' families, the boys have difficulty in finding an emotionally sympathetic adult as a symbol for emulation, a person around whom ideals and standards of behavior can be woven by the child to form the core of his own character. Such facts — and there are other relevant ones — suggest that fundamental changes should be made in curricula, teacher-training, and school teaching-patterns.

As to curricula, forcing certain types of children into the traditional mold results in increased tension, frustration, and displacement of frustration onto acts of revolt, delinquency and a mask of defiant "toughness." Much greater flexibility in school curricula and in the length of school lessons is therefore called for. A rich variety of school programs and experiences must be devised that will enlist the interests of pupils of different physical and temperamental types. To make one suggestion, it may be useful to set up school programs in which half the day is spent in classroom activities and half in paid work of various kinds outside the school. To make such a scheme practical, it would be necessary to enlist the cooperation of various industries and shops in offering opportunity for systematic part-time employment, and to provide sympathetic and ingenious overseers of the experiment.

But there are other relevant improved educational patterns. This has been recognized in the District of Columbia.

> Children who begin to display possibly predelinquent behavior in school such as truancy, aggressive acts toward the teacher or other pupils, or vandalism, must be given special attention. This attention may take the form of auxiliary counseling or casework, special teaching within the regular class, or separation into separate classes with other troubled or misbehaving youngsters. In the District of Columbia these services are provided by (1) Pupil Personnel Services; (2) social adjustment classes; (3) Twilight Schools; (4) boys' and girls' Junior-Senior High Schools; and (5) the STAY [School-to-Aid-Youth] programs for dropouts.[25]

All such imaginative special educational projects call for imaginative teachers. To supply instructors with the necessary equipment for coping with the emotional problems of childhood, teacher selection will have to be improved through the inducements of a more dignified status of the teacher in our society, as well as of better pay. Teacher training will have to be modified to include liberal elements of dynamic psychology and opportunities to participate in clinical conferences. Practice-teaching of the various traditional subjects in the curriculum cannot replace the need for an understanding of the troubles and tensions of children as they wrestle with the problem of adjusting to the restraints of the adult world.

More important, school authorities will have to take into account the role of the teacher as a parent-substitute and ego-ideal. Planned experiments in the best use of teacher personnel and assistants are called for. Perhaps young-adult male teachers are needed in much greater number, even in the kindergarten and elementary grades. Perhaps husband-wife teams of teachers would provide a more natural and wholesome emotional climate in the classroom and present to many pupils a previously unknown standard of parental relations. At all events, experiments are needed to test various patterns of teacher–child relationships from the point of view of their effect on the dynamics of temperament and the formation of integrated personality and acceptable character.[26]

4. *Use of leisure.*

We have spoken of special characteristics of individual delinquents and predelinquents, of the home and family life, and of the school. In a comprehensive attack on the roots of delinquency, the furnishing of constructive outlets for leisure must also be taken into account. In their life in the city streets, as well as in other respects noted, we have seen that the delinquent boys were worse off during their growing up than the nondelinquents in ways related to use of leisure. Their families moved about more frequently, interfering with whatever stabilizing influences might be found in attachment and loyalty to a definite community and familiar neighbors, and increasing the hazards of readjustment. To a greater extent than the nondelinquents, the juvenile delinquents had worked in street trades where they were subject to the risks attending unsupervised employment at an impressionable and inexperienced age. Their preferences were, on the whole, for risky and adventurous energy outlets, such as hopping trucks, keeping late hours, bunking out, running away from home, destroying property, and the like, and seeking play-places at great distances from their homes, such as waterfronts and railroad yards.

These adventure-seeking tendencies were also shown in the greater extent to which the delinquents suffered serious street accidents and, vicariously, in their more frequent movie attendance. Most of the juvenile delinquents, it will be recalled, ultimately became members of gangs, and many preferred companions older than themselves. There is also strong evidence that the delinquents disliked the confinement of playgrounds, supervised recreation, attendance at clubs or other such group centers, which they rarely joined on their own desire or initiative. Finally, they were more neglectful of church attendance than the nondelinquents.

As noted in the follow-ups, many of these tendencies persisted well into adulthood. Some of them, such as love of adventure, are not bad in themselves; but constructive channels must be found for them so that boys can be properly habituated in youth.

The foregoing summary comprises a network of attitudinal and behavioral tendencies which suggest that settlement houses, schools, community centers, church organizations, boys' clubs, and other such agencies must, in planning their programs and selecting their personnel, take into account the characteristics and preferences of especially adventure-thirsty boys who dislike intensive, mechanical supervision and tend to delinquency as an exciting or congenial outlet. Such agencies need to experiment with various means of attracting and guiding youngsters of this type into at least socially harmless, if not positively constructive, channels of energy release. In a busy, exciting urban community of individualists "on the make" and bent on reaching materialistic goals with least effort, such boys drift among the general population unattached to loyalties except to those of similar energy drive and consuming interests. There is thus a pressing need for a systematic coping with the leisure-time problem through carefully designed community action based upon surveys of local conditions, facilities, and liabilities. A number of communities have been concerned with this problem, although it would seem that such a device as employment of clean-minded athletes with a special flair for understanding and influencing youngsters has not been sufficiently appreciated or resorted to.

INTEGRATION OF COMMUNITY FACILITIES: THE WASHINGTON EXPERIMENT

It should not be supposed, in considering the foregoing suggestions, that we believe that any one social agency, clinic, school, or church can focus *exclusively* on any of the target-areas discussed. Reflection upon the very complex nature and interrelation of the influences at various levels involved in the prevention and treatment of predelinquency and delinquency shows that, while each group has its own focus in the total task, the specific traits and factors in individual and family life and in the life of the community that need attention do not fall neatly into separate compartments. In general, all that can be said is that either an overall directive and coordinating agency is called for in a community,[27] or the community-clinic system, or some other agency with a general child-and-parent orientation, should be charged with a leading, if not the primary, responsibility for the total problem. But, just as the separate identity of each factor or target does not destroy the organic unity of the interrelated person-situation, so the specialization of each agency in one group of factors does not eliminate the harmonious participation of all community agencies in a well-conceived *general* plan of attack.

In most communities it will be found that there are not enough clinics or similar facilities; that some clinics and other agencies are "choosy" and will not accept predelinquents and delinquents; and that efforts of public and private agencies are not methodically planned so as to provide a *coordinated network* of services directed discriminatively to various needs in a total situation. It is therefore advisable for each community to set up a committee of informed persons to study the unplanned and haphazard mélange of public and private "helping agencies" that have grown up over the years, to assess their operations in method and result, and to develop a plan for a more comprehensive and cooperative apparatus of preventive and therapeutic action focused on continuing improvement of family life in the context of the community.

It may well be that the system being developed in Washington, D. C., will have appeal to other communities. There the Commissioners' Youth Council, since its inception in 1943 as an agency of the municipal government of the District of Columbia, has been aware of the tragedy and waste involved in attempting to deal with multiform problems of the socially pathological family through disconnected agencies and a piecemeal attack on fragments of the total situation. Recently a concerted and concentrated approach to eliminate "fragmentation" of social services has been undertaken.

> Fragmentation of responsibility among agencies leads inevitably to fragmentation of services to families, and even to fragmented perception of problems within one family.[28]

On the basis of much varied experience by dedicated workers, the Youth Council, in collaboration with other community agencies, is applying the following principles in dealing with families presenting numerous difficulties.

> 1. We assess the problem in terms of what the *city* — not the agency — needs to do. 2. We survey the total family as a single unit. 3. We decide on a plan of action. 4. We undertake that plan ourselves immediately, and right in the neighborhood without referral elsewhere. 5. We assign *one* worker to be responsible for *all* treatment as it applies to that family, although the specialized services of many agencies may be used. 6. We stimulate neighborhood action for self-improvement. 7. We use community development as part of the treatment process in order to absorb the problem family more quickly into the mainstream of neighborhood activity.

> "We" in this project are a voluntary association of some thirty groups. Among them are two hospitals, the social science departments of two universities, the home extension service of another university, Planned Parenthood, an elementary school, the Council of Churches, a consumer education bureau, the Family Life Association, a number of private agencies, and the Youth Council.[29]

The reader will be inclined to agree that such a strategy is justified by both the troubles and pathologies of the multiproblem urban family and by the need of coordinating and focusing preventive, therapeutic and reconstructive efforts on the family as a unit if there is to be any hope of preventing delinquency.

A WORD OF PARTING

A vast task of implementation of aid-giving agencies of all kinds awaits us as we confront the age-long hazards of a poverty-tainted segment of a galloping affluent society. To sustain our efforts we have one source of comfort that should stimulate both preventive-therapeutic activity and needed experimental and evaluative researches: namely, that determinism in human affairs does not mean fatalism; it simply describes the observed fact that nature tends to present a routine series of events linked together in what is referred to as "causal sequence." This, however, does not mean — and medicine has proved this again and again — that it is useless to intervene, to change a familiar sequence by prophylactic and therapeutic measures. As we have previously observed, and despite the discouraging scroll of delinquency and recidivism revealed in the present study, we continue to believe that in antisocial behavior we are dealing, *not so much with predestination as with destination*. Skillful, painstaking, and patient effort with individuals and groups has shown that there is a comforting probability that, in more instances than one might suppose, destination can be redirected through timely, kindly, intelligent intervention. We believe that not a few of the delinquent boys who continued their anti-social escapades from early childhood into adulthood might have been directed into law-abiding channels if their parents and others who had dealt with them all along the line had taken the time and thought necessary to give them therapeutic aid in a friendly and patient manner. In reflecting upon the numerous cases of delinquency and criminality we have investigated over the years we get the feeling that the art of discouraging delinquency and dealing with it effectively is still, at best, in an amateur state; that is, for all except those politicians who are convinced that massive provision of huge sums of money will in itself "cure" all social ills.

And so we come to the end of the story. The major theme of the account, borne in upon us by the facts, is the original and persisting difference between those persons who, over the years, pursued stumblingly an antisocial career and those who managed to abide by the "rules of the game" of conventional, relatively law-abiding society. In this final chapter we have set forth some suggestions for possibly decreasing the incidence of social rebels or antisocial human driftwood. We have shown that the task we all — especially parents and teachers —

must face, is both enormous in scope and complex in content. But it certainly can and should be attacked with more forethought, intelligence, and patience than — according to the bleak evidence we have laid before the reader — it has thus far received.

Notes

1. *The Challenge of Crime in a Free Society, A Report by the President's Commission on Law Enforcement and Administration of Justice* (Washington: Government Printing Office, February 1967). These problems, focused on the capital city area, have also been ably discussed in the *Report of the President's Commission on Crime in the District of Columbia* (Washington: Government Printing Office, 1966). A significant omission in the two reports is any reference to the potentialities of predictive devices in aid of judges and parole boards in sentencing and releasing offenders.

2. For discussions of the problems involved, and references to various crime surveys and other relevant sources, see S. Glueck, *Crime and Justice* (Boston: Little Brown, 1936; Cambridge, Mass.: Harvard University Press, 1945; New York: Kraus Reprint, 1966). A basic omission of the two reports by the President's Commissions is a recommendation for the greatly needed fundamental new profession of specially trained Social Problem Lawyer: to serve criminal, juvenile, and family courts as public defenders and prosecutors and as specialized judges; to take the leadership in various reforms called for at the different stages of criminal procedure and administration; to serve as informed members of governmental commissions concerned with such problems; to staff parole boards; and to improve the public image and status of the criminal bar generally. Bills for setting up special Academies of Criminal Justice with such aims have been introduced in the U. S. Senate by Senator Edward M. Kennedy of Massachusetts, and in the House of Representatives by Congressmen James C. Corman of California and Spark M. Matsunaga of Hawaii. Simultaneously with the study of the traditional legal subjects, the students in such a "West Point of Criminal Justice" would be studying relevant disciplines in the individual and social behavioral fields, such as psychiatry, psychology, sociology, cultural anthropology, and the like, and would be given practical experience in clinics, courts, and correctional establishments. See S. Glueck, "Law and the Stuff of Life," *Harvard Law School Bulletin*, 14:3-6 (June 1963) ; "A Federal Act to Establish the Roscoe Pound Academy of Criminal Justice," *Harvard Journal on Legislation*, 2:131-145 (1964) ; and S. Glueck "Wanted: A New Legal Profession," *The Police Chief*, August 1965, pp. 24-32.

3. G. Aschaffenburg, *Crime and Its Repression*, trans. A. Albrecht (Boston: Little, Brown, 1913), p. 228.

4. In Chapter XVI we have discussed the weaknesses of unilateral theories in explaining delinquency and recidivism.

5. Edwin J. Lukas, "Prevention of Crime," in Vernon C. Branham, M.D. and Samuel B. Kutash, *Encyclopedia of Criminology* (New York: Philosophical Library, 1949), p. 333.

6. *Ibid.*

7. "The most productive appproach for both the potential offender and the community is to prevent delinquency before it begins." *Report of the President's Commission in the District of Columbia*, p. 733.

8. The recent interest in biological implications of social problems has been discussed in Chapter XVI. See also H. J. Eysenck, *Crime and Personality* (London: Routledge & Kegan Paul, 1964), esp. chap. iv, "The Biological Roots of Personality."

9. In recent years, Dr. William Sheldon, a leading authority on somatotyping, has greatly improved the objectivity of the technique of somatotyping and has given proof of the relative unchangeability of the somatotype. See W. Sheldon, "Brief Communication on Objectification of the Somatotype and on the Primary Psychiatric Components," Maudsley Bequest Lecture; paper read by Emil M. Hartl, Ph.D., at the Royal Medico-Psychological Association, London, England, May 13, 1965 (mimeographed). See also Herbert Rowell Stolz and Lois Meek Stolz, *Somatic Development of Adolescent Boys* (New York: Macmillan, 1951).

10. We have tentatively related various traits often involved in delinquent behavior to various somatotypes. We welcome further research along such lines by other investigators — anthropologists, psychologists, sociologists. Compare S. and E. T. Glueck, *Physique and Delinquency* (New York: Harper, 1956; Kraus Reprint, 1965) and *Family Environment and Delinquency* (London: Routledge & Kegan Paul; Boston: Houghton Mifflin, 1962).

11. During the past few years there has been considerable expansion of Federal preventive programs through the Department of Health, Education and Welfare, including such projects as job-training for delinquents, stimulation of further education for school drop-outs (it will be recalled, for example, that there is an excess of "hand-minded" boys among our delinquents, and that such boys prefer manual training and dislike verbal disciplines), programs for coping with youthful gangs, and devising alternatives to formal juvenile court referral "to give delinquents the support and counseling they do not get from their families" (*The Challenge of Crime in a Free Society*, p. 283). Some of the Government's recent programs further removed from delinquency and from special concern with delinquency-prone children are the Neighborhood Youth Corps, the Job Corps, the Youth Opportunity Centers, the Elementary and Secondary Education Act, Head Start programs for pre-school children, in which, in some regions, a special effort is made to draw parents into the picture (*ibid.*, p. 284). Some of these programs might benefit from the use of delinquency prediction and follow-up devices which would accumulate data showing the varied prophylactic and therapeutic indications for different types of children and families.

12. This exceedingly significant fact requires emphasis and re-emphasis. "Once a juvenile is apprehended by the police and referred to the Juvenile Court, the community has already failed; subsequent rehabilitative services, no matter how skilled, have far less potential for success than if they had been applied before the youth's overt defiance of the law." *Report of the President's Commission on Crime in the District of Columbia*, p. 733. See also S. and E. T. Glueck, *One Thousand Juvenile Delinquents* (Cambridge, Mass.: Harvard University Press, 1934; New York: Kraus Reprint, 1965), esp. chaps. x and xiii.

13. The more successful cases had the following characteristics: (1) boys whose delinquent behavior did not occur until relatively late and who were examined at the Judge Baker Guidance Clinic soon thereafter; (2) boys who were not retarded in school; (3) boys who had not misconducted themselves in school; (4) cases in which there was a wholesomely affectionate relationship between the offender and his parents; (5) cases in which the disciplinary practices were sound; (6) cases in which there was an absence of mental disease or defect in the families of the delinquents; (7) cases in which the clinical recommendations were followed by the court (particularly true of the recommendations pertaining to other matters than where the delinquent should reside); (8) cases supervised by certain probation officers. *One Thousand Juvenile Delinquents*, pp. 242 and 243.

14. See "Does Failure Run in Families?," by A. D. Ullman, H. W. Demone, Jr., and A. W. Stearns, *American Journal of Psychiatry*, 107:667-676 (March 1951).

15. See C. S. Chilman, "Poverty and Family Planning in the United States," *Welfare in Review*, 5:3-15 (April 1967).

16. *Report of the President's Commission on Crime in the District of Columbia*, pp. 756-757. See, also C. Downing Tait, Jr., M.D., and Emory F. Hodges, Jr., M.D., *Delinquents, Their Families, and the Community* (Springfield, Ill.: Charles C. Thomas, 1962).

17. We are of course not unmindful that in adolescence, also, there are often special psychological problems to be understood and coped with; but the earliest and major opportunity is presented when the child first has to face authority, routine, and discipline outside the home.

18. See E. T. Glueck, "Toward Improving the Identification of Delinquents," *The Journal of Criminology and Police Science*, 53:168 (June 1962); "Toward Further Improving the Identification of Delinquents," *ibid.*, 54:178 (June 1963); "Identification of Potential Delinquents at 2-3 Years of Age," *The International Journal of Social Psychiatry*, 12:5 (1966).

19. A basic problem involved is to diminish as much as possible the ambiguous middle category of cases in which the indicated probabilities are about equally divided between the extremes. We are constantly working on this problem, and progress is being made. In the meantime, the cases of children who, according to the factors involved in a prediction table, have a relatively equal chance of delinquency or nondelinquency should present a challenge

to clinicians and social workers to "pull them over the line" so that they in fact do not become delinquent.

20. For details of the original tables, see *Unraveling Juvenile Delinquency*, chap. xx. For results of validation experiments, see M. M. Craig and S. J. Glick, "Ten Years' Experience with the Glueck Social Prediction Table," *Crime and Delinquency*, 9:249-261 (July 1963) ; Craig and Glick, "Application of the Glueck Social Prediction Table on an Ethnic Basis," *ibid.*, 11:175-185 (April 1965) ; Craig and Glick, *A Manual of Procedures for Application of the Glueck Prediction Table* (New York: The New York City Youth Board, 1964) ; N. B. Trevvett, "Identifying Delinquency-Prone Children," *Crime and Delinquency*, 11:186-191 (April 1965) ; Trevvett, "Treatment Planning for Multiproblem Families," *ibid.*, 13:307-316 (April 1967). See also dissertation for Doctorate of Jurisprudence (Faculty of Law, Johannes Gutenberg University, Mainz, West Germany, 1967) by Hermann Elmering, "Die Kriminologische Frühprognose." This is a validation of the Glueck Social Prediction Table on 100 Juvenile Court boys in Munich and Aschaffenburg, West Germany. Ninety-two percent of these delinquents would have been identified as serious potential delinquents at school entrance. The dissertation is to be published in *Kriminologische Schriftenreihe*, ed., Armand Mergen, Professor of Criminal Law, University of Mainz, and President, German Criminological Society.

21. E. T. Glueck, "Distinguishing Delinquents from Pseudodelinquents," *Harvard Educational Review*, 36:119-130 (Spring 1966). For answers to such criticisms, see S. Glueck, "Ten Years of *Unraveling Juvenile Delinquency*," *The Journal of Criminal Law, Criminology and Police Science*, 5:283 and 306 (September–October 1960).

22. *The Challenge of Crime in a Free Society*, p. 59.

23. In S. and E. Glueck, *Predicting Delinquency and Crime* (Cambridge, Mass.: Harvard Mass.: Harvard University Press, 1960), pp. 44, 81-82, it is shown that in 18 out of 30 prediction tables dealing with adult offenders and 3 out of 10 concerned with juvenile delinquents during all forms of sentence and treatment and for 15 years thereafter, the factor of *age at onset of antisocial behavior* had to be included as a differentiative indicator because of its strong predictive involvement as between successes and falures under correctional treatment. In all but four of the tables dealing with adult offenders, *the earlier the onset* of the delinquency, the higher the failure score under one or another form of peno-correctional treatment and during a significant test period thereafter; or, to state it differently, the deeper the roots of childhood maladjustment, the smaller the chance of adult law-abiding adjustment. In this connection, it will be recalled that the mean age at onset of misbehavior among the delinquents of *Unraveling Juvenile Delinquency*, whose careers are traced well into adulthood in the present work, was 8.35 years (S. D. ± 2.39), and that 87.6% were 10 years or younger (48.4%, 7 years or younger) at the onset of definitive acts of misconduct (*Unraveling*, p. 28). The antisocial acts involved so early in life include stealing, truancy, destructive mischief, running away from home, stealing rides, stealing junk, sex affairs, tantrums, disobedience, stubbornness.

24. *Report of the President's Commission on Crime in the District of Columbia*, p. 757. Similar encouraging results have been obtained in the New York City prediction experiment. See Craig and Glick, *A Manual of Procedures for Application of the Glueck Prediction Table*, pp. 14-15. See also Trevvett, "Treatment Planning for Multiproblem Families," pp. 307, 313, 315. Significant results have also been obtained in many small-sample studies elsewhere in the United States and abroad. See Glueck, "Ten Years of *Unraveling Juvenile Delinquecy*," pp. 304-305.

25. *Report of the President's Commission on Crime in the District of Columbia*, p. 736.

26. Although published a long time ago, valuable suggestions are still to be found in S. and E. Glueck (Editors), *Preventing Crime* (New York: McGraw-Hill, 1936; New York: Kraus Reprint, 1966). See also E. T. Glueck, *The Community Use of Schools* (Baltimore: Willimas & Wilkins, 1927).

27. The need of a *general planning and coordinating organ* to bring order into the chaos of disparate agencies concerned with prevention and treatment of delinquency has recently been emphasized in the *Report of the President's Commission on Crime in the District of Columbia* (pp. 772-792) : "A Youth Commission should be established in the District of Columbia to develop and administer a comprehensive anti-delinquency program for the

entire city, coordinating and reviewing the activities of all public and private agencies in the field and assuming central responsibility for the handling of all delinquency-prone children as well as the treatment of all delinquents referred by the police or committed to its custody by the Juvenile Court. . . . The Youth Commission should assume responsibility for coordinating the activities of private agencies in the anti-delinquency field so that they can most effectively utilize their resources and so that duplication of services will be avoided" (p. 790).

28. Trevvett, "Treatment Planning for Multiproblem Families," *Crime and Delinquency,* 13:307-316 (April 1967).

29. *Ibid.*, pp. 314-315. The need of coordinated community action is now being recognized in England. See R. G. Andry, "The Relationship between Criminology and Other Disciplines Including Psychology and Education." Lecture delivered at UNAFEI, Tokyo, Japan, 1966 (mimeographed).

APPENDICES   INDEX

Appendix A   The Case of Henry W

(Illustrating Method of Social Investigation)

When Henry was 16 years old he was included among the cases of *Unraveling Juvenile Delinquency*.[1] Part I of the present appendix covers the social history of Henry W as prepared when he was first included for study among the cases of *Unraveling*. The investigation, though completed before 1948, was not actually published until 1962 in *Family Environment and Delinquency*.[2]

We appreciate the permission granted by Routledge & Kegan Paul to reproduce the case investigation (with slight modifications) so that we might unite it with Part II which describes the follow-up of Henry W through the two periods of study (ages 17-25, 25-31). Part III records the sources of information regarding Henry W from his 16th birthday (January 1941) until he was 31 (January 1956), as well as a summary of the findings. In Part IV are presented the detailed findings on each one of the factors incorporated in this book for each of the two follow-up periods (ages 17-25 and ages 25-31), wherever pertinent and known; it should be noted that the data are listed in the order of presentation of the tables in the book and the relevant table number is provided in the first column of Part IV.

Part I of the Case of Henry W was prepared by Mildred P. Cunningham and George F. McGrath, and edited by Virginia G. Atchley; Part II was prepared by John E. Burke and edited by Rose W. Kneznek.

All place and agency names and dates have been disguised to assure against identification. The following key to the abbreviations used may be helpful: *BCW*, Boston Child Welfare Agency No. 1; *B. Hosp.*, Boston Hospital; *BSA*, Boston Social Agency No. 1; *MH & H*, Maternity Home and Hospital No. 1; *Bradwood CWA*, Child Welfare Agency; *Bradwood SA*, Social Agency; *BPD*, Boys' Parole Division; *BVS*, Bureau of Vital Statistics; *CPA*, Child Placing Agency No. 1; *DMH*, Dept. of Mental Health; *FM*, Feeble-Minded; *H of C*, House of Correction; *PO*, Probation Office; *RA*, Relief Agency No. 1; *SSI*, Social Service Index; *SH*, Settlement House.

PART I.   *Initial Consultation of Social Service Index*

Henry was selected for the original research at a Massachusetts Correctional School in January 1941. The investigation was begun by securing from the

---

1. Sheldon and Eleanor Glueck (New York: The Commonwealth Fund, 1950; Cambridge, Mass.: Harvard University Press, 1951.
2. Sheldon and Eleanor Glueck (London: Routledge & Kegan Paul, 1962).

school the boy's birthdate, names of parents and siblings, and their approximate birthdates and last address. It was learned that Henry had a stepfather and three half-brothers, and that his real father was a man about whom nothing was known, except that he was thought to have been a machinist named James S. J., who had never married the boy's mother.

With this meager identifying data, inquiry was made of the Social Service Index in Boston for contacts of the boy, his mother, and his stepfather with social welfare agencies, and for any data available on the maternal and paternal grandparents and their children. Attention was also drawn to Henry's alleged father in the hope that the Index could throw more light on the boy's paternity. Photostatic copies of the Index's file cards on several family members were soon received.

These revealed that Henry's mother, Rose P. W, and stepfather, Leo W, had been known to at least twenty agencies either before or after their marriage.

A Red Cross Agency
A Red Cross Supervisors' Office
A Welfare Committee for Men
A U.S. Veterans' Clinic
Mental Hospital No. 1, OPD
Social Service Department of Maternity Home and Hospital No. 1
Social Service Department of a Boston Hospital
Boston Social Agency No. 1
A Vocational Aid Society
Relief Agency No. 1
Relief Agency No. 2
Boston Child Welfare Agency No. 1
A Veterans' Agency
Relief Agency No. 3
A Boston Health Agency
A Church Relief Society
Legal Assistance Bureau
Child Placing Agency No. 1
A Welfare Agency for Transients
A State Child Placing Agency

Addresses of the family in the years 1919, 1921, 1926, 1928, 1936, 1938, and 1940 were given, plus the information that the mother was born in 1906 in Everett, Mass., and worked in a factory; that the father (whom we knew to be the stepfather) was born in 1890 and was a teamster; and that Henry's siblings (whom we knew to be half-siblings) were Arthur, born in 1927, Kenneth, born in 1934, and Charles, born in 1937. The name of James S. J., born in 1901, of Stoughton, Mass., was given as a reference, but there was no indication that he was Henry's father.

The maternal aunt, Florence P, was reported by the Social Service Index (or central repository of public and private agency contacts in the Boston area) to be known to three agencies.

Girl Welfare Agency No. 1

Boston Social Agency No. 1
Relief Agency No. 1

Addresses of the maternal aunt were also listed, and a comparison of these with the addresses of the boy's family indicated that the aunt frequently lived with them. In addition, it was learned that the aunt was born in Everett, Mass., in 1908, and was single.

The maternal grandparents were found to have been known to ten agencies.

Boston Child Welfare Agency No. 1
A State School for Feeble-Minded
Maternity Home and Hospital No. 2
Child Placing Agency No. 2
Relief Agency No. 1
Veterans' Relief Agency No. 1
Boston Social Agency No. 1
Boston Social Agency No. 2
Relief Agency No. 3
Mental Hospital No. 1

Addresses of the maternal grandparents between the years 1910 and 1934 were given, plus the information that the maternal grandmother was born in New Hampshire in 1879, the maternal grandfather in Connecticut in 1873, and that they had two children: Florence, born in 1908, and Rose (the mother of Henry), born in 1906.

The paternal step-grandparents and step-relatives were also shown to be known to several agencies, but as they were not Henry's blood relatives these data were not of interest to us.

A couple named Mr. and Mrs. W, cross-indexed with the boy's stepfather, was known to a number of agencies. The stepfather was listed as a reference, but no details were given. The contents of this card were regarded as probably irrelevant for the inquiry, but were kept available for possible use later.

Initial Clearance through the Massachusetts Board of Probation

The court records of Henry, his mother, stepfather, and older half-bother were secured by mail from the Massachusetts Board of Probation. (The court records of the two other half-siblings were not checked, as they were only about six and three years old, respectively.) Neither the mother nor the older half-brother, Arthur, had a court record; but a possible record of the stepfather was found, containing insufficient identifying data. Further investigation showed that this was not his record.

Henry himself was found to have the following record.

2/9/36 Larceny, 2 counts, W District Court. Correctional School on each count, appealed. 4/11/36, C Superior Court, probation 2 years on each count.

9/28/36 Assault and battery, D District Court. Adjudged delinquent. Filed. 10/3/36, surrendered on probation of 4/11/36, C Superior Court. Committed to Correctional School. Paroled, 11/30/37. Returned to

Correctional School, 2/7/38. Paroled, 10/9/38; expiration of sentence, 1/16/46.

12/1/38 Breaking and entering nighttime, Y Court. Adjudged delinquent. Filed. Parole revoked, returned to Correctional School. Paroled, 12/28/39; expiration of sentence, 1/16/46.

8/18/40 Larceny, W District Court. Filed. 8/24/40, parole revoked, returned to Correctional School.

Home Interview

On 2/10/41, the home investigator went to 17 P Street, Dorchester, the home address for Henry's family given in the records at the Correctional School. Here the family interview was carried out with Henry's mother. It lasted about two hours, during which the investigator took no notes except for recording the boy's health history toward the close of the interview. The information obtained was recorded as follows:

(1) a running account of the interview was dictated; (2) data were entered in red ink on the social investigation schedule (to distinguish them from data obtained from other sources); and (3) a memorandum was prepared for the case collator indicating which factors needed to be verified, amplified or initially secured.

Following is the dictated report of the interview with the boy's mother.

In the late afternoon of 2/10/41, the home investigator called at 17 P Street, Dorchester. This address turned out to be an old wooden tenement house. The investigator did not know on which floor the family lived, and after trying all bells and getting no response, he went into the front hallway and knocked on a door on the second floor. A woman, who proved to be the boy's mother, answered the door, and the investigator explained that he wished to talk with her about her son, Henry. Without any hesitation or questioning, she invited him into the home and preceded him through the length of the apartment to the kitchen in the rear. Coming into the kitchen, he observed that she was slicing apples for applesauce. Throughout the first part of the interview she continued her work, finally sitting down at the kitchen table when the sauce was on the stove. The interview was carried out in the kitchen and there were no interruptions or distractions.

In appearance the boy's mother is tall and strongly built, with a dark complexion and dark brown hair. Her hands showed no evidence of hard work and were well kept, with brightly polished nails. Her attitude was one of grudging cooperation. She volunteered little in the discussion and had to be questioned closely; though not unfriendly, she was more or less indifferent. The investigator got the impression that she is an "old hand" at being interviewed by social workers and others and has cultivated an attitude of appearing to be cooperative but at the same time giving only the barest amount of information. He felt that her statements could not be accepted as completely reliable, as she resisted giving any information derogatory to the family.

In the course of the discussion, Mrs. W allowed the investigator to infer that her husband was Henry's father. After the investigator informed her that he knew Henry was adopted by her husband, she readily admitted that he was not the real father. Under questioning she stated that Henry true father, Mr. J, was so adjudged in B District Court, and later in C Superior Court, and was ordered to pay $6.00 a week for the boy's support. This he did for two or three years through the Probation Office of the C Superior Court. Regular payments continued until Henry was about two years old, when his father made a settlement of $250 in a lump sum, and the case was closed. Mrs. W stated that this arrangement, which was entirely agreeable to her, was suggested by Mr. J because he had remarried.

According to the mother, Henry's father had always been a resident of Randolph, Mass., and was employed there in a shoe factory. In discussing her association with him, she said that they "kept company" for some time, although forbidden to do so by her father (no reason for this parental disapproval was proffered). Henry's father has not seen him and has taken no interest in him other than sending the financial support ordered by the Court. Mrs. W herself has not seen Mr. J since the court proceedings and has no idea where he is now living. He was an only child, four years older than herself, and came of "nice people." The paternal grandfather, when she knew him, had been injured and was unable to work. He got some sort of compensation at the time she kept company with Henry's father.

Mrs. W, first in a family of two children, was born in Everett, Mass., in 1906. Asked about her nationality, she said her parents were born in this country, one in New Hampshire and one in Connecticut. Leaving school in the eighth grade, she did factory work until her marriage to Mr. W.

Since her mother's death in 1932, her sister, Florence, who is two years younger, has been living in the W household. Florence was described as being unable to work because she is an epileptic. Before coming to live with the W's, she had spent much time at the Q State Infirmary, the P State Hospital and a State School for the Feeble-Minded.

The investigator was unable to get a very clear picture of Henry's stepfather as Mrs. W obviously did not wish to talk about him. When they were first married, he was a factory worker; but after he lost his job, they were obliged to apply for relief. For nearly fourteen years, according to her, he has worked steadily for the X Public Utility Company as a laborer, earning almost $30 a week. She claims that during this period they have never received any public aid. (This seems doubtful in view of the information already received from the Social Service Index.) Mrs. W said that he was born in Jamaica Plain, Mass., but she constantly referred to Pennsylvania and Delaware, giving the impression that her husband spent most of his youth in these two states. When asked if this was true, however, she said that it was not, that he was brought up in Boston. He was aware of Henry's presence at the time of their marriage and shortly thereafter legally adopted him. Until recently, she said, her husband had been quite a heavy drinker who would "drink anything," but now contents himself with buying a small bottle of wine every pay day. He was never abusive, she said, to her or the children: "I've got no kick coming. He's been a good provider." This statement was made without a great deal of conviction, however, and the investigator got the impression that there is considerable friction in the home.

Mrs. W said that she had seen her father-in-law only a few times when he paid visits to her home; and she would say nothing about his personal or family history, or, as she called it, "his personal affairs," which she said she does not "pry into." When she last heard, he was living in Michigan. Her father-in-law owns his own business, she said, although she would not admit any knowledge of its nature or size.

Two of Henry's half-brothers were attending school and all three were living at home.

Henry's chief interests seem to have been in group athletics. He was a member of Settlement House No. 1, and, according to his mother, spent most of his leisure time there. His hobby has been making model airplanes and he hopes some day to become an airplane pilot. Toward that end he intends to complete a high school education and then make application to join the U.S. Army in the Air Corps section. Mrs. W visits Henry regularly at the Correctional School and is hopeful that he will be home before Easter time.

Most of the above information, as well as other specific data gathered in the home interview, were recorded in the social investigation schedule.

The investigator's memorandum to the case collator read as follows.

1. Obtain stepfather's court record at Board of Probation. The one sent to us previously is not that of stepfather. He probably has a long court record for drunkenness.

2. Get further identifying data on the boy's true father and clear through the Board of Probation for his court record.

3. What is true father's nationality or descent? Mother is "Old American."

4. Obtain true father's birthplace and date. Is he still living? Did he marry?

5. What is the religion of the boy and his parents? Interviewer did not get this information.

6. Correctional School records may be incomplete on the boy's half-brothers. Send requests for court records on any additional half-siblings. Stepfather seems to have been married previously. Were there any children of this marriage?

7. Mother says her sister has been in the Q State Infirmary, the P State Hospital, and a State School for the Feeble-Minded; and that she is an epileptic. Suggest this be verified.

8. Data concerning delinquency, alcoholism, mental dullness, mental disease and education of the boy's true father and his family largely unknown to the boy's mother.

9. Why was the boy first placed out in a foster home?

10. Was the boy's parole to the same foster home on his second as on his first parole from Correctional School?

11. Exact length of time the family has been living at the present address needs to be determined.

12. Health history is unreliable. Verify the boy's mild attack of epilepsy in 1928.

Verifying and Amplifying Data Obtained and Securing New Data

With the results of the home visit in hand, the case collator mapped out the next steps with a view to amplifying and verifying the data thus derived and securing additional information on Henry and his family. Many clues had already been provided by consulting the Massachusetts Board of Probation and the Social Service Index.

Boys' Parole Division. First, Henry's record at the Boys' Parole Division in Boston was consulted. A field investigator summarized the information in the boy's folder, omitting data previously obtained at the Correctional School. He found a copy of a home investigation report made by a parole agent following Henry's first commitment to the Correctional School in 1936. The address visited by the agent at this time was noted. (New addresses were constantly being discovered, so that by the time the field work was finished, a complete record had been obtained of all the addresses where Henry had lived from birth to the time he was taken on for study.) There was a report of another home visit in September 1938, when conditions were described as much better than before. However, on a later visit in December 1939, the agent stated that home conditions were not improved: "The mother was still in bed near noon. She claimed to be sick but a plate of cigarette butts by her side shows she must be an excessive smoker." (This statement tended to support the home visitor's observation that the household routine was not well planned.) As a result, the parole agent recommended foster home placement, but Henry was allowed to return home, and it was from home that he was sent back to the Correctional School for the term during which we examined him on 1/5/41. Henry was then in the graduating class at the F School and had expected to enter high school in the fall.

The Boys' Parole Division record also contained a statement from Mental Hospital No. 1 to the effect that Henry had no physical abnormalities; that blood tests for syphilis were negative; and that one of his lungs was weak. (The mother had told the home visitor that Henry had had pneumonia at three years of age and that one lung had been weak ever since.) The hospital psychiatrist added that he felt Henry's irregularities of behavior were probably the result of unhealthy family atmosphere or heredity.

While taking these notes, the field investigator copied the name, approximate birthdates and birthplaces of Henry's mother and stepfather; their address in August 1940; the names of their children; and so on. He noted that there was much less family information in the folder than was usually the case.

State Bureau of Vital Statistics. At this point the case collator felt it advisable to verify certain names, birthplaces, and so on, and to seek additional data. A field investigator therefore checked the birth of Henry's true father at the State Bureau of Vital Statistics. His approximate age and place of birth being already known, the record was readily found, and as there was only one of that name and age, it was, without doubt, that of the father. He was born 5/16/01 in Spencer, Mass. The birth certificate provided the names and birthplaces of the paternal grandparents, and the information that the paternal grandfather was born in Norwell, Mass., and the paternal grandmother in Spencer. As it had already been determined that the maternal grandparents were native-born, and it was now confirmed that both the parents were native-born, the factor, dominant stock (#5 on the schedule), was established as Old American. This information answered in part questions 2, 3, and 4 of the home visitor's memorandum to the collator.

The birth of Henry himself was also verified. It was recorded under his mother's maiden name. Residence of mother was given as 12 A Street, Roxbury. (The mother had told the home visitor that she had been living a 120 A Street, Roxbury, with her parents at that time.) Such slight inaccuracies in a mother's statements were frequent throughout the study and usually indicated lapse of memory rather than any attempt to falsify.

Massachusetts Board of Probation. There was now enough identifying information for an investigator to obtain from the files of the Massachusetts Board of Probation the court record of Henry's true father and stepfather. Following is that of the true father:

10/3/24 Bastardy, B District Court. Adjudged father, appealed. 3/13/25, illegitimate child, C Superior Court. Probation two years.

2/30/26 Illegal parking, B District Court. $5.00 paid.

3/14/29 Nonsupport of child, H District Court. Probation, 7/10/29. Defaulted. (Refers to daughter, Anne, Henry's half-sister.)

The Board of Probation also provided the additional information that in 1929, when last arrested, James S. J had a wife, Helen, and was living in Stoughton, Mass. All this information was now inserted under items previously recorded by the home investigator as *unknown.*

The court record of the stepfather included twenty arrests for drunkenness and one conviction for grand larceny. Two weeks before Henry was returned to the Correctional School on 8/24/40 (the particular term of confinement during which he was selected for inclusion in the study), his stepfather was surrendered on a suspended sentence and sent to the C House of Correction for one month. (This information was recorded in the schedule, not under factor #31, family background, as the stepfather was not a blood relative of the boy, but under factor #A17, moral standards of home, because the stepfather was living in the household of which Henry had been a part.)

Boston Social Service Index. Now that so much information on the true father had been secured, the Boston Social Service Index was again consulted concerning him and his wife, Helen. A photostatic copy of the Index card indicated that the wife was known to the Bradwood Social Service Index (3/8/33) and a Bradwood Child Welfare Agency (10/10/39); that they had a daughter, Anne, born in 1928; and that the wife and child were living in Bradwood in March 1933. This information added a new half-sister to the list. Attached to this photostat was a card on Henry, questioning his connection with the J family and indicating that he was known to Mental Hospital No. 1, as a house patient. It also gave Henry's addresses in 1935 and 1939.

Relief Agency. Reference to the data derived initially from the Social Service Index in Boston concerning Henry's' mother and stepfather indicated that the agencies most likely to have the fullest records for our purposes were Relief

Agency No. 1, Boston Child Welfare Agency No. 1, and Boston Social Agency No. 1.

From the records of Relief Agency No. 1, the field investigator learned that Mr. and Mrs. W were first referred to this agency in October 1927. There were two children in the home at that time, Henry and his half-brother, Arthur W, born 6/12/27 in Boston. The stepfather was receiving veterans' compensation of about $30 a month for a disability. He had been laid off one month before from a factory. Grocery orders for $3 a week were given until November 1927, when he secured work. In December 1927 he was again laid off and again received $3 grocery orders until January 1928, when he was re-employed. He was aided again, off and on, between June 1928 and October 1928; and then was not heard from again until 1940 when the mother reapplied, because he had just been committed to the House of Correction. There were now three children in the home (Henry had just been sent to the Correctional School). In addition to Arthur, there were Kenneth, born 7/5/34 in Boston, and William, born 6/5/37 in Boston (who had been incorrectly recorded as Charles at the Index). The stepfather now had a permanent job as a laborer at the X Public Utility Company and last worked there 8/10/40. The maternal aunt, Florence, was living in the home. Emergency aid was given until the stepfather's release from the House of Correction and his return to his job with the utility company. A list of addresses in the record extending from 1924 through 1928 and for the year 1940 were noted for inclusion in the final listing of places of residence of Henry.

Though Henry's mother had not indicated to the home investigator the extent to which she had had relief, the periods during which the family received aid, according to Relief Agency No. 1, were not long enough to change the *marginal* economic status of the family as recorded by the home investigator. The records of this agency also supported the mother's statement that her husband was a permanent employee of the X Public Utility Company.

While at Relief Agency No. 1, the field worker secured information about the maternal grandparents, who were known to that agency in 1928 and 1933. He learned that the maternal grandfather was Arnold P, born in Bridgeport, Conn., 9/18/73; and that the maternal grandmother was Margaret C, born in Keene, N.H. She had died 1/16/32 (verified) at the M. C. Hospital of "aortic stenosis." This confirmed the mother's statement about her mother's death. There was a maternal aunt, Florence, born 1/3/08, in Everett, Mass., who was living with the maternal grandfather. This grandfather had not received aid, according to this particular record, until July 1933, and was last assisted in January 1934, to the extent of $8 a week. He had worked for the City of Boston as a janitor and was discharged for drunkenness. This information supported the mother's statement to the home visitor that the status of her parents had been *marginal* with occasional dependence (factor #40, economic status of maternal family).

Massachusetts Board of Probation. With the above definite information on the maternal grandparents and aunt, the case collator sent for their court records at the Massachusetts Board of Probation which revealed the following information.

The maternal aunt had been committed to jail on 4/5/33 for fornication, from the N District Court. She was listed as single and was living with the W's at this time. The fact of her criminal behavior helped to confirm the home visitor's judgment that the moral standards of Henry's home were poor.

The maternal grandfather had the following court record.

10/1/29 Drunk, B District Court. Filed.
5/19/32 Drunk, V District Court. Released.

The names of his parents were listed in the record as well as his address and birthdate.

The maternal grandmother had no court record in Massachusetts.

This information from the Board of Probation corroborated the mother's statement to the home visitor that her father had been arrested for drunkenness (factor #32). The maternal aunt's conviction for fornication provided data for the factor, Delinquency in Maternal Family, which was previously *unknown*.

Boston Child Welfare Agency. A field investigator now visited Boston Child Welfare Agency No. 1 and summarized its long record on the family, keeping in mind those factors especially needed for the social schedule. The complainant to this agency, in July 1928, was Henry's true father who felt that the mother and stepfather were neglecting his son. The BCW agent made frequent visits to the boy's home between 1928 and 1935, when final arrangements were effected for Henry's placement in a foster home away from the unfavorable environment of his own home. The BCW record revealed early-morning drinking parties, entertainment of men at all hours by the mother and the aunt, brief separations of the mother and stepfather, the birth of a child, Kenneth, whose paternity the stepfather denied, and abuse of the children. It was clear from the BCW record that Henry was fully aware of what was going on.

The following data derived from the BCW record were used in the social investigation schedule.

The mother's statement that she never married the true father of the boy was confirmed by the BCW (factors #19-21). The circumstances surrounding the birth of the half-brother, Kenneth, on 7/5/34 in Boston, were recorded. Mrs. W had given the home investigator the impression that this child was legitimate, but the BCW record stated not only that the stepfather denied the paternity of this child, but that the mother had admitted it was not his. Moreover, Henry had vividly described to the BCW worker the frequent visits of men to the home around the time that Kenneth was conceived. The landlady, who wished to evict the family, made similar complaints. Though the mother had no court record, according to the Board of Probation, it was now clear that she had been delinquent (factor #31). She had one illegitimate child at least (Henry), and probably another as a result of adultery. She had been brought into court with her husband for neglect of her children on 5/31/35 through the efforts of the BCW but, after several continuances, was found not guilty. There was no indication in the BCW record that she was an excessive drinker (factor #32). The BCW noted that Henry's half-brother, Arthur, was guilty of considerable petty stealing (factor #31).

The BCW record confirmed the mother's statement that the maternal aunt, Florence, was epilepic and had been at P State Hospital. It further stated that the mother had been treated for gonorrhea in 1934 at a Boston hospital (factors #35-36). The mother herself had made no mention of this in discussing her own health. The BCW record also contributed to the list of addresses at which Henry had lived, clarified with whom he had lived, and why the family had to move so frequently — for example, because the mother and stepfather separated and the mother returned to maternal relatives, or because the landlady evicted the family for misconduct.

The mother had told the home visitor that Henry shared a room with his half-brother. Though this was a fact at the time of Henry's admission to the Correctional School, it was clear from the BCW record that he had often slept in the same bed with his mother, mainly to keep the stepfather out of it, or with his aunt (factor # 62). The aunt in this way introduced Henry to bad sex practices at the age of ten years, according to the stepfather. This item was noted in the schedule under sex habits of boy (factor #A42). The mother had not mentioned this.

The BCW record supplemented the description of the home and of the mother's housekeeping habits (factors #65-67). It contained statements that in 1928 the home was well furnished, upset but not untidy; that in 1932 it was untidy and neglected-looking and that the children were brought to school in very unkempt condition; that in 1934, however, the home was cleaner than usual (factors #65-66). On the whole, the mother was not a good manager, according to the district nurse's report to the BCW. The nurse felt her main difficulty was laziness. This corroborated the home investigator's impression that she was not planful (factor #A10). According to the BCW record, in addition to poor moral standards (factor #A17), as already indicated, the family showed little self-respect (factor #A18) by allowing a "steady stream" of men callers at all hours regardless of the protests of neighbors and landlords and the comments of their own children. The stepfather did protest at times but his own behavior gave this action little weight.

As to the methods of control and discipline (factors #A24, A26), the BCW reported that the stepfather knocked the children about rather brutally when in a half-drunken condition; that he tried to discipline Henry but that his wife opposed it. She had stated that the father took little or no part in control of the children.

Though Mrs. W told the home investigator that she and her husband had never separated (factor #A29, conjugal relations of parents), the BCW record stated that they had separated once; that the stepfather was planning to divorce his wife; and that she had returned to her mother's home with Henry, complaining that her husband was boorish and uninteresting, and became quarrelsome when she refused to have sex relations with him. As for affection for the boy (factor #A30), she had told the home investigator that the stepfather was indifferent; he accepted the boy in the home, but had no affection for him. The BCW felt that the stepfather was inclined to "pick" on the boy, but that Henry's relationship with his half-brother, Arthur, was good — Henry was fond of him (factor #A32).

From the BCW record some data about Henry's health were gleaned: he had his tonsils and adenoids removed at the P Q Hospital in 1935, though his mother had said that he had not had any operations (factor #A38). She also stated that

Henry had never had scarlet fever, but the BCW had learned from school that he was home with this contagious disease in 1934 (factor #A39).

As for bad habits of the boy (factors #A42-A43), Henry's mother had apparently withheld or not recalled information at the time of the home investigator's visit, for she had revealed to the BCW a much earlier onset of bad habits. These old records have often been found to be far more valuable and reliable than a mother's memory in ascertaining such important items as the earliest misbehavior of a boy. For example: Mrs. W told the home investigator that Henry started smoking when he was about thirteen or fourteen years old; but, according to the BCW record, he was smoking at ten years. By her account, Henry began to steal rides and hop trucks at twelve or thirteen years; according to the BCW, he began at ten years. The BCW record shows that he used vile language at ten years; in the interview his mother did not acknowledge any. She said she did not consider him pugnacious but, according to the BCW record, he was complained of for striking girls on the street at nine years; at eight years he was guilty of destructive mischief (which consisted of breaking many windows in houses and automobiles). At this age, he also snatched things from store counters and set small fires. The last alarmed the landlady, and the stepfather became "panic-struck," but the mother minimized the matter, according to the BCW. She had not mentioned the fire-setting at all to the home investigator, though he specifically questioned her about this.

When she had been asked for her explanation of why Henry became delinquent, she tended to place the blame on the particular circumstances surrounding each of his delinquencies rather than on the boy himself or home conditions; but to the BCW in 1935 she said that Henry did not seem to be able to withstand temptation (factors #A53-A54).

The BCW record also contained digests of records of other agencies which were sufficiently full and mutually corroborative to eliminate the need for seeking the original sources. The advantage of this is obvious when one recalls that the mother and stepfather alone were known to at least twenty agencies. For example:

The BCW had made a contact with a Veterans' Clinic that had known the stepfather and was told that his statements regarding his wife were unreliable.

A Legal Assistance Bureau had stated that the stepfather was so drunk when he asked for a divorce in 1933 that he could hardly walk; yet he vowed he never drank. This organization had reported that both the stepfather and mother were low grade mentally and the children in danger of becoming neglected.

A worker from Settlement House No. 2 had reported in 1933 that Henry was stealing from other boys at the club (factor #A43) and that he had begun to attend this settlement club at the age of seven years (factor #A46).

The out-patient department of Mental Hospital No. 1, to which Henry was taken by the BCW worker in 1934, had reported that an intelligence test had been given him (intelligence quotient of 96) and that, following the test, he stole a fountain pen from the psychologist (factor #43). On 9/13/34, the chief of the out-patient department of this hospital had reported that Henry's history indicated a mild form of epilepsy (factor #A38). "If allowed to remain longer with parents, he will undoubtedly develop into a delinquent boy." The mother had denied convulsions or any other epileptic symptoms or extreme nervousness in the boy in her interview with the home investigator. Henry had been a house patient at this same hospital from 2/22/36 to 4/11/36 after appearing in the W District Court and was found to be "not psychotic." The stepfather had also been examined at the out-patient department of this hospital in 1933, where it was noted that he had a mental age of only nine years and where he was diagnosed as a neurosyphilitic. As he was not a blood relative, this significant information had no place in the social investigation schedule except as it threw light on the home atmosphere.

A Children's Clinic had also reported to the BCW in February 1934 that Henry's physical examination was negative except that he seemed nervous (factor #A40-41).

A Boston Hospital had reported to the BCW that the mother was seen there in August 1932, because of "fainting spells." The diagnosis was "question of neurasthenia." This was recorded (factor #34) with the hope of getting further evidence of psychoneurosis from some other agency to help in making a judgment on the mental health of the mother.

A State School for the Feeble-Minded had reported to the BCW that Henry's maternal aunt had been an inmate there for three years and had an intelligence quotient of 55 (factor #33). The mother had not mentioned this serious mental defect in her family to the home interviewer.

While securing information on the immediate family at the BCW, the field investigator also examined the record of the maternal grandparents, dating back to 1910. This revealed the alcoholism of the grandfather; also the adultery of the grandmother, for which offense she was committed on 6/30/10 to a House of Correction. Their children, including Henry's mother, were committed to the care of the state but returned to their parents in 1911. There was now no doubt that both delinquency and alcoholism existed in the maternal family (factors #31-32). (The court record of the maternal grandmother was obtained from an old social service record and not from the Board of Probation which was not functioning for all Boston until 1916, and for the rest of the state until 1924.)

In 1927, the BCW had again received a complaint that the family was degenerate, that the maternal aunt was teaching neighborhood children perversions. Investigation at that time had revealed that the maternal aunt had epileptic fits and could not work (factors A#35-36); but that the maternal grandfather was now working steadily as a janitor for the city (factor #40).

Boston Social Agency. The field investigator now consulted the records on Henry's mother and stepfather and his maternal grandparents at the central office of Boston Agency No. 1. Mr. and Mrs. W had asked for aid occasionally between 1927 and 1940, receiving a few grocery orders from time to time and a pair of trousers for Henry. No intensive work was done with the family, however, because after learning of the previous experiences of other agencies, the agency decided for the most part to refer the family back to Relief Agency No. 1.

The BSA folder contained the answer to the home investigator's questions about a possible earlier marriage of the stepfather and whether there were any children by this marriage. He had been previously married and divorced; there were no children.

The following data derived from the BSA records were used for the social investigation schedule:

To the BSA, Mrs. W quite readily revealed occasional adultery (factor #31); and she was also considered by them to be "low grade mentally" (factor #33). Beside the BCW record of petty stealing by the half-brother, Arthur, the BSA mentioned his habit of truancy (factor #31); he could thus be considered an incipient delinquent, though his actual court record did not begin until after the completion of Henry's social investigation. The BSA also verified Henry's adoption by his stepfather on 12/1/26, when his surname was changed. The addresses mentioned in this record were added to the list of Henry's places of residence. The BSA augmented the home visitor's description of Henry's home (factors #65-66) by stating in 1934 that it was an untidy, badly-cared-for tenement; and in 1935 that the mother was in bed at all hours and "not always alone in bed," the baby was filthy, and so on. As to work habits of the stepfather (factor #A4), he was laid off jobs from time to time, probably because of drinking, until in 1931 he got a job on a public utility truck. This gave Mr. W at most nine years of steady employment rather than fourteen years, as his wife had said. Even from this job he had temporary layoffs. He frequently came to the BSA office with a "strong odor of liquor about him."

Henry's mother had told the home investigator that the family had no savings (factor #A9). This was confirmed by the BSA, which said that, in the past at least, they had no credit, were behind in the rent, and were generally hard up. The stepfather complained of the way his wife spent the income, but he drank a lot of it up himself. This tended to confirm the home visitor's observation (factor #A10) that the family "lived from day to day."

Under moral standards of the home (factor #17), it was noted from the BSA record that the immoral, alcoholic maternal aunt had lived a great deal with the family and was a bad influence on Henry. The BSA substantiated the home visitor's feeling that the family had little if any self-respect (factor #A18): Mrs. W had begged aid of the agency just after collecting her husband's pay in 1939; and he had asked aid of Relief Agency No. 3 in 1933 when he was earning $29 a week. Though the home investigator had recorded Mrs. W's statement that her husband was uninterested in disciplining Henry (factor #A26), the BSA told of a neighbor's complaint that he sometimes beat Henry severely.

Beside having a summary of the BCW records, the BSA had information from the Veterans' Clinic and the Red Cross about the stepfather's early history. Relief Agency No. 3 had reported to the BSA that they had aided the family in 1928 with food and clothes. Child Placing Agency No. 1 also had talked the problem over with the BSA; but the field investigator decided to get the details from that agency directly as specific information about the foster home placements was especially needed.

The maternal grandparents' record at the BSA mostly concerned Henry's aunt, Florence, who went to live with Henry's mother and stepfather after the maternal grandmother had died, 1/16/32 (verified). This was a second confirmation of Mrs. W's statement that her mother had died of heart trouble in 1932 (factor #35). The aunt at this time, according to Henry's mother who took her in, was "tearing around with men and drinking and picking up strange men and bringing them home." The mother made clear to the BSA that she also was having "a good time" and leaving her husband home to take care of the children.

Bradwood Social Service Index. While the above information was being secured in the Boston area, information was sought from agencies with whom contact was best made by correspondence. Consultation of the Bradwood Social Service Index revealed that Henry's real father and his legal wife had been known to a Bradwood Social Agency and a Bradwood Child Welfare Agency.

The brief report of the Bradwood Social Agency was received with the Bradwood SSI card. James S. J's wife had come to the office in 1933 to ask for some clothing for their child, Anne (half-sister of Henry). Her husband had deserted her four and a half years before, in 1929, and she had returned to her parents in Bradwood. She received the clothing but never returned to the agency.

Bradwood Child Welfare Agency. A letter was sent to the Bradwood Child Welfare Agency asking for a summary of their contact, in the hope of learning Mr. J's present whereabouts. Unfortunately, their record was mostly concerned with the behavior of his wife, Helen, with whom the inquiry was not concerned. However, the record did mention the "wild" behavior of Henry's half-sister, Anne J, and gave her exact birthdate as 4/15/27/8 in Bradwood. Also it contained the verified date of James J's marriage to Helen (7/8) and the date of her divorce from him (1934), at which time she was given the care and custody of Anne. It stated in 1941 that the father had never been located. As search in Bradwood, Stoughton, Randolph and Boston directories and in Massachusetts death records proved unavailing, the case collator had to content herself for factors #6 and #23 with the fact that, though it was known that Henry's father was living in Stoughton in 1929 when he defaulted in H District Court, it had not been determined whether he was alive or dead in 1940. Henry's mother did not know either, according to her statement to the home investigator.

Maternity Home and Hospital No. 1, which had known Henry's mother in 1924, was also consulted by letter. The hospital report confirmed her birthdate and her religion as Protestant (factor #18), and her delivery of a male child there, Henry, on 1/16/25 ("normal delivery and no complications"). The mother had also told the home investigator that delivery was normal (factor #A38). She was said to be "willing and easy to manage." Over a year later she wrote to the hospital that she had married Leo W.

Superior Court. Further information about Henry's true father was sought from his probation record in C Superior Court. (As an example of the specific instructions given by the collator to the field investigators, the following are typical: "We know very little about Henry's real father, James S. J, so please get all you can about him, his parents and siblings, if any; habits; comments on intelligence, personality, and so on.")

At the probation office of the C Superior Court, the field investigator learned that James S. J had pleaded not guilty to the charge of bastardy in B District Court on 10/3/24, but was adjudged to be the father of the mother's unborn child and appealed the case. The mother, interviewed by the probation officer in C Superior Court in March 1925, said that Mr. J claimed he could not marry her because he was already married; but he proved to the court that he had been divorced from his first wife in Chicago, Illinois, on 5/5/21 (verified). According to the probation officer, Henry definitely resembled the defendant, who on 3/13/25 (about two months after Henry was born) was ordered to pay $5 a week for the boy's support and the confinement expenses, and was placed on two years' probation on an illegitimate child charge. At that time Mr. J was living in Stoughton and earning $26 a week in a machine shop, but he worked very irregularly during his probation and was soon in arrears. The probation officer said he never was inclined to work, kept his jobs only a short time, and that although the mother wanted to marry him, he was in no financial condition to do so. On 5/10/26 the mother married Leo W, and they and Henry continued to live with her parents. Mr. W was earning $27 a week and was anxious to adopt Henry. Shortly after this, on 6/2/26, Mr. J married Helen B in Bradwood. In October 1925, very little money having been paid by him to Henry's mother, the probation officer persuaded the paternal grandmother ("a respectable woman" — factor #31) to advance the father some money to cover all payments. On 2/12/27 the adjudication was vacated and the complaint dismissed.

The early addresses of Henry, his mother, and stepfather as contained in the C Superior Court record were noted.

Lower Court. At this point a copy of the Y Court probation record on Henry himself was received. Henry had made only one appearance in this court, on 12/1/38, for breaking and entering a variety store. He was found delinquent and the case was filed, since he was turned over to his parole officer for return to the Correctional School. Even this brief record added a few items to the social investigation schedule: according to the Y Court, Henry was a Methodist (factor #3) and his mother a "Protestant" (factor #18). His stepfather was employed as a laborer by a public utility company at $29.50 a week (factor #A7), and had been in court with Henry, resentful that the boy was causing so much trouble (factor #A30). Henry was convicted of stealing at thirteen years of age (factor #A43). He was attending Settlement House No. 1 in 1938 when thirteen years old (factor #A46); in fact, he stated that the reason he went into town and got into trouble was because there were no activities at the Settlement House that day.

Child Placing Agency. A field investigator then went to Child Placing Agency No. 1 and consulted its long record on Henry.

On 6/18/35, the BCW asked CPA No. 1 to place Henry in a foster home, as his mother and stepfather were not well adjusted to each other and could not control the boy, who had a tendency to petty theft, truanted, was on the street at all hours, and had also set a fire. A charge of neglect against the parents had been dismissed with a warning by the judge. The CPA was assured, however, that Henry's intelligence quotient was fairly high. After some hesitation because of the family background, and upon receipt of a second request from the BCW, the CPA finally agreed to place him, particularly since his examination at the PQ Hospital was negative; the doctor had found him in fine condition except for his teeth. Henry was back and forth in CPA foster homes from 11/6/35 until he was committed to the Correctional School in 1936.

The following data derived from the CPA records were used for the social investigation schedule.

The record indicated grave doubt as to the paternity of Mrs. W's last child, William, born 6/5/37, because during 1936 the neighbors considered her "everybody's wife," and Mr. W himself doubted that the expected baby was his (factors #28, 31).

Mrs. W told the CPA in 1935 that Henry's true father was alcoholic; he "worked one day and drank the next" (factor #32). She herself did not appear "bright" to the CPA visitor (factor #33), to whom she gave a lively description of her attempt at suicide. She said she took poison and was saved when her sister called a doctor. This item, added to those already listed under factor #34 on the mother, indicated emotional instability. On one call the CPA found the home clean and neat; on another, not very clean (factor #65). When the worker called to take Henry to his foster home, as planned with his mother, she not only did not have him dressed but had not given him any breakfast; while the social worker waited, she gave the boy (ten years old) three doughnuts and two cups of coffee (factor #66). It was clear that she had not been supervising him adequately, as he was on the street at all hours (factors #A6, A27). Her method of punishing him was to whip him or deprive him of supper or the movies (factor #A25). The stepfather also resorted to these methods, but he was usually drunk when home weekends, and alternately quiet and noisy, erratic and unpredictable in his handling of Henry (factor #A26).

The mother and stepfather had separated several times (factor #A29). She told the CPA that she returned to her husband following these periods of separation only for financial reasons. (She had apparently chosen to forget these incidents when talking to our home investigator in 1941.) According to the CPA, Henry knew he was adopted but knew nothing of his father. The stepfather's favorite child was Arthur, the only one he felt sure was his own (factor #A30). The mother, too, considered Arthur her favorite, and Henry felt this. But she also showed considerable fondness for Henry, giving him a bicycle in 1935 (factor #A31); and she avoided court action against her husband for fear the children might be taken from her. As to household duties of the boy (factor #A33), the CPA confirmed her statement that they were not regular. She sent Henry to the store occasionally on errands and considered him quite reliable on such jobs. "He rarely stole more than a few pennies from me." The CPA record illustrated the disunity in the family (factor #A37), for beside considerable evidence of the parents' neglect of their children and their lack of affection for each other, Henry's stepfather and maternal aunt, Florence, "fought like cats and dogs" (factor #A37). Mrs. W insisted, however, on keeping Florence in the home as it was her mother's "dying wish."

At the time of Henry's foster home placement in 1935, the CPA gave him a physical examination, in connection with which some of the early health information was probably supplied by his mother. It confirmed her statement to our home investigator that Henry was a full-term baby, normally delivered, and not a late walker or talker (thirteen months and fifteen months, respectively) (factor #A38). However, though she denied any history of convulsions to the home investigator, it was here recorded that he had had two convulsions, one at six months and the other at one year (factor #A38). He had had his tonsils and adenoids removed in 1935 (factor #A38); and had had pneumonia and frequent colds (factors #A40-A41). His mother also denied to the home visitor that he had recurrent headaches, though Mental Hospital No. 1 reported infrequent headaches and dizziness to the CPA; and although she denied enuresis, his foster mother complained of it in 1936 when he was eleven years old (factors #A40-A41). Henry's mother could give no evidence of extreme nervousness, though the P Q Hospital reported to the CPA that at ten years of age he was nervous, had nightmares after seeing thrilling movies, and didn't sleep well (factors #A40-A41).

According to the CPA, Henry was already a problem as a truant at ten years of age, though his mother told the home visitor that he had truanted "once or twice" since he was fourteen. She also told the CPA that Henry was "truck hopping" and keeping late hours at ten years, and that he had been unmanageable since infancy (factors #A42-A43).

Mrs. W had not said much to the home visitor about Henry's foster home placements, but an accurate account was obtained from the CPA, which revealed that on 11/6/35 Henry was placed with Mrs. M. Q in Canton, Mass. On 1/15/36, Henry was returned to his own mother at her request (the stepfather was paying his board), and Mrs. M. Q stated that she did not want him back, as he had been stealing. He remained at home in Roxbury with his stepfather, mother, maternal aunt, and half-brothers until he was arrested and appeared in W District Court on 2/9/36 for larceny from a department store, for which offense he was committed to the Correctional School. The sentence was appealed, and while awaiting a hearing in C Superior Court, he was kept in a State Child Placing Agency temporary home until 2/22/36. At this time the Court placed him in Mental Hospital No. 1 for a period of observation, because the out-patient department examination had indicated that there was some question of psychotic tendencies. On 4/10/36, the hospital reported that the boy was restless and emotionally unstable, with violent outbreaks of temper if he could not have his own way (factors #40-A41); that he had an intelligence quotient of 103 (an I.Q. of 96 had been reported in 1934), and a mental age of 12 yrs., 8 mos.; and that he was not insane or feeble-minded. Re-placement in a foster home was recommended. (The fact that this full report had been secured from Mental Hospital No. 1 by the CPA, plus previous summaries, made a separate visit by a field worker to the hospital unnecessary.)

On 4/11/36, Henry was given two years probation in the C Superior Court and placed by the CPA. After five days in a temporary home, he went to live with a Mr. and Mrs. J. F, on the outskirts of Medway, Mass. (his stepfather paying the board). The CPA was enthusiastic about these foster parents but indicated that the foster mother was a rather rigid disciplinarian. They had a farm of several acres with pigs, cows and chickens, and a large garden (factor #51). After an enjoyable summer of swimming, fishing, and small chores, Henry's behavior began to deteriorate on return to school in the fall. He was rude to the teachers, exhibited a violent temper, stole bicycle fixtures from a store, and ran away several times. Finally he attacked a boy with a knife, seriously injuring him. In consequence of the assault, Henry was sent to the Correctional School.

Henry showed no concern over the condition of the boy, nor did he seem to realize the seriousness of what he had done, according to the CPA. The CPA then closed the case and future placements were made by the Boys' Parole Division.

State Department of Mental Health. With the vital statistics now complete on all members of the boy's family, both on the paternal and maternal side, a field investigator checked through the files of the Massachusetts State Department of Mental Health, finding a record only for Henry's aunt, Florence, who, while a patient at one of the state mental hospitals, had been diagnosed as suffering from "psychoneurosis." This diagnosis provided data for factor #34.

School History

The gathering of Henry's school history was a task largely separate from the rest of the social investigation.

From Henry himself and from the Correctional School records, it was learned that he had last attended the F Intermediate School in Roxbury, being in the eighth grade in June 1940; then he was arrested and returned to the Correctional School before examination for this study. A school investigator went to the F School to obtain Henry's record there and as much of his previous school record as possible. The ADP card (see *Unraveling Juvenile Delinquency*, Chapter VII) was available but incomplete, beginning only with his experience in the F School. He had attended here twice: first, in the seventh grade from October 1938 to December 1938, when he was returned to the Correctional School; and again, when paroled from the Correctional School, in the eighth grade from January 2, 1940 to the end of June 1940. His scholarship record in the last term of the eighth grade was as follows: A in Physical Education and Hygiene; B's and C's in Reading, Literature, English, Spelling, Penmanship, Arithmetic, Geography, and History; D's or E's in Music, Drawing and Conduct (factors #A64-A65).

The school investigator then interviewed Henry's eighth grade teacher, who checked the following characteristics as applying to him (factors #A71-A74, #A76): stealing, obscene notes and talk, truancy, cheating, unreliableness, lack of interest in work, laziness, smoking, unhappiness, depression, easy discouragement, carelessness at work, inattention, slovenliness in appearance, suspiciousness, and thoughtlessness. The investigator also had a conversation with the Principal, who felt that Henry's behavior difficulties resulted from a combination of home conditions and his own attitude toward life. The family was careless and inadequate; the boy was "slippery," untrustworthy, and had poor associations; and, the Principal understood, the stepfather was a drinker. He gave as the reason for retardation (factor #A77) "lack of interest plus many changes of schools"; as the reason for truancy (factor #A78) "influence of bad companions plus lack of interest in school." As for adjustment to schoolmates (factor #A29), he said Henry tended to bad associations. The boy, he said, did not participate in extracurricular activities (factor #A80).

The investigator now needed to complete the history of Henry's earlier schooling. Noting that on his original commitment to the Correctional School Henry had come from a Medway, Mass., elementary school, he wrote to the superintendent of schools in that town, enclosing a questionnaire. The prompt reply happily included an ADP card listing the schools attended by the boy from kindergarten to his first Correctional School commitment, as follows:

School Year	School	Grade
1/17/31 to 12/31	N School, Boston	1, 1
12/31 to 6/33	D School, Boston	1, 2
9/33 to 3/34	P School, Boston	3
3/34 to 6/35	S School, Boston	3, 4
9/35 to 11/35	B School, Boston	5
11/35 to 1/36	F School, Canton	5
1/36 to 2/36*	B School, Boston	5
4/36 to 9/36	R School, Medway	5, 5

* Between 2/36 and 4/36 Henry was in a temporary foster home and in Mental Hospital No. 1 for observation and did not attend school.

Data on scholarship were not included in the reply; but Henry's conduct was given as "fair to poor." There were no absences, no tardiness, no truancy. His intelligence quotient was 112 on a Binet-Simon Test, but his school achievement was one to three years below his chronological age. As the boy's outstanding problem (factor #A80) the Superintendent had commented "obedience and dependability were both subaverage."

The investigator next wrote to the F School in Canton, and received an identical ADP card covering all experiences through that school. A copy of Henry's fifth-grade report card was enclosed with his marks for the 1935-36 period, ranging from A to D. His mark in conduct was D.

From these ADP cards it was clear that, except for these two out-of-town experiences, all the schools Henry had attended before his commitment to the Correctional School were in Boston. The investigator therefore consulted the B and P Schools in Roxbury and the South End district of Boston and learned that Henry's school misbehavior began in the fifth grade at ten years of age, in the B School. He was unruly, truanted on at least three occasions, and stole. There was no record of misconduct at the P School and the investigator therefore did not consult any previous schools.

At this point the case collator observed a gap between the date 10/36 when Henry left the R School in Medway and 10/38 when he entered the F School. This period was found in the Boys' Parole Division records to be covered as follows: 10/36 to 12/37 at the Correctional School; 12/37 to 2/38 on parole in a foster home, attending the sixth grade in South Holyoke, Mass.; 2/38 to 10/38 at the Correctional School.

There was now available a complete chronological list of Henry's school experiences, from which the following facts were gleaned. He started the first grade at just six years of age (factor #A56). He had between nine and ten years of schooling (factor #A57). He attained the eighth grade in school (omitting the Correctional School) at fifteen years (factor #A58). He repeated grade one and grade five (factor #A59). He was retarded two years at the time he left school (factor #A61). He did not attend any special class or the Disciplinary Day School (factor #A62). He had ten school experiences in all, not counting the Correctional School (factor #A63). His first serious misbehavior (factor

#A66) was recorded as truancy, unruliness in class, and stealing. The age and the grade in which his first serious misbehavior was evident (factors #A67-A68) were given as ten years in grade five. The age truancy started (factor #A69) was recorded as ten years; the frequency of truancy (factor #A70) was recorded as occasional at first, but persistent in his last year.

Completing the Investigation

During the course of gathering Henry's family and personal history, the collator frequently reviewed the progress of the case, mapping out new sources of information and redirecting the field investigators to old sources as the need became evident. When it appeared that all the data were in hand, she reread the home interviewer's suggestions for further exploration and found that they had been successfully completed. She then reviewed the detailed schedule, into which the results of the investigations had been entered, to make certain that every factor was accounted for and that there were no contradictions between factors (except in instances where she felt that the authors of *Unraveling Juvenile Delinquency* would have to resolve them, there being no additional data available). After this final check, the social investigation schedule on Henry was ready to be reviewed by the authors and prepared for statistical treatment.

SUMMARY OF INFORMATION AS RECORDED IN THE
SOCIAL INVESTIGATION SCHEDULE

Below are presented: (A) a detailed statement of Henry's places of residence, entered on the schedule under the heading *Chronological Summary of Boy's Whereabouts from Birth to Present* (which provided the basis for completing factors #42-56); (B) a summary, factor by factor, of all data derived from the home interview and from the field investigations, as they were finally assembled in the schedule.

A. CHRONOLOGICAL SUMMARY OF HENRY'S WHEREABOUTS FROM BIRTH TO PRESENT
(Including breaks in home life and departures from home)

Deteriorated Area	Whereabouts	With Whom	Dates	Reason for Change
Yes	12 A Street, Dorchester	Mother, maternal grandparents, occasionally maternal aunt	1/16/25–4/3/26[a]	Maternal grandparents moved
Yes	209 B St., Roxbury	Mother, maternal grandparents, occasionally aunt and, after 5/26, stepfather	4/3/26–8/26	Mother and stepfather moved to own place
No	10 Y Street, Dorchester	Mother and stepfather	8/26–11/26	Mother and stepfather returned to maternal grandparents

[a] Actually boy and mother at Maternity Home and Hospital No. 1 (1/16/25–2/4/25).

(Continued)

Deteri-orated Area	Whereabouts	With Whom	Dates	Reason for Change
Yes	209 B St., Roxbury	Mother, stepfather, maternal grand-parents, occasionally aunt and, after 6/27 half brother	11/26–1928	Mother and step-father moved to own place
Yes	211 B St., Roxbury	Mother, stepfather and half-brother	1928–30	Unknown
Yes	213 B St., Roxbury	Mother, stepfather and half-brother	1930–32	Unknown
Yes	211 B St., Roxbury	Mother, stepfather, half-brother and aunt	1932–12/11/32	Mother left stepfather
Yes	29 S Street, Dorchester	Mother, half-brother, and maternal relatives (maternal grand-mother had died)	12/11/32–6/33	Mother and step-father reunited
No	81 N St., Boston	Mother, stepfather, half-brother and aunt	6/33–12/12/33	Unknown
Yes	67 C St., Boston	Mother, stepfather, half-brother and aunt	12/12/33–3/25/34	Family put out for disorderly con-duct
Yes	539 M Street, Roxbury	Mother, stepfather, half-brothers and aunt	3/25/34–10/21/34	Unknown
Yes	286 J St., Roxbury	Mother, stepfather half-brothers and aunt	10/21/34–7/35	Unknown
Yes	13 L St., Roxbury	Mother, stepfather, half-brothers, aunt and boarder (stepfather out of home part of time)	7/35–11/6/35	Placed in foster home by Child Placing Agency No. 1
No	66 S Street, Canton	Foster mother, Mrs. M.Q.	11/6/35–1/15/36	Stole, and foster mother did not want him back
Yes	13 L St., Roxbury	Mother, stepfather half-brothers and aunt	1/15/36–2/9/36	Arrested and appealed
	Temporary home of State Child Placing Agency		2/9/36–2/22/36	Sent by court to Mental Hospital No. 1 for ob-servation
	Mental Hospital No. 1 as patient		2/22/36–4/11/36	Placed in temporary home by Child Placing Agency No. 1
	Temporary home of Child Placing Agency No. 1		4/11/36–4/16/36	Placed in foster home by CPA No. 1
No	J Street, Medway	Foster parents, Mr. and Mrs. J. F.	4/16/36–9/27/36	Assaulted a boy and ran home
Yes	21 Y St., Roxbury	Mother, stepfather, half-brothers and aunt	9/27/36–10/3/36	Arrested and com-mitted

(Continued)

226

Deteri-orated Area	Whereabouts	With Whom	Dates	Reason for Change
	Correctional School	Confined	10/3/36– 11/30/37	Placed out by Boys' Parole Division
No	S Ave., South Holyoke	Foster mother, Mrs. M	11/30/37– 2/6/38	Ran away
	Bunking out		2/6/38– 2/7/38	Caught and returned to Correctional School
	Correctional School	Confined	2/7/38– 10/9/38	Paroled to mother and stepfather
Yes	17 P Street, Dorchester	Mother, stepfather, half-brothers and aunt	10/9/38– 12/1/38	Returned to Correctional School
	Correctional School	Confined	12/1/38– 12/28/39	Paroled to mother and stepfather
Yes	17 P Street, Dorchester	Mother, stepfather half-brothers and aunt	12/28/39– 8/18/40	Arrested, but got away
	Bunking out on runaway		8/18/40– 8/24/40	Caught and returned to Correctional School
	Correctional School	Confined	8/24/40	

B. FACTOR-BY-FACTOR PRESENTATION OF DATA FROM HOME INTERVIEW AND FROM FIELD INVESTIGATIONS

Family Background

Factor	Home Interview	Field Investigation [a]
1. Birthplace	Boston	Boston (verified by BPD in 1936; verified in detail by field worker at BVS).
2. Legitimacy	Conceived out of wedlock, parents never married	Illegitimate (BPD in 1936, BSA, BCW, CPA).
3. Religion	Not determined	Protestant (BPD); Methodist (Y Court).
4. Age (at date of examination)	16 years	16 yrs. Calculated on the basis of verified birthdate 1/16/25 (BVS) and date of examination 1/5/41.
5. Dominant stock	Parents native-born; maternal grandparents native-born (N.H. and Conn.)	Old American. Father native-born (verified at BVS). Paternal grandparents native-born (stated on birth certificate of father, BVS). Mother native-born (SSI, RA, BCW, BSA, etc.). Maternal grandmother native-born (verified on death certificate, BVS). Maternal grandfather native-born (SSI, RA, B of Prob).

[a] Includes correspondence.

(*Continued*)

Factor	Home Interview	Field Investigation[a]
6. Whereabouts of father	Unknown; never lived with boy	When he defaulted, according to H District Court in 1929, he was living in Stoughton, Mass. (B of Prob). Whereabouts unknown (BPD, 1936, 1940). Whereabouts unknown (Bradwood SA, 1933). Father had deserted true wife in 1929 (Bradwood SA, 1933). Whereabouts unknown, as never located (Bradwood CWA in 1940). No trace of father in 1940 directories or telephone books of Randolph, Bradwood, Stoughton, and Boston, Mass.
7. Whereabouts of mother	With boy	With boys (BPD).
8. Birthplace of father	Spencer, Mass.	Spencer, Mass. (verified at BVS).
9. Birthplace of mother	Everett, Mass.	Everett, Mass. (SSI, RA, BCW, BSA).
10. Disparity in age of parents	Birthdate of father, 1901; of mother, 1906	4 yrs., 7 mos., 18 days. Birthdate of mother 1/4/06 (verified MH & H) minus birthdate of father 5/16/01 (verified BVS).
11. Age of father at birth of boy	Not calculated because date unverified	23 yrs., 8 mos.; birthdate of boy 1/16/25 (verified at BVS by BPD) minus birthdate of father (see # 10).
12. Age of mother at birth of boy	Not calculated because date unverified	19 yrs., 12 days. Birthdate of boy (see #11) minus birthdate of mother (see #10).
13. Nativity of parents	Native-born (see #8 and #9)	Both native-born (see #8 and #9).
14. Nativity of parents and boy	Native-born (see #1, #8 and #9)	Parents and boy native-born (see #1, #8 and #9).
15. Date of arrival of boy in U.S.	Native-born (see #1)	Native-born (see #1).
16. Date of arrival in U.S. of father	Native-born (see #8)	Native-born (see #8).
17. Date of arrival in U.S. of mother	Native-born (see #9)	Native-born (see #9).
18. Religion of parents	Not determined	Father Protestant? (divorced twice, C Superior Court and Bradwood CWA); Mother Protestant (MH & H, Y Courts).
19. 20. Date and place of marriage of parents	Never married	Parents never married (BCW, BSA). Y Court assumed step-father was true father but made no investigation on this brief case.
21. Civil condition	Parents never married	Parents never married.
22. Date of remarriage of parent with whom living	Not determined, but both parents have remarried	Mother married for first time 5/17/26 (verified, BCW) when the boy was slightly over one year of age.

(Continued)

228

Factor	Home Interview	Field Investigation [a]
23. Date of death of father	Unknown if living or dead	Unknown whether dead or alive (Bradwood CWA, 1940). No record of father's death in Mass. (BVS).
24. Date of death of mother	Still living	Living (BPD, Correctional School).
25. Size of father's family	Only child	No information.
26. Size of mother's family	Mother one of two children	Mother one of two children (SSI, BCW, BSA).
27. Siblings of boy 28.	Three half-siblings by mother	Four living: 3 half-siblings by mother (SSI, BSA, BCW) and one half-sibling by father and his second legal wife (Bradwood CWA). Father had no children by his first legal wife (C Superior Court).
29. Rank of boy among siblings	First child	First child (SSI, BCW, BSA).
30. Time between birth of boy and next older child	Boy is oldest	Boy is the oldest child (SSI, BCW, BSA).
31. Delinquency in paternal family	Negative, as far as mother knows; father came from "nice people"	Paternal grandparents were respectable (social agencies by implication). Paternal grandmother respectable woman (C Sup. Ct. PO). Paternal grandparents were too old for clearance through the B of Prob for court records as their town did not report till 1924. There were no aunts and uncles.
Delinquency of father	Placed on probation when adjudged father of boy at time of his birth; otherwise unknown	Father convicted of offense of illegitimate child and nonsupport of child (B of Prob).
Delinquency in maternal family	Negative, according to mother	Maternal grandmother was committed to H of C for adultery in 1910 (BCW). Maternal aunt convicted of fornication (BCW, B of Prob).
Delinquency of mother	Boy is illegitimate	Mother had illegitimate child, Henry, and possibly two of her children allegedly by stepfather were illegitimate (BCW, CPA). Mother admits occasional adultery (BSA). Mother in court 5/31/33 for neglect of children but found not guilty (BCW).
Delinquency among siblings of boy	Negative, according to mother	Half-brother, Arthur, engaged in petty stealing (BCW); a frequent truant (BSA); no court record (B of Prob). Half-sister, Anne, "wild" and stays out late (Bradwood CWA). Other half-siblings too young to have court records.
32. Alcoholism in paternal family	Negative, as far as mother knows	Unknown. Court records before 1924 for Randolph, Mass., not available at B of Prob.

(Continued)

Factor	Home Interview	Field Investigation[a]
Alcoholism of father	Negative, according to mother.	Father alcoholic, according to the mother: "He worked one day and drank the next" (CPA).
Alcoholism in maternal family	Mother admits her father has been arrested for drunkenness	Maternal grandfather in court for drunkenness at least twice and convicted once (B of Prob.). Maternal grandfather alcoholic (BCW).
Alcoholism of mother	Mother claims she does not drink to excess	No agencies record that mother drank to excess, though BCW describes early morning drinking parties in mother's home.
Alcoholism among siblings of boy	Half-siblings too young	Half-siblings too young to drink to excess.
33. Mental dullness in paternal family	Mother considered paternal grandparents "normal"	Unknown (no comment by any agency).
Mental dullness of father	Father was of average intelligence, according to mother	Unknown, but probably within normal range, judging by his schooling and by the C Sup. Ct. size-up of him.
Mental dullness in maternal family	Question about Aunt Florence (see dictated report)	Maternal aunt's I.Q. 55 (State School for FM to BCW).
Mental dullness of mother	Impressed investigator as low average	Mother "low grade mentally" (BSA). Appears mentally "low grade" (BCW). Not bright (CPA).
Mental dullness among siblings of boy	No information	Half-siblings appear mentally retarded; their father a moron (CPA).
34. Mental disease in paternal family	Negative, as far as mother knows	No mental disease or distortion indicated by agency records. Paternal grandparents not known to Mass. DMH.
Mental disease of father	Considered normal by mother	Father not known to DMH, No mental examination at C Sup. Ct., but PO commented that behavior was rather irresponsible. He made a good superficial impression, however.
Mental disease in maternal family	Aunt Florence epileptic; has been in state institution (see dictated report)	Maternal aunt: diagnosis, "psychoneurosis" (DMH). Maternal aunt had epileptic fits (BCW).
Mental disease of mother	Seems quite normal	Mother had fainting spells. Diagnosis was "question of neurasthenia" (B Hosp. to BCW). Mother said she attempted suicide in 1933 (CPA).
Mental disease among siblings of boy	Negative, according to mother	Half-siblings not known to DMH.
35, 36. Health of paternal family	Grandfather had been injured and unable to work	No information from agencies.
Health of father	Had always been good, according to mother	Father's health negative in 1925 according to the C Sup. Ct. Unknown since then.
Health of maternal family	Maternal grandmother had heart trouble prior to her death in 1932; maternal aunt had epileptic fits	Maternal grandmother died of "aortic stenosis" at 53 (BVS to BSA). Maternal aunt had epileptic fits (BCW).

(Continued)

Factor	Home Interview	Field Investigation [a]
Health of mother	Negative	No illnesses mentioned by agencies except gonorrhea in 1934 B Hosp. to BCW).
Health of siblings	Negative	No illness mentioned except deafness of half-brother, Arthur (CPA).
37. Education of paternal grand parents	Unknown; were literate	Unknown, although undoubtedly both paternal grandparents had some common schooling, as born and grew up in Mass.
Education of maternal grandparents	Grandparents had few years of schooling	No information.
38. Education of father	Went to H. S.; unknown if graduated	No information.
Education of mother	Went through the seventh grade	No information.
39. (Dropped from study)		
40. Economic status of paternal grandparents	Grandparents received "some kind of compensation" at time of boy's birth as grandfather unable to work	Paternal grandfather a shoe worker (directory and BVS). Paternal grandparents could afford to pay enough to cancel debt of their son in 1926 (C Sup. Ct.). Bradwood SSI has no registration for paternal grandparents.
Economic status of maternal grandparents	Marginal, occasionally dependent, according to mother	Maternal grandfather on a pension (RA about 1933); drank and gambled his money away BCW, 1911); formerly a teamster and janitor who got "relief" for only a few months in 1933 (RA). Mother and her sister cared for by the state 1910-1911, when maternal grandmother in jail (BCW).
41. (Dropped from study)		
42. Age first left home	11 yrs., 3 mos.	10 yrs., 10 mos. (CPA, BCW).
43. Reason first left home	Not determined	Delinquency of boy, and home considered unsuitable by agency (BCW, CPA).
44. Nature of first departure from home	To foster home	To foster home (BCW, CPA).
45. Summary of abnormal environmental experiences	Foster homes and correctional school; family moved many times	Correctional School, four times (BPD). Foster homes, not relatives (CPA, BPD). Running away and bunking out (CPA and BPD). Excessive moving (RA, BSA, BCW, CPA, school records, directories).
46. Nature of first break in family life	Boy illegitimate, no father in home	Boy illegitimate, father not in home since before birth of the boy.
47. Age of boy at first break	Before birth of boy	Before birth of boy.

(Continued)

Factor	Home Interview	Field Investigation [a]
48. Summary of breaks in family life	Parents not married and did not live together since before boy's birth	Parents not married and did not live together since before birth of boy. Mother and stepfather separated on and off (BCW, CPA).
49. Household changes	Not determined	5 (all agencies).
50. Parent substitutes	One step-parent and foster parents	Stepfather (BCW) and foster parents (nonrelatives) (CPA).
51. Length of time lived in urban area	Predominantly urban	Predominantly urban (agencies and directories).
52. Age at change from rural to urban area	Usually lived in city	Premoninantly urban (agencies and directories).
53.a Frequency of moving	Not determined	More often than once a year (summary of agencies, BPD, schools, and directories).
53b. Frequency of moving (number of times)	Not determined	19 moves (summary of agencies, schools, BPD, directories).
54. Nature of mobility	Not determined	Excessive moving to different parts of one city (agencies, schools, BPD, directories).
55. Length of time in slum areas	Not determined	On and off throughout (agencies, schools, etc.).
56. Length of time family lived at present address	Nearly 3 yrs.	2½ years (CPA and directories).
57. 58. Composition of household	Boy, mother, stepfather, maternal aunt and three half-siblings	Boy, mother, stepfather, 3 half-siblings, maternal aunt (BPD, 1940 directory, RA).
59. Type of house	Old 6-family house	Old 6-family house (BPD).
60. Crowding of home	4 rooms, 3 bedrooms, 7 occupants	7 occupants (BPD, 1940 directory, RA).
61. Rental (monthly average per room)	$5.00	No information.
62. Sleeping arrangements for boy	Shares room with half-brother, Arthur	Had slept in same bed with mother or aunt when 9 yrs. old; boy and half-brother sleep with stepfather (BCW, 1933).
63. Sanitary facilities	All but central heat	No information.
64. Furnishing of home	Radio, some books, pictures, lamps; fairly well furnished	Home well furnished (BCW, 1928).
65. Orderliness of home	Rather disorderly; mother seems careless in housekeeping habits	Upset but not untidy (BCW, 1928); untidy and neglected home (BCW, 1931); untidy, badly-cared-for tenement (BSA, 1934); cleaner than usual (BCW, 1934); clean and neat (CPA, 1935); not very clean (CPA, later in 1935).

(Continued)

232

Factor	Home Interview	Field Investigation [a]
66. Household routine	Some semblance of routine; not a well ordered household, however	Children brought to school very unkempt (BCW, 1932). Mother in bed all hours. Baby in filthy condition (BSA, 1935). Boy not dressed and hadn't breakfasted when called for by social worker, by appointment; then mother gave him three doughnuts and 2 cups of coffee (CPA, 1935). Mother in bed near noon with plateful of cigarette stubs beside her (BPD, 1939).
67. Summary of physical home	(to be filled in by coder)	
68. Neighborhood type	Second-class tenement district, one block removed from a business artery	Fairly good location. Family has moved frequently but generally in this same neighborhood (BPD, 1936).
69. Street life	Crowds hang around nearby corners	No information.
Barrooms	2 or 3 within 2 blocks of home	No information.
Empty lots	On street near home	No information.
Supervised indoor recreational facilities	Boys' club, and Settlement House No. 1 in neighborhood	Settlement House No. 1 in contact with boy (Y Ct., 1938).
1A. Breadwinners	Stepfather	Stepfather (BPD). (His commitment to H of C two weeks before boy's commitment not counted.)
A2. Present occupation of father or substitute	Stepfather a laborer for X Public Utility Co.	Stepfather a laborer for X Public Utility Company (BPD, 1940; RA). (See #A1.)
A3. Usual occupation of father or substitute	Stepfather working on same job for past 14 yrs., according to mother	Stepfather a laborer (1940 Boston directory, BPD); a teamster for X Public Utility Co. (Y Ct., 1938); employed by X Public Utility Co. since 1932 (BSA).
A4. Work habits of father or substitute	Stepfather has worked for X Public Utility Co. for past 14 yrs.; boy's mother states that his drinking has not interfered with his work	Stepfather working last 9 yrs. as laborer for X Public Utility Co. (BSA, RA, Y Ct.); has been laid off occasionally, probably for drunkenness (BSA); works steadily (CPA, 1935); employment record very irregular between 1927 and 1928 (RA).
A5. Usual occupation of mother or substitutes	Housewife; did factory work after birth of boy and before marriage; no work outside the home since then	Housewife (all agencies).
A6. Supervision of children	Mother says she supervised closely (this may be questioned)	Boy on street at all hours (CPA, 1935).

(Continued)

Factor	Home Interview	Field Investigation[a]
A7. Sources of family income	Stepfather's wages $28 a week	Stepfather's earnings plus his veterans' compensation. Stepfather in 1934 paid $30 a week by X Public Utility Co. (BCW); receiving veterans' compensation of about $30 a month for mental disability (RA, BCW); earns $25.95 a week and gets $30 a month from the Veterans' Clinic for "shell shock" (CPA, 1935).
A8. Average weekly income of household per person	Not determined	$4.44 ($28 a week plus $7.50 a week from veterans' compensation).
A9. Family savings	None	Family has no credit, behind in rent, and generally hard up (BSA, 1927).
A10. Planfulness in management of family income	No savings (see #9); live from day to day; mother admits she uses very little "system" in her management of her income	Mother is lazy (Veterans' Clinic to BCW, 1933). Stepfather complains of way mother spends income, but drinks a lot of it up himself (BSA, 1935).
A11. Economic condition of family at present	Marginal	Marginal. Stepfather permanent employee of X Public Utility Co. (RA, 1940).
A12. Usual economic condition of family	Marginal; received aid in early married life but none for 15 yrs. according to mother	Marginal. Family received public welfare aid only for short periods in 1927 and 1928 and not again till 1940 when emergency aid received for 3 weeks while stepfather at H of C (RA, 1927-1940). Supplementary aid granted of clothing and very occasionally a grocery order between 1926 and 1940 (BSA). Relief Agency No. 2 aided family in 1928 only, with food and clothing (BSA).
A13. Reasons for dependency of family	Not dependent (see #A12)	Family not usually dependent (see #A12).
A14. Number of agencies knowing family since marriage of parents	Not determined	At least 16 agencies, since conception of boy, as parents never married (SSI).
A15. Type of social agencies interested in family	Not determined	Straight relief, public and private (RA, BSA); family welfare (BSA, Relief Agency No. 1); child welfare (CPA, BCW); physical health (MH & H, CPA, BCW); mental health (Ment. Hosp. No. 1, to agencies); recreational (Y Ct., BCW); vocational (Voc. Aid Soc.).
A16. Age of boy at first social service contact with family	Not determined	Before birth of boy (MH & H).

(Continued)

	Factor	Home Interview	Field Investigation[a]
A17.	Moral standards of home	Stepfather a heavy drinker until recently, according to mother	Stepfather has long record for B & E, drunkenness, etc.; was committed to the H of C in August 1940 (B of Prob). Stepfather also in court for A & B on wife, and he and wife in court for neglecting the children (BCW). (See #31 on delinquency of mother and half-brother). Immoral, alcoholic maternal aunt lives with family and is a bad influence on boy (BSA, B of Prob).
A18.	Self-respect of family	Mother not greatly concerned about family reputation or boy's delinquency	A steady stream of men callers at all hours according to neighbors, landlady and stepfather (BCW, 1935). Mother begged for aid when she had just collected the stepfather's pay (BSA, 1939). Stepfather asked for aid of Relief Agency No. 2 while being paid wages by the X Public Utility Co. (BSA). Mother says the stepfather has told boy to "pick up things," *i.e.*, steal (BCW, 1934). Neighbors considered mother "everybody's wife" (CPA).
A19.	Ambition of family	Mother has no ambition; seems resigned to live from day to day without thought of the future; is making no effort to improve the home situation	No indication in agency records that family had ambition.
A20.	Plans of family for boy's future	Stepfather and mother willing to allow boy to follow through his own plans but have decided nothing for him; boy wants to complete high school education and join the Air Corps of the U.S. Army	No information.
A21.	Recreational facilities for children in the home	Facilities confined to a few "funny books" and toys; mother admits making no special effort to encourage children to spend their leisure time at home	Mother says boy has toys of his own but that even so he steals toys from others (CPA, 1935).
A22.	Provision for children to entertain friends at home	Children are allowed to have friends in the home but no special efforts made in this direction	No information.
A23.	Family group recreations	Mother states that she and boy often go to the movies together	Stepfather sometimes takes boy and half-brother to the movies, but apt to be too drunk to be a companion (BCW).
A24.	Method of control of children by father or substitute	Stepfather takes very little part in the rearing of the children, leaving the discipline of them to mother, according to her	Stepfather knocks the children about rather brutally. Boy states stepfather hit him and made him do what he wanted (BCW, 1932). Stepfather whips or deprives of supper or movies CPA, 1935.

(Continued)

	Factor	Home Interview	Field Investigation[a]
A25.	Method of control of children by mother or substitute	Physical punishment when boy younger; later, deprivation of privileges and threat of law	Mother also whips or deprives of supper or movies (CPA, 1935).
A26.	Discipline of boy by father or substitute	Stepfather uninterested in boy's welfare, on the whole; feels little sense of responsibility for his actions, according to mother	Stepfather beats boy till he screams all over the neighborhood (BSA, 1934). Stepfather alternately quiet and noisy, erratic and unpredictable, in his handling of boy (CPA, 1935).
A27.	Discipline of boy by mother or substitute	Mother says she may not have been firm enough in disciplining boy	Boy on street at all hours (CPA, 1935). Mother can't control boy (BCW to CPA, 1935).
A28.	Dominant parent	Stepfather's role in home seems to be little more than bringing home the pay check; mother makes all the decisions and assumes the responsibility; she seems more dominant	Stepfather believes three of the children are not his and refuses to feel responsible for them (BCW, 1934 and CPA, 1935). Mother insisted on keeping the maternal aunt in the house against the stepfather's wishes (CPA).
A29.	Conjugal relation of parents or substitute	Mother has "no kick coming," the stepfather a good provider and never abused her; this statement, however, was made without any enthusiasm	Mother says she and stepfather quarrel but seldom fight (BCW, 1928). Separated from Dec. 1932 to May 1933, in 1935 and again later. Mother says she returned to stepfather for financial reasons only. Both contemplated divorce from time to time (CPA, BCW, BSA). Stepfather says mother drove him to drink (BCW, 1934).
A30.	Affection of father or substitute for boy	Stepfather is indifferent; has little interest in him, takes no responsibility for his actions, has never shown boy any affection, according to mother	Stepfather really fond only of half-brother, Arthur. Stepfather resentful that boy is causing trouble (Y Ct., 1938); abusive to boy (BSA, 1934); inclined to "pick" on the boy (BCW, 1932). Stepfather willing to and did contribute to boy's board (CPA, 1935).
A31.	Affection of mother or substitute for boy	Seems genuine; is boy's regular visitor and correspondent at the Correctional School; finds excuses for his misbehavior	Half-brother, Arthur, is mother's favorite also and boy feels this. Mother fears having her children taken from her; gave boy a bicycle; requested boy be returned to her from foster home (CPA, 1935).
A32.	Relations of siblings to boy	Younger brother looks up to boy; no antagonism, according to mother	Boy is fond of half-brother, Arthur (BCW, 1935).
A33.	Household duties of boy	Only occasional duties, no regularly assigned tasks; boy has not had to feel responsible for anything at home	Mother sends boy to store occasionally (CPA).
A34.	Potentials for culture conflict in home	Inapplicable, because parents and boy native-born	Inapplicable as parents and boy native-born.
A35.	Culture conflict in home	Inapplicable (see #A34)	Inapplicable (see #A34).

(Continued)

Factor	Home Interview	Field Investigation [a]
A36. Evidences of cultural refinement	Home lacks evidence of good taste or love of beauty; stepfather and mother show no indication of aesthetic appreciation	None (see #64, #65, #66).
A37. Cohesiveness of family group	Stepfather is chief factor in family's lack of unity because of his drinking habits and lack of affection for the children; home is more than "just a place to hang your hat" chiefly because of the mutual attachment between mother and the children	Stepfather and maternal aunt fight "like cats and dogs," yet mother insists on keeping aunt in the home (CPA). Stepfather and mother in court for neglecting children, but children were left in their care after a warning by the judge (BCW, 1935). Stepather believes two of the other children are not his and refuses to feel responsible for them (CPA, BCW). Mother does not want to lose any of the children; no indication of hostility between the children (all agencies).
A38. Birth and infancy of boy	Weighed 6 lbs. at birth; good health in first 2 yrs.; all other items negative, according to mother	A full-term baby (CPA). Normal delivery, no complications (MH & H, 1925; CPA). Breast-fed till 7 mos. Convulsions twice, one at 6 mos. and one at 1 yr. (CPA). Treated for a mild form of epilepsy in OPD of Ment. Hosp. No. 1 in 1934 (BPD). Had tonsils and adenoids removed in 1935 (PQ Hosp. to CPA). Walked at 13 mos. and talked at 15 mos. (CPA).
A39. Contagious diseases	Only contagious disease was a mild case of measles at 10 yrs. according to mother	Scarlet fever in 1934 (school, BCW).
A40, A41. Specific susceptibilities	Frequent chest colds since recovery from pneumonia at 3 yrs. "One lung weak since"; has had boils at the Correctional School, none at home; all other items negative, according to mother	Frequent colds, croup, and pneumonia once before 10 yrs. (CPA, 1935). Infrequent headaches and dizziness, sometimes refuses breakfast (Ment. Hosp. No. 1 to CPA). Enuresis at 11 yrs. in foster home (CPA, 1936). Boy nervous, has nightmares after seeing thrilling movies and doesn't sleep well (PQ Hosp. to CPA, 1935). Nervous, smokes a lot; complete physical examination negative except for nervousness (RS Hosp. to BCW, 1934). History indicates mild form of epilepsy (Ment. Hosp. No. 1 to BCW, 1934). Restless and very emotional with violent outbursts of temper (Ment. Hosp. No. 1 to BPD, 1936). One lung "weak" (BPD, 1940). Mother says boy started school late because of ill health (BCW, 1932).

(Continued)

Factor	Home Interview	Field Investigation[a]
A42, A43. Bad habits (and age began)	*Smoking:* since 13 or 14 yrs. — at home since 14 yrs.; *Training:* "once or twice" since 14 yrs.; *Stealing rides and truck hopping:* since 12-13 yrs.; *Stubbornness:* often disobedient and argumentative with parents; *Impulsive stealing* (when arrested)	Mother says boy unmanageable since infancy (CPA). Mother says boy set fire in the house only once, age 8 (BCW, 1933). Stepfather complains that maternal aunt has taught boy (age 10) bad sex practices (BCW, 1935). Mother says boy stole a bus ride to Wellesley (BCW, 1935). *Smoking:* age 10 (RS Hosp. to BCW, police to BCW). *Runaway from foster home:* age 11 (CPA). *Truanting:* age 10 (CPA, school). *Impulsive lying:* age 8 (school to BCW). *Vile language:* age 10 (neighbors to BCW). *Pugnacity:* struck girls on street, age 9 (BCW); threatened schoolmate with knife, age 12 (CPA); attacked boy with knife, age 11 (BPD); *Destructive mischief:* broke many windows in houses and autos, age 8 (landlady to BCW). *Tantrums:* wild outbursts of temper, age 10 (Ment. Hosp. No. 1 to BPD). *Late hours:* on the street at all hrs., age 10 (CPA). *Impulsive stealing:* from stores, age 8 (school to BCW); stealing from other boys in club, age 8 (S.H. No. 2 to BCW). *Planful stealing:* age 9 (Ment. Hosp. No. 1 to BCW); age 13 (Y Ct.). *Indecent exposure:* age 10 (girl accused boy, BCW).
A44. Agreement between statement of boy and parents	(to be filled in by coder)	
A45. Frequency of movie attendance	Once or twice a week	No information.
A46. Play places	Own neighborhood, distant neighborhood streets, settlement house; mother states boy spent most of his leisure time at Settlement House No. 1	Began to attend S.H. No. 2 toward end of 1932 (BCW, 1933). Attending S.H. No. 1 (Y Ct., 1938).
A47. Church or Sunday School	Occasionally	No information.
A48. Nature of companionships	Few friends; delinquent, younger boys	Boy tended to bad associations (school, age 15).
A49-A52. Agreement between statement of boy and parents	(to be filled in by coder)	

(Continued)

Factor	Home Interview	Field Investigation[a]
A53, A54. Family's reason for boy's conduct	Although boy has been stubborn and hard to handle at times, mother is quite satisfied with his behavior at home; she blames circumstances surrounding each of his delinquencies rather than boy himself or home conditions; does not consider boy in need of correction or adjustment and finds excuses for all the trouble he has gotten into in the community	Mother says boy can't withstand temptation; he is sorry after he misbehaves (BCW, 1935).

SCHOOL HISTORY[a]

Factor	Field Investigation[b]
A56. Age started school	6 yrs. (chronological list of school experiences based on ADP card from Medway, Mass.).
A57. Number of years in school	Between 9 and 10 yrs. (chronological list of school exeperiences based on record cards from Medway, Canton, F School and BPD).
A58. Grade attained	Grade 8 (F School records).
A59. Grades repeated	Grade 1 and grade 5 (sources same as #A57).
A60. Grades skipped	None (sources same as #A57).
A61. Amount of retardation	2 yrs. (see Boston Public Schools Scale).
A62. Attendance in special classes Attendance in Disciplinary Day School	None (sources same as #A57). None (sources same as #A57).
A63. Number of school experiences	10 (sources same as #57), not counting correctional school.
A64. A65. Scholarship in last full year	A in Physical Education and Hygiene; B's or C's in Reading, Literature, English, Spelling, Penmanship, Arithmetic, Geography, and History; D's or E's in Music, Drawing, Conduct (yellow sheet school records).
A66. Nature of first misbehavior in school	Truancy, unruliness in class, and stealing (records of B school, Boston).
A67. Age at which first school misbehavior occurred	10 yrs. (records of B School, Boston).
A68. Grade in which first misbehavior occurred	Grade 5 (records of B School, Boston).
A69. Age truancy started	Grade 5 (records of B School, Boston).
A70. Frequency of truancy	Occasional at first, later persistent (sources same as #A57).

[a] The home interviewer obtained no information on school history. This was done entirely through field investigation.

[b] Includes correspondence.

(Continued)

Factor	Field Investigation[b]
A71. Teacher's estimate of char- A74. acteristics of boy	Stealing, obscene notes and talk, truancy, cheating, unreliableness, lack of interest in work, laziness, smoking, unhappiness, depression, easy discouragement, carelessness in work, inattention, slovenliness in appearance, suspiciousness, thoughtlessness (8th grade teacher of F School).
A75. Summary of school behavior	(to be filled in by coder).
A76. Dropped from study	
A77. Reasons for retardation	Lack of interest plus many changes of schools (Principal of F School).
A78. Reason for truancy	Influence of bad companions and lack of interest in school (Principal of F School).
A79. Adjustment to schoolmates	Tended to bad associations (Principal of F School).
A80. Participation in extracurricular activities	Did not participate (Principal of F School).
Boy's outstanding problems	Boy's problems result from home conditions plus his own attitude toward life; family careless and inadequate; stepfather drinks; boy is slippery, untrustworthy, and has poor associations (Principal of F School).

PART II • SUMMARY OF INVESTIGATION OF HENRY W

FROM 16TH TO 31ST BIRTHDAY

In July 1941 Henry was paroled from a correctional school and went to live in a foster home in rural Massachusetts. He was viewed regularly by a supervisor from the Boys' Parole Department of the Massachusetts Department of Correction, who reported favorably on his progress. He attended the local public school, where he was in the ninth grade, and played on the local basketball team.

In October 1941, because of his good record in the school, the community, and the foster home, Henry was allowed to visit his own home, which was now in Roxbury. Once back in his old environment he was loath to return to the foster home and asked permission to remain with his mother, stepfather, maternal aunt, and half-brothers. This request was granted by the Boys' Parole Department because investigation revealed that the home conditions were better than previously: the stepfather was working regularly, and neither he nor Henry's mother was drinking as much.

Since by now he was almost 17 years old, Henry was no longer legally obliged to return to school and refused to do so. Hence his schooling was formally terminated in October 1941. Although free of classes, he did not feel obliged to work. According to his own statement to the investigator, he spent part of his spare time in his favorite sports — gym exercises and swimming — at a settlement house, where he also played basketball, badminton, and table tennis. Except for minor misconduct which did not bring him into conflict with the law, Henry — despite his record of unemployment — remained a satisfactory parolee.

Pressured by his parole supervisor and his mother to find work, Henry tried to get a job but was unsuccessful. So he decided to enlist in the Civilian Conservation Corps as a laborer in January 1942. He remained in the Corps until April, when he was given an honorable discharge and went to a State forestry camp. While in the camp he temporarily dropped the name of his stepfather and assumed that of his own father. He rejoined his mother, and after three weeks of loafing, went to work as a laborer for a National Youth Administration farm project in May 1942; but two months later he was dismissed from the project on suspicion of stealing clothing.

Again Henry returned to his mother's home, and at the end of July 1942 he secured work as a messenger boy for Western Union. But within a few weeks he decided to quit work and leave home to find another job. When he reached Washington, D.C., he told a welfare agent for transients that he had "bummed" his way to New York City, Raleigh, Miami, and Washington, where he was picked up by police as a vagrant. With the help of an agency for transients and a Boston agency, he was returned to Boston. When asked how he had obtained enough money to support himself, he made vague references to odd jobs and restaurant work.

Again goaded by his mother to get a job, he enlisted (in October 1942) in the United States Navy, remaining there for eighteen months. The Navy records show that during this enlistment he was twice absent without leave — the first time in 1943, when he disappeared for ten days, was picked up by the Navy Shore Patrol, and was placed on probation for six months. A month after the second absence (March 1944), he was given a bad conduct discharge. He admitted heavy drinking episodes and occasional gambling for high stakes during leaves.

Within two weeks of his discharge from the Navy, Henry secured work with a Boston drug company, where he was assigned to the shipping room as a laborer at $31 a week. In July 1944 dissatisfied with this low pay and anxious to make use of his Navy experience, Henry joined the United States Maritime Service and was given the rating of able-bodied seaman. Between boat trips he returned to his mother's home. His excessive drinking continued, both at sea and at home. Henry soon began to experience difficulty in finding ship asignments, so in January 1945 he took a job as a helper on an express truck. He worked at this for about two weeks, and then transferred to a job in the warehouse, where he was considered a satisfactory worker; his weekly wages ranged from $35 to $38. He held these positions from January 14 to March 20, 1945, and then left of his own accord. He loafed for about three weeks, in the course of which, he told the investigator, he and some delinquent companions stole a car and started to drive to New York City, where he planned to rejoin the Maritime Service. But the youths were apprehended a short distance from Boston, and (after a short stay in a local jail) in May 1945 Henry was given an indefinite sentence of five years in the Massachusetts Reformatory.

While at the Reformatory Henry was brought before the Superior Court on charges of robbery and assault and battery with intent to rob which had occurred while he was still in the Navy. The offense involved an assault on a

State Department employee, who lost an eye as a result. In November 1945 Henry received two concurrent sentences to the Massachusetts State Prison for nine to twelve years and nine to ten years, to be served "from and after" the five-year Reformatory sentence. In January 1946 the Appellate Division of the Superior Court increased the "from and after" sentence to twelve to fifteen years, to be "served forthwith and notwithstanding the Massachusetts Reformatory sentence." Therefore, on January 26, 1946, Henry was re-sentenced and committed to the State Prison, to which he was transferred from the Reformatory. In February 1949, he was transferred to the State Prison Colony.

In January 1954, after serving eight years and eight months, Henry was paroled and allowed to return home. Almost immediately he shipped out as an able-bodied seaman in the Maritime Service, where he earned $317 per month. Henry worked regularly and sent periodic letters or reports to his parole officer from Japan, Korea, Venezuela, and Panama. About November 1954, however, he reported that shipping was slow and he asked to be allowed to get a driver's license so that he could work ashore as a truck driver in the Boston area. When the license was denied him Henry decided to try to get back into the Maritime Service, despite the slow shipping. In order to return to New York City, where he sought a billet, he stole a car on December 10, 1954, but was apprehended by the Boston police and lodged in a local jail pending trial. While in jail, on December 16, 1954, he attempted suicide and was sent to a state hospital for observation. He was diagnosed as "without psychosis" and was therefore returned to the jail.

On February 20, 1955, all the charges connected with the car stealing were filed and Henry was returned to the State Prison as a parole violator; he was still there on his 31st birthday (January 16, 1956).

PART III • SOURCES OF INFORMATION —

JANUARY 1941–JANUARY 1956

The first step in our follow-up investigation was to clear this case with the Social Service Index of Boston. Other sources of information used were directories and telephone books of Boston and Bradwood; interviews with Henry and his mother; and an interview with a cousin of Henry's father, held in an effort to locate him. Inquiry was the next made of each of the agencies, either by a personal interview or by examination of the recorded information pertaining to Henry W.

Armed Forces Information Service

On the records of the draft board, Henry was reported as having enlisted in the Navy at the Receiving Station in Boston on 10/1/42, under the name of his real father, which he exhibited on his birth record. He took this action so that the recruitment office would be unable to trace his juvenile record.

The draft board had information that Henry was given a bad conduct discharge from the Navy at Norfolk, Virginia on 4/28/44. His offenses in the Navy were as follows:

1. Absent without leave, 3/2/43-3/12/43. Sentence: six months probation.
2. Missing muster, shirking duty, and using obscene language. Sentence: five days' solitary confinement on bread and water.
3. Having emergency flashlight. Sentence: four hours of extra duty.
4. Using obscene and profane language. Sentence: three days on bread and water.
5. Shirking duty. Sentence: five days on bread and water.
6. Absent without leave, 3/20/44-3/28/44. Sentence: bad conduct discharge.

The records of the Armed Forces Information Service revealed that on 5/17/44 he registered as a bad-conduct Navy discharge. He stated that he had completed the first year at a Boston high school; he was employed as a shipper by a drug company at $31 per week; he had passed the physical examination for the United States Maritime Service. He listed his mother as a dependent.

Welfare Agency for Transients

In September 1942 the Washington branch office of this agency reported that Henry was stranded there and needed funds for transportation to Boston. The agency learned that Henry was on parole from a juvenile correctional institution in Massachusetts and that if he returned to Massachusetts he would probably be surrendered as a parole violator. The agency's Boston representative found Henry's mother unable and unwilling to help him, and described her as difficult, aggressive, and fault-finding. Relief Agency 1 authorized Henry's return to Boston at its expense, so he was brought back, was met by his parole officer, and was allowed to continue on parole.

Relief Agency 1

Henry's mother came to this agency in April 1942 to request financial aid. She stated that she had recently moved to 26 C Street in Roxbury. The agency gave her a grocery order to tide her over. In September 1942 the agency refused the mother's request for a food order because Henry's maternal aunt, Florence, was living in the house and was receiving a pension of $12 a month, as her father was a Spanish War veteran; and also because Henry was in Florida. Eventually, the agency gave the mother a $2 food order.

In November 1942 the mother again visited the agency to seek additional aid. Relief Agency 1 was at this time giving her $6.83 weekly. The mother stated that Henry was in the Navy but was not sending her any money. The maternal aunt was still with her. A $2 food order was given her and on 12/6/42, a $3 food order.

On 3/5/43 the mother returned to the agency and asked for another food order. She informed a social worker that she had heard from Henry's commanding officer that he had deserted the Navy. A half-brother was reported to be working in a hotel. The mother said that she had been legally separated from the stepfather since January 1943 and that he was in a state hospital for alcoholics. The family income, she stated, was $15 a week for five people. She was given a $4 food order and shoes for the children.

On 7/1/45 Henry's mother sought help from the Red Cross. Henry's half-brother Arthur had enlisted in the Armed Forces on 3/18/45 and was sending an allotment. (Henry on this date was at the Massachusetts Reformatory.) The mother was also reported as having received soldiers' relief. She informed the Red Cross that she owed money for groceries and that the rent of her apartment was $23 a month. The Red Cross referred Henry's mother to Relief Agency 1 and she was given $14.

Massachusetts Department of Correction

In February 1950 the records of the Massachusetts Department of Correction were consulted by a field worker. They stated that Henry had been in the State Prison Colony since 2/19/49 and would be eligible for parole on 1/27/54. He was still single. Henry was visited at the Prison Colony by his mother and half-siblings.

The Department of Correction authorities confirmed that Henry had received a bad-conduct discharge from the Navy on 4/28/44 and that he had served in the Maritime Service for six months. Prior to his Navy and Maritime service, he had been in the Civilian Conservation Corps for less than three months and had been employed as a trucker's helper for a brief period. The Department also verified the fact that Henry completed the ninth grade at a Boston public school. At the Massachusetts State Prison his initial medical examination on 1/27/46 was negative.

The Department of Correction records further stated that while in the Maritime Service Henry worked on several vessels sailing from Boston or New York. In 1944 he was reported as an able-bodied seaman for the M. Steamship Line in Boston. He drank moderately but denied using drugs. He admitted having been arrested on his way to New York to rejoin the Maritime Service in May 1945.

On 4/28/46 a Department of Correction worker reported that she had talked with Henry's mother in Dorchester. During this interview, the mother asserted that the stepfather had worked steadily for the City of Boston, but that he drank heavily. They had separated in January 1943 and he had not supported the family since that time. All of Henry's half-siblings were living: one brother had entered the Army in March 1945, and the younger brothers were still in school. The mother was working in a chocolate factory. The worker described the home as a very poor tenement house located in a disadvantaged district. The interior was neat and well furnished and looked as though the occupants were interested in its maintenance. The mother said that she was receiving an allotment of $79 per month from Henry's half-brother.

According to the Department of Correction records for 1950–1955, Henry was in Massachusetts penal institutions from May 5, 1945, until January 27, 1954, at which time he was released on parole from the State Prison Colony. While there he completed some high school courses by correspondence, received high marks, and had an excellent attitude toward his school work. In December 1951 he was rated as a below-average worker in the shop, but the following

June he was considered of average efficiency in maintenance work. In February 1953 he was transferred to the farm gang, where he apparently remained until his release.

In December 1952 there seemed to be strong values in the family ties. While in the State Prison Colony Henry wrote regularly to his mother and received regular visits from his half-brothers.

In January 1954 Henry was released on parole to his mother in Dorchester, where the family lived in five rooms on the second floor of an old three-decker in a run-down area. With the mother were the aunt, and Henry's two half-brothers, Kenneth and William.

Before Henry's release from the State Prison Colony a letter had been received from an auto wash company promising Henry a job. However, after his release, Henry returned to the Boston office of the Maritime Service and signed up as an able-bodied seaman aboard a steamer bound for the Far East. His salary was $317 per month, with board and room. He made an allotment to his mother of $50 every two weeks. On 3/8/54 he reported from Yokohama. Five weeks later he reported from Pusan, Korea, that he had been paid off with the sum of $648. On 5/5/54 he reported that he was working on a tanker plying between Venezuela and Panama, at a salary of $355 per month. In July 1954 he reported from Venezuela, and two months later he was en route to Tampa, Florida, after having returned home for a brief visit in September. In November 1954 he reported that he was on another steamer and was working regularly for the Maritime Service.

Late in November 1954 Henry returned to Boston and asked his parole officer for permission to get a driver's license so that he could get a job as a truck driver for the rest of the winter, since shipping was "slow." On December 10, 1954, he was arrested for using an automobile unlawfully and for driving after his license had been suspended, and was confined in a local jail awaiting trial. While there he attempted to commit suicide, because he was "disgusted with the stupid act" that had caused his arrest and because he had broken faith with people, including his girl friend.

Henry appeared in a municipal court, but his case was held over so that he could be sent to a state hospital for observation following his suicide attempt. In January 1955 the hospital reported to the court that Henry was unreliable, impulsive, and antisocial; it gave its diagnosis as "without psychosis; personality disorder; sociopathic personality-disturbance; antisocial reaction."

On 2/20/55 Henry was returned to the Massachusetts State Prison as a parole violator. While there he was rated as an average worker in the paint shop and on the farm gang. He was a voracious reader and was interested in sports, the prison's education committee, football, and field events. He attended no religious services. On 11/15/55 his work rating was "below average," and the notation was made that he "would rather sleep than work."

In January 1956 (just before his 31st birthday) Henry's request for transfer to a forestry camp was denied. He claimed that his record, which was the basis for the denial, was misleading; he insisted that his four juvenile arrests should not have been on the record, and that his Navy court record was not a criminal one. He concluded, therefore, that he was a "first offender."

Relief Agency 2

In a further effort to locate Henry's father, a field worker visited Relief Agency 2, where the paternal grandparents were known. On the suggestion of the agency's social worker, the field worker visited a nephew of the paternal grandfather at his home. This nephew said that he knew nothing definite about Henry's father, but that he was supposed to have ben working as a mechanic in California during World War II. At another time a relative told the nephew that the father had been seen in New York City, but he could not be located at the time of death of either of the paternal grandparents (in 1942 and 1950).

Massachusetts Bureau of Vital Statistics

The date of the stepfather's death was recorded by this source as 8/29/47 at the Boston City Hospital. His last address was in Dorchester, where he was born. His age was given as 54. He was listed as a laborer but was an employee of a restaurant chain at the time of death. The cause of death was given as cirrhosis of the liver and alcoholism. Henry's mother was the informant.

Massachusetts Department of Mental Health

The records of this department stated that following a suicide attempt in jail while awaiting court sentence, Henry was committed to a State hospital on December 16, 1954, and was discharged from there on January 22, 1955, and was returned to the municipal court. A diagnosis was given of antisocial reaction, personality disorders, primary behavior disorders, and conduct disturbance.

Interview with Henry's Mother

Henry's mother and maternal aunt were living at 15A N Street, Dorchester, at the end of the second follow-up period. This section was probably one of the worst in Dorchester. A coal company was nearby, and railroad tracks ran in the rear of the brick blocks which lined the upper part of the street. The mother and aunt occupied part of the second floor of one of these blocks. The block was rapidly becoming a slum. The house needed repairs inside and out. The ceiling and floors were dirty and cluttered. The same was true of the living room, which had a dirty and worn linoleum; the overstuffed chairs were protected by faded slip-covers. There were no curtains on any of the windows, and the Venetian blinds were dirty. The whole impression was that of a drab, bare, and unattractive apartment.

The mother, who was in her early fifties, wore a soiled housedress. Her hair was carelessly pulled behind her ears, and she gave the impression of being worn out by worry and trouble. During the interview the mother spoke dispassionately of Henry, but was careful to give what she thought was a good report of his activities. She did not discount some of his earlier criminal activities, although she claimed that the revocation of his parole at the end of 1954 was unjustified and unnecessary. She exhibited an Internal Revenue Service withholding slip in order to prove that he had been working fairly steadily. She pointed out the souvenirs which Henry had sent home during his trips with the USMS, and spoke in an offhand manner about his obligations to her. Between his 25th and 31st birthdays, Henry had been at large for less than 11 months, during which time he was in the Maritime Service and visited the Orient, South America, and Panama.

The mother described Henry as weak and suggestible, despite his relatively good intelligence; when with his delinquent friends, he was sure to get into trouble. She had encouraged him to go to sea in order to avoid associating with them. When asked about his education, the mother asserted that he was always "sending away for courses in electronics, but he never goes through with any of them that I know of."

When the subject of Henry's religion came up, his mother said that he is a Protestant, but that when he was at home on Sundays he sometimes went to a Roman Catholic church in the neighborhood.

All in all, the mother seemed fairly reliable in her statements and was co-operative — at least on the surface.

From already recorded sources of information and from data gathered by the case collator (through correspondence) and by the field investigator, the following summaries were compiled:

1. Chronological summary of Henry's whereabouts
2. Summary of Henry's schooling
3. Summary of Henry's employment
4. Henry's criminal history
5. Criminal history of Henry's close relatives.

1. Chronological Summary of Henry's Whereabouts. January 1944–January 1956 (including breaks in home life and departures from home)

Deteri-orated Area	Whereabouts	With Whom Living	Dates	Reason for Change
—	Correctional School	Correctional School	1/16/41–7/23/41	Left Correctional School for foster home
No	Rural foster home	Foster mother	7/23/41–10/24/41	Home on visit and remained there
Yes	26 C St., Roxbury	Mother, step-father, maternal aunt, half-siblings	10/25/41–1/18/42	Enrolled in Civilian Conservation Corps
No	Civilian Conservation Corps	Other camp workers	1/18/42–4/3/42	Honorable discharge
No	State Forestry Camp	Other workers	4/3/42–4/21/42	Returned home
Yes	26 C St., Roxbury	Mother, maternal aunt, and half-siblings	4/21/42–5/12/42	To work at National Youth Administration Project
No	National Youth Administration Project	Other workers	5/12/42–7/10/42	Discharged for stealing

(Continued)

247

Deteri-orated Area	Whereabouts	With Whom Living	Dates	Reason for Change
Yes	26 C St., Roxbury	Mother, maternal aunt, and half-siblings	7/10/42–8/10/42	Left home "to find work" and violated parole
—	On Runaway — in N.Y. City, Raleigh, N.C., Washington, D.C., Miami, Fla.	Alone	8/10/42–10/1/42	Returned to Boston via Washington Police Dept. and Welfare Agency for Transients
Yes	26 C St., Roxbury	Mother, maternal aunt, and half-siblings	10/1/42–10/20/42	Enlisted in Navy
—	U. S. Navy	In Navy	10/20/42–4/28/44	Bad-conduct discharge
Yes	15A N St., Dorchester	Mother maternal aunt, and half-siblings	4/28/44–7/31/44	To enroll in USMS
No	USMS	USMS	7/31/44–1/14/45	Resigned from USMS
Yes	15A N St., Dorchester	Mother, maternal aunt, and half-siblings	1/14/45–3/20/45	Left home
—	Stealing cars in Massachusetts, in various towns, and trips in stolen cars	Two other car thieves	3/20/45–5/5/45	Arrested and jailed
—	County jail; held for Superior Court	In jail	5/5/45–5/22/45	Committed to Mass. Reformatory
—	Reformatory	In reformatory	5/22/45–1/26/46	Committed to State Prison on new sentence and transferred
—	State Prison	In state prison	1/26/46–2/19/49	Transferred to State Prison Colony
—	State Prison Colony	In state prison colony	2/19/49–1/27/54	Paroled
Yes	15A N St., Dorchester, between trips	Mother, maternal aunt, and half-siblings	1/27/54–12/10/54	Arrested and jailed
—	County jail	In jail	12/10/54–2/20/55	Committed to State Prison
—	State Prison	In prison	2/20/55–1/16/56	31st birthday

2. Summary of Henry's Schooling: January 1941–January 1956

Academic

Rural school in Massachusetts, 9th grade, 1941.

No further academic schooling while subject was in the community, but some academic courses while at State Prison Colony. No further academic schooling according to Armed Forces Information Service.

Vocational

Subject took a State-sponsored correspondence course in navigation while at the Massachusetts Reformatory in 1945. Took a course in practical electricity at State Prison Colony in 1953.

3. Summary of Henry's Employment since Age 16

Dates	Employment
1/18/42–4/3/42	Civilian Conservation Camp in Western Massachusetts: satisfactory work; given honorable discharge
5/12/42–7/10/42	NYA farm project: dismissed when authorities found clothing missing
7/20/42–8/10/42	Messenger boy: left employment — did not like work.
10/20/42–4/28/44	Armed Forces
May 1944	Shipper for U Drug Company
7/31/44–1/14/45	USMS as able-bodied seaman
1/14/45 3/20/45	Trucker's helper for storage warehouse company: left of his own accord
2/3/54–11/22/54	Shipped out through the National Maritime Union and was employed as able-bodied seaman on tankers

4. Criminal History of Henry W: January 1941–January 1956

Date	Court	Charge	Disposition	Dates of Correctional Experiences
5/5/45	Municipal	Larceny	Reformatory	5/22/45–1/26/46
1/26/46	Superior	Robbery and assault and battery with intent to rob	State Prison	1/26/46–1/27/54; Paroled until 1/26/57

Date	Court	Charge	Disposition	Dates of Correctional Experiences
12/10/54	Municipal	1) Using auto without authority 2) Operating auto after right to do so suspended 3) Operating to endanger	Held over	
2/20/55	Superior	Above three counts	Filed 2/20/55	
2/20/55	Superior	Violation of parole	State Prison	2/20/55–31st birthday

5. Summary of Criminal History of Family: January 1941–January 1956[a]

Family Member	Date	Court	Offense	Disposition
Stepfather	1/1/42	Y District	Drunkenness	Filed
	4/13/42	A District	Drunkenness	Filed
				Surrendered on an earlier drunk charge; committed to State Farm
				Paroled 4/12/43
	6/11/43	W District	Drunkenness	Filed
				Parole revoked 7/9/43; committed to State Farm
				Paroled 4/27/44
Arthur	4/25/42	W District	Breaking and entering and larceny	Probation to 5/5/43
	2/15/47	W District	Drunkenness	Filed
	6/7/47	W District	Drunkenness	Released
	9/3/47	W District	Assault and battery	3 months House of Correction, suspended
			Malicious destruction	Filed

[a] Except for those of the stepfather and one half-brother, no additional entries were made on the records secured from the Massachusetts Board of Probation.

PART IV

DETAILED FINDINGS FOR FOLLOW-UP PERIODS

Table No.[b]	Factor	Information for First Follow-Up Period[a]	Information for Second Follow-Up Period
IV-1	Number of sources of information	Nineteen	Six
IV-2	With whom interviews held	Subject; mother; cousin; agencies; records	Mother; records
V-1	Whereabouts on 17th birthday	26 C St., Roxbury, Mass.	—
	Whereabouts on 22nd birthday	State Prison	—
V-2	With whom living on 17th birthday	Mother, stepfather, maternal aunt, and half-siblings	—
	With whom living on 22nd birthday	Inapplicable, as in penal institution	—

[a] Some of the information for this period covers the 17-25 age-span, whereas other items deal with the 20-25 age-span. This is clear in the chapter texts.

[b] The Roman numerals refer to chapters in which the data on the cases were presented.

(Continued)

Table No.[b]	Factor	Information for First Follow-Up Period[a]	Information for Second Follow-Up Period
V-3	Whereabouts at end of period	State Prison Colony	State Prison
V-4	With whom living at end of period	Inapplicable, as in penal institution	Inapplicable, as in penal institution
V-5	Departures from home	Two	Two
V-6	Nature of departures from home during period	To wander about; to correctional institution	To sea; to correctional institution
V-7	Frequency of moves	Inapplicable, as not in community for 12 consecutive months	Inapplicable, as not in community for 12 consecutive months
V-8	Nature of mobility	Inapplicable, as not in community for 12 consecutive months	Inapplicable, as not in community for 12 consecutive months
V-9	Kind of neighborhood in which resident at end of period	Inapplicable, as in penal institution	Inapplicable, as in penal institution
V-10	Time spent in underprivileged areas	Inapplicable, as not in community for 12 consecutive months	Inapplicable, as not in community for 12 consecutive months
V-11	Evaluation of neighborhood influences surrounding home at end of period	Inapplicable, as in penal institution	Inapplicable, as in penal institution
V-12	Nature of poor neighborhood influences surrounding home at end of period	Inapplicable, as in penal institution	Inapplicable, as in penal institution
V-13	Size of household of which a member at end of period	Inapplicable, as in penal institution	Inapplicable, as in penal institution
V-14	Crowding of home at end of period	Inapplicable, as in penal institution	Inapplicable, as in penal institution
V-15	Furnishings of home in which living at end of period	Inapplicable, as in penal institution	Inapplicable, as in penal institution
V-16	Orderliness and cleanliness of home at end of period	Inapplicable, as in penal institution	Inapplicable, as in penal institution
V-17	Household routine during period	Inapplicable, as not in community for 12 consecutive months	Inapplicable, as not in community for 12 consecutive months
VI-1	Physical health at end of period	Good	Good
VI-2	Severe illness or physical disabilities during period	None	None
VI-3	Type of mental pathology during period	Psychoneurotic	Psychopathic
VI-4	Social inefficiency	Mild	—
VII-1	Age first left school	16 years, 9 months	—

(Continued)

Table No.[b]	Factor	Information for First Follow-Up Period[a]	Information for Second Follow-Up Period
VII-2	Age at final academic attainment	Unknown	—
VII-3	Attitude toward further academic studies at end of period	Attended school at the State Prison Colony; 10th grade English, history, civics, mathematics	—
VII-4	Major reason for stopping school	Own volition	—
VII-5	Educational attainment end of period	Tenth grade	—
VII-6	Special skills, trades, vocations, or professions acquired during period	Some	—
VII-7	Highest skills, trades, vocations, and professions attained during period	Able-bodied seaman rating in USMS	—
VII-8	How special skills acquired	USN and USMS experience; correspondence course in navigation at correctional institution	—
VII-9	Utilization of special skills	Very briefly in USMS	—
VII-10	Attitude toward further specialized training at end of period	Some interest	—
VIII-1	Civil condition of subject at end of period	Single	Single
VIII-2	Number of marriages	None	None
VIII-3	Age of subject at first marriage	Inapplicable, as subject still single	Inapplicable, as subject still single
VIII-4	Age of wife at marriage	Inapplicable, as subject still single	Inapplicable, as subject still single
VIII-5	Length of courtship	Inapplicable, as subject still single	Inapplicable, as subject still single
VIII-6	Forced marriage	Inapplicable, as subject still single	Inapplicable, as subject still single
VIII-7	Character of wife with whom marriage contracted	Inapplicable, as subject still single	Inapplicable, as subject still single
VIII-8	Relationship between subject and wife	Inapplicable, as subject still single	Inapplicable, as subject still single
VIII-9	Assumption of marital responsibilities	Inapplicable, as subject still single	Inapplicable, as subject still single
VIII-10	Wife's employment	Inapplicable, as subject still single	Inapplicable, as subject still single
VIII-11	Number of children at end of period	Inapplicable, as subject still single	Inapplicable, as subject still single
VIII-12	Legitimacy of children born during period	Inapplicable, as subject still single	Inapplicable, as subject still single

(*Continued*)

Table No.[b]	Factor	Information for First Follow-Up Period[a]	Information for Second Follow-Up Period
VIII-13	Whereabouts of children at end of period	Inapplicable, as subject still single	Inapplicable, as subject still single
VIII-14	Cohesiveness of family unit	Inapplicable, as not in community for 12 consecutive months	Inapplicable, as not in community for 12 consecutive months
IX-1	Age subject first began to work	17 years	—
IX-2	Highest degree of industrial skill attained	Semi-skilled; able-bodied seaman in USMS	—
IX-3	Work habits	Inapplicable, as not in community for 12 consecutive months	—
IX-4	Industrial training provided by correctional institutions	None	—
IX-5	Use of industrial training provided by correctional institutions	Inapplicable, as none provided	—
IX-6	Reason for unemployment occurring during last three years of period	Inapplicable, as in penal institution	Committed to penal institution
IX-7	Length of employment on most recent job	Inapplicable	8 months
IX-8	Efforts to improve occupational status	Inapplicable, as in penal institution	Inapplicable, as in penal institution
IX-9	Amount of weekly income at end of period	Inapplicable, as in penal institution	Inapplicable, as in penal institution
IX-10	Type of dependents at end of period	None	None
IX-11	Contribution to support of dependents at end of period	Inapplicable	Inapplicable
IX-12	Illicit occupations during period	Inapplicable, as not in community for 12 consecutive months	—
X-1	Usual economic condition during period	Inapplicable, as not in community for 12 consecutive months	Inapplicable, as not in community for 12 consecutive months
X-2	Comparison of economic conditions during period with economic conditions during childhood	Inapplicable, as not in community for 12 consecutive months	Inapplicable, as not in community for 12 consecutive months
X-3	Value of property acquired	Inapplicable, as not in community for 12 consecutive months	—
X-4	By whom insurance paid	Inapplicable, as not in community for 12 consecutive months	—
X-5	Indebtedness during period	Inapplicable, as not in community for 12 consecutive months	—

(Continued)

Table No.[b]	Factor	Information for First Follow-Up Period[a]	Information for Second Follow-Up Period
X-6	Size of debts	Inapplicable, as not in community for 12 consecutive months	—
X-7	Social services required during period	Inapplicable, as not in community for 12 consecutive months	Yes
X-8	Nature of social services	Inapplicable, as not in community for 12 consecutive months	Mental health
X-9	Number of dependents at end of period	None	None
X-10	Trend in economic conditions during last three years of period	Inapplicable, as not in community for 12 consecutive months	Inapplicable, as not in community for 12 consecutive months
X-11	Extent of self-support at end of period	Inapplicable, as in penal institution	Inapplicable, as in penal institution
XI-1	Amount of leisure time spent in home during period	Inapplicable, as not in community for 12 consecutive months	—
XI-2	Suitability of home for leisure time activity	Inapplicable, as not in community for 12 consecutive months	—
XI-3	Family group recreation	Inapplicable, as not in community for 12 consecutive months	—
XI-4	Nature of leisure activities at home	Inapplicable, as not in community for 12 consecutive months	—
XI-5	Other places of recreation	Inapplicable, as not in community for 12 consecutive months	—
XI-6	Type of companions	Inapplicable, as not in community for 12 consecutive months	—
XI-7	Type of newspapers read	Inapplicable, as not in community for 12 consecutive months	—
XI-8	Frequency of newspaper reading	Inapplicable, as not in community for 12 consecutive months	—
XI-9	Magazine reading	Inapplicable, as not in community for 12 consecutive months	—
XI-10	Frequency of magazine reading	Inapplicable, as not in community for 12 consecutive months	—
XI-11	Type of magazine reading	Inapplicable, as not in community for 12 consecutive months	—
XI-12	Book reading	Inapplicable, as not in community for 12 consecutive months	—

(Continued)

Table No.[b]	Factor	Information for First Follow-Up Period[a]	Information for Second Follow-Up Period
XI-13	Frequency of book reading	Inapplicable, as not in community for 12 consecutive months	—
XI-14	Type of books read	Inapplicable, as not in community for 12 consecutive months	—
XI-15	Frequency of movie attendance	Inapplicable, as not in community for 12 consecutive months	—
XI-16	Type of movies preferred	Inapplicable, as not in community for 12 consecutive months	—
XI-17	Attendance at burlesque shows	Inapplicable, as not in community for 12 consecutive months	—
XI-18	Participation in civic affairs	Inapplicable, as not in community for 12 consecutive months	—
XI-19	Attendance at clubs	Inapplicable, as not in community for 12 consecutive months	—
XI-20	Nature of clubs attended	Inapplicable, as not in community for 12 consecutive months	—
XI-21	Change in frequency of church attendance	Inapplicable, as not in community for 12 consecutive months	—
XII-1	Contentment with lot in life	inapplicable, as confined for most of period	—
XII-2	Economic ambition at end of period	Inapplicable, as in penal institution	—
XII-3	Nature of economic ambition at end of period	Inapplicable, as in penal institution	—
XII-4	Realism of economic aims at end of period	Inapplicable, as in penal institution	—
XII-5	Occupational ambitions at end of period	Inapplicable, as in penal institution	—
XII-6	Nature of work ambitions during period	Inapplicable, as confined for most of period	—
XII-7	Realism of occupational aims at end of period	Inapplicable, as in penal institution	—
XII-8	Educational ambition at end of period	Inapplicable, as in penal institution	—
XII-9	Nature of educational ambitions at end of period	Inapplicable, as in penal institution	—
XII-10	Family ambitions at end of period	Inapplicable, as not married	—
XII-11	Nature of family ambitions	Inapplicable, as not married	—

(Continued)

Table No.[b]	Factor	Information for First Follow-Up Period[a]	Information for Second Follow-Up Period
XII-12	Realism of family ambitions	Inapplicable, as not married	—
XIII-1	Service in Armed Forces up to 25th birthday	Yes	—
XIII-2	Branch of service	Navy	—
XIII-3	Reasons for deferment	Inapplicable	—
XIII-4	General classification test scores	Unknown	—
XIII-5	Method of first entering service	Enlistment	—
XIII-6	Age at first enlistment	17 years, 8½ months	—
XIII-7	Length of service in Armed Forces up to 25th birthday	18 months	—
XIII-8	Highest rating achieved	Unknown	—
XIII-9	Conduct in Armed Forces	Brought up on charges	—
XIII-9A	Number of times brought up on charges	Six	—
XIII-10	Nature of offenses for which brought up on charges	Being AWOL; disobedience of orders; shirking duty; using obscene language	—
XIII-11	Nature of dispositions of offenses for which brought up on charges	Probation; solitary confinement; extra duty; bad conduct discharge	—
XIII-12	Character of discharge from service	Dishonorable	—
XIII-13	Reason for discharge from service	Misconduct — general court martial	—
XIV-1	Frequency of arrests	Two	Two
XIV-2	Nature of arrests	Robbery and assault and battery with intent to rob; larceny	Using auto without authority; operating auto after right to do so suspended; operating to endanger; violation of parole
XIV-3	Number of court appearances	Two	Two
XIV-4	Nature of dispositions	Committed to reformatory; committed to state prison	Filed; committed to state prison
XIV-5	Number of convictions	Two	Two
XIV-6	Seriousness of conduct	Serious offender	Serious offender
XV-1	Number of all types of correctional experiences	Three	Three
XV-2	Length of time for all correctional experiences	67 months	Entire period

(Continued)

Table No.[b]	Factor	Information for First Follow-Up Period[a]	Information for Second Follow-Up Period
XV-3	Number of extramural correctional periods	One	One
XV-4	Length of time under extramural supervision	9 months	10 months
XV-5	Number of probation experiences	None	None
XV-6	Length of time on probation	Inapplicable	Inapplicable
XV-7	Number of probations on which surrendered	Inapplicable	Inapplicable
XV-8	Number of parole experiences	One	One
XV-9	Length of time on parole	9 months	10 months
XV-10	Number of paroles revoked	None	One
XV-11	Number of intramural correctional experiences	Two	Two
XV-12	Length of incarceration	58 months	62 months
XV-13	Legal status at end of period	In correctional institution	In correctional institution

Appendix B

COMPARISON OF 500 DELINQUENTS AND
500 NONDELINQUENTS OF *UNRAVELING JUVENILE DELINQUENCY*
WITH THE FOLLOW-UP SAMPLE OF 438 DELINQUENTS
AND 442 NONDELINQUENTS

Prepared by Rose W. Kneznek

	U.J.D. Sample			Follow-Up Sample		
	Delin-quents	Nondelin-quents	Dif-ferences	Delin-quents	Nondelin-quents	Dif-ferences
No. of Cases	500	500	—	438	442	—
Developmental Health History						
Poor Health in Infancy	14.6%	9.6%	5.0%	13.6%	8.8%	4.8%
Extreme Restlessness in Early Childhood	59.6	30.0	29.6	57.9	27.6	30.3
Enuresis	28.2	13.6	14.6	26.4	12.6	13.8
Neurologic Findings						
Irregular Reflexes	34.0%	38.6%	— 4.6%	33.1%	38.9%	— 5.8%
Cyanosis	41.4	43.4	— 2.0	43.0	44.6	— 1.6
Absence of Dermographia	54.9	41.6	13.3	52.6	40.0	11.8
Tremors	18.4	20.4	— 2.0	17.8	21.5	— 3.7
Other Physical Findings						
Genital Underdevelopment	11.6%	13.2%	— 1.6%	11.8%	13.6%	— 1.8%
Strength of Handgrip	51.5	43.9	7.6	53.8	49.0	4.8
Some Aspects of Intelligence						
Low Verbal Intelligence	28.4%	16.2%	12.2%	27.8%	12.6%	15.2%
High Performance Intelligence	39.6	42.2	— 2.6	39.7	43.8	— 4.1
Originality	27.6	25.4	2.2	28.0	27.2	0.8
Banality	26.2	31.2	— 5.0	26.1	30.4	— 4.3
Poor Power of Observation	36.3	29.3	7.0	36.2	29.5	6.7
Intuition	16.5	15.4	1.1	17.2	16.8	0.4
Tendency to Phantasy	39.0	32.4	6.6	39.9	33.2	6.7
Lack of Common Sense	25.0	19.1	5.9	23.2	19.2	4.0
Unmethodical Approach to Problems	79.0	64.8	14.2	77.7	64.0	13.7
Absence of Potential Capacity for Objective Interests	55.6	45.6	10.0	55.5	44.0	11.5
Basic Attitudes to Authority and Society						
Social Assertiveness	45.2%	20.5%	24.7%	46.9%	21.1%	25.8%
Defiance	50.4	11.5	38.9	48.3	11.6	36.7
Nonsubmissiveness to Authority	73.4	20.4	53.0	72.7	20.5	52.2
Ambivalence to Authority	40.8	19.6	21.2	39.0	19.3	19.7

(*Continued*)

	U.J.D. Sample			Follow-Up Sample		
	Delin-quents	Nondelin-quents	Dif-ferences	Delin-quents	Nondelin-quents	Dif-ferences
Feelings of Resentment Anxiety, Inferiority, and Frustration						
Absence of Feeling of Insecurity	81.6%	71.2%	10.4%	83.0%	71.5%	11.5%
Marked Feeling of not Being Wanted or Loved	84.2	88.0	— 3.8	83.6	87.2	— 3.6
Feeling of Not Being Taken Care Of	28.8	24.2	4.6	30.1	24.3	5.8
Absence of Marked Feeling of Not Being Taken Seriously	55.8	48.3	7.5	56.9	49.0	7.9
Absence of Feeling of Helplessness	57.9	45.5	12.3	57.8	45.5	12.3
Feeling of Not Being Appreciated	36.1	24.5	11.6	37.2	25.6	11.6
Absence of Fear of Failure and Defeat	56.2	36.9	19.3	56.1	35.8	20.3
Feeling of Resentment	73.9	50.7	23.2	73.3	50.3	23.0
Feelings of Hostility						
Poor Surface Contact with Others	8.2%	3.3%	4.9%	8.2%	2.8%	5.4%
Hostility	79.5	55.9	23.6	79.1	55.4	23.7
Marked Suspiciousness	51.1	26.4	24.7	50.7	27.2	23.5
Destructiveness	48.4	15.3	33.1	47.8	16.0	31.8
Feeling of Isolation	45.1	36.2	8.9	46.9	37.6	9.3
Defensive Attitude	56.0	44.4	11.6	54.4	42.9	11.5
Dependence and Independence						
Absence of Marked Dependence on Others	31.1%	14.4%	16.7%	31.3%	13.9%	17.4%
Feeling of Being Able to Manage Own Life	73.2	63.7	9.5	72.9	64.8	8.1
Goals of Strivings						
Narcissistic Trends	23.0%	14.2%	8.8%	24.5%	15.6%	8.9%
Receptive Trends	30.0	13.5	16.5	30.4	15.1	15.3
Absence of Masochistic Trends	84.7	63.3	21.4	83.8	62.4	21.4
Destructive-Sadistic Trends	48.7	15.8	32.9	48.1	16.5	31.6
Some General Qualities of Personality						
Emotional Liability	43.5%	18.5%	25.0%	41.8%	19.5%	22.3%
Lack of Self-Control	61.5	34.3	27.2	59.0	33.5	25.5
Vivacity	50.6	23.2	27.4	49.4	22.8	26.6
Absence of Compulsory Trends	79.3	69.8	9.5	79.6	70.8	8.8
Preponderance of Extro-versive Trends	54.5	35.1	19.4	53.1	34.3	18.8
Preponderance of Intro-versive Trends	27.3	24.5	2.8	27.8	26.5	1.3
Deep-Rooted Emotional Dynamics						
Sensitivity	31.7%	35.6%	— 3.9%	32.1%	35.3%	— 3.2%
Suggestibility	59.6	26.2	33.4	61.0	24.4	36.6
Feeling of Inadequacy	84.9	69.3	15.6	84.6	67.1	17.5
Stubbornness	41.3	8.2	33.1	43.1	9.0	34.1
Adventurousness	55.2	18.0	37.2	55.5	18.3	37.2
Uninhibited Motor Re-sponses to Stimuli	56.6	28.4	28.2	57.3	29.2	28.1
Emotional Instability	81.7	50.1	31.6	81.4	48.9	32.5

(Continued)

	U.J.D. Sample			Follow-Up Sample		
	Delin-quents	Nondelin-quents	Dif-ferences	Delin-quents	Nondelin-quents	Dif-ferences
Appetitive–Aesthetic Tendencies						
Absence of Aestheticism	82.7%	61.5%	21.2%	83.9%	62.8%	21.1%
Sensuousness	19.8	6.0	13.8	20.6	6.1	14.5
Acquisitiveness	20.6	14.0	6.6	21.1	14.9	6.2
Personality Orientation						
Unconventionality	75.3%	51.5%	23.8%	74.0%	51.2%	22.8%
Lack of Self-Criticism	28.7	10.6	18.1	27.2	9.7	17.5
Lack of Conscientiousness	91.1	45.6	45.5	90.5	45.8	44.7
Impracticality	80.5	65.1	15.4	80.7	63.0	17.7
Some Aspects of Mental Pathology						
Emotional Conflicts	74.6%	37.5%	37.1%	75.0%	37.2%	37.8%
Absence of Neuroticism	75.4	64.2	11.2	77.2	65.6	11.6
Psychopathy	24.1	6.2	17.9	24.5	6.6	17.9
Nativity of Parents						
One or Both Parents Foreign-Born	57.8%	61.1%	− 3.3%	58.4%	62.8%	− 4.4%
Pathology of Parents						
Delinquency of Father	66.2%	32.0%	34.2%	65.7%	32.3%	33.4%
Alcoholism of Father	62.8	39.0	23.8	60.5	38.2	22.3
Emotional Disturbance of Father	44.0	18.0	26.0	42.6	18.5	24.1
Serious Physical Ailment of Father	39.6	28.6	11.0	39.7	28.9	10.8
Delinquency of Mother	44.8	15.0	29.8	43.3	15.1	28.2
Alcoholism of Mother	23.0	7.0	16.0	22.1	7.4	14.7
Emotional Disturance of Mother	40.2	17.6	22.6	38.8	17.4	21.4
Serious Physical Ailment Mother	48.6	33.0	15.6	48.6	33.0	15.6
Economic Conditions						
Financial Dependence of Family	36.2%	14.6%	21.6%	37.8%	15.1%	22.7%
Poor Management of Family Income	66.3	43.8	22.5	65.5	44.8	20.7
Erratic Employment of Mother	26.6	14.6	12.0	24.4	14.3	10.1
Physical Aspects of Home						
Crowded Home	32.6%	24.8%	7.8%	32.2%	23.3%	8.9%
Unclean and Disorderly Home	51.3	34.5	16.8	50.8	33.8	17.0
Careless Household Routine	75.6	50.9	24.7	75.1	50.6	24.5
Lack of Cultural Refinement in Home	91.7	81.8	9.9	91.2	80.8	10.4
Instability of Home and Neighborhood						
Rearing in Broken Home	60.6%	34.2%	26.4%	58.9%	34.1%	24.8%
Boy Less than 5 Years of Age at First Breach in Family Life	56.7	47.3	9.4	56.5	45.0	11.5
Rearing by Parent Substitute	47.4	12.0	35.4	47.9	11.7	36.2
Frequent Moving	53.6	18.6	35.0	51.8	18.3	33.5

(Continued)

	U.J.D. Sample			Follow-Up Sample		
	Delin-quents	Nondelin-quents	Dif-ferences	Delin-quents	Nondelin-quents	Dif-ferences
Atmosphere of Family Life						
Dominance of Mother in Family Affairs	50.7%	51.9%	− 1.2%	50.8%	50.3%	0.5%
Lack of Family Self-Respect	43.2	10.0	33.2	42.9	10.0	32.9
Lack of Family Ambition	89.3	69.8	19.5	88.8	69.1	19.7
Poor Conduct Standards of Family	90.4	54.0	36.4	89.7	52.7	37.0
Poor Work Habits of Father	62.4	28.9	33.5	62.4	28.3	34.1
Evidence of Family Disunity						
Incompatibility of Parents	63.1%	34.7%	28.4%	61.8%	33.8%	28.0%
Lack of Family Group Recreations	67.4	37.9	29.5	66.8	38.3	28.5
Parents Uninterested in Boy's Companions	79.5	61.8	17.7	80.6	63.0	17.6
Meager Recreational Facilities in Home	53.3	35.8	17.5	53.9	36.5	17.4
Lack of Family Cohesiveness	83.9	38.2	45.7	82.8	37.7	45.1
Affection of Family for Boy						
Rank of Boy among Siblings: Middle Child	60.0%	48.2%	11.8%	59.5%	48.6%	10.9%
Indifference or Hostility of Father for Boy	59.7	19.3	40.4	59.3	18.3	41.0
Indifference or Hostility of Mother to Boy	27.8	4.4	23.4	27.0	4.5	22.5
Indifference or Hostility of Siblings to Boy	28.1	7.2	20.9	27.9	6.1	21.8
Feeling of Boy for Parents						
Indifference or Hostility of Boy to Father	67.2%	34.8%	32.4%	68.5%	34.2%	34.3%
Unacceptability of Father to Boy for Emulation	30.6	7.0	23.6	31.3	6.1	25.2
Indifference or Hostility of Boy to Mother	35.1	10.2	24.9	34.1	10.4	23.7
Supervision and Discipline of Boy						
Unsuitable Supervision of Boy by Mother	63.8%	13.0%	50.8%	61.4%	13.3%	48.1%
Unsuitable Discipline of Boy by Father	94.3	44.4	49.9	94.2	45.0	49.2
Physical Punishment of Boy by Father	67.8	34.5	33.3	68.3	34.1	34.2
Supervision and Discipline of Boy (Concluded)						
Threatening or Scolding of Boy by Father	32.1%	31.4%	0.7%	32.7%	30.9%	1.8%
Unsuitable Discipline of Boy by Mother	95.7	34.4	61.3	95.4	34.3	61.1
Physical Punishment of Boy by Mother	55.6	34.4	21.2	55.3	33.4	21.9
Threatening or Scolding of Boy by Mother	46.8	36.9	9.9	44.8	35.0	9.8

Appendix C

CLASSIFICATION OF CRIMES IN ORDER OF SERIOUSNESS

Serious Offenses

A. Homicide (murder; voluntary and involuntary manslaughter)

B. Grave sex crimes
    1. Violent and deliberate, sexually motivated attacks (rape, attempt to rape, assault with intent to rape; excluding technical rape)
    2. Pathologic sex expressions (incest, sodomy, indecent assault, carnal knowledge or abuse of female child)

C. Violent property crimes (involving force or threat of force)
    1. Robbery (including attempted robbery, armed robbery, accessory before fact to robbery, assault to rob, conspiracy to rob, possession of weapons)
    2. Arson
    3. Extortion

D. Other serious property crimes
    1. Burglary (including attempted breaking and entering in day or night; possessing burglar's tools)
    2. Larceny (from person; other larcenies, including stealing of motor vehicle)
    3. Receiving stolen goods
    4. Other theft crimes (embezzlement, obtaining property by false pretenses, forgery and uttering, bribery)

E. Other serious offenses
    1. Kidnaping
    2. Serious violations of motor vehicle laws (operating under influence of liquor, leaving scene of accident after injuring person)
    3. Escape or rescue (not including murder or some other felony committed in the course of escape or rescue)
    4. Perjury

Less Serious Offenses

A. Offenses involving domestic relations
    1. Desertion, assault on wife, fathering illegitimate child, polygamy, abandonment of wife and/or child
    2. Nonsupport; neglect

B. Simple assault

C. Malicious mischief

D. Offenses involving drugs or alcohol (including violation of liquor laws, keeping and exposing)

E. Offenses against public order (vagrancy, disturbing the peace, profanity and threats, affrays; registering bets; lottery)

F. Less serious sex offenses
    1. Homosexual acts
    2. Adultery, fornication, technical "rape," lewd and lascivious cohabitation

G. Violation of minor technical motor vehicle laws

H. Juvenile offenses (being stubborn child, truancy, associating with bad companions)

I. Violation of probation (if violation consists of new crime, classification is by crime)

Index